NORTHSTAR

LISTENING AND SPEAKING

High Intermediate

SECOND EDITION

Tess Ferree
Kim Sanabria

Series Editors
Frances Boyd
Carol Numrich

Longman

NorthStar: Listening and Speaking, High Intermediate, Second Edition

Pearson Education, 10 Bank Street, White Plains, NY 10606

Pronunciation consultant: Linda Lane
Development director: Penny Laporte
Project manager: Debbie Sistino
Development editor: Andrea Bryant
Vice president, director of design and production: Rhea Banker
Executive managing editor: Linda Moser
Production coordinator: Melissa Leyva
Senior production editor: Kathleen Silloway
Associate art director: Tracey Cataldo
Director of manufacturing: Patrice Fraccio
Senior manufacturing buyer: Dave Dickey
Cover design: Rhea Banker
Cover art: Detail of Wandbild aus dem Tempel der Sehnsucht\dorthin/, 1922,
    30 Mural from the temple of desire\there/ 26.7 × 37.5 cm; oil transfer
    drawing and water color on plaster-primed gauze; The Metropolitan
    Museum of Art, N.Y. The Berggruen Klee Collection, 1984.
    (1984.315.33) Photograph © 1986 The Metropolitan Museum of Art.
    © 2003 Artists Rights Society (ARS), New York / VG Bild-Kunst, Bonn
Photo research: Aerin Csigay
Photo credits: see page 253
Text design: Quorum Creative Services
Text composition: ElectraGraphics, Inc.
Text font: 11/13 Sabon
Text art: pp. 17, 123, Ron Chironna; pp. 71, 193, Lloyd Birmingham;
    p. 162, Tracey Cataldo
Text credits: see page 253

Wandbild aus dem Tempel
der Sehnsucht ↖ dorthin ↗
Paul Klee

Library of Congress Cataloging-in-Publication Data

Ferree, Tess
    NorthStar. Listening and speaking, high intermediate/Tess Ferree,
Kim Sanabria.—2nd ed.
        p. cm.
    Includes index.
    1. English language—Textbooks for foreign speakers. 2. English
language—Spoken English—Problems, exercises, etc. 3. Listening—
Problems, exercises, etc. I. Title: Listening and speaking, high
intermediate. II. Sanabria, Kim III. Title.

PE1128.F425 2004
428.3'4—dc21
                                                            2003044469

ISBNs: 0-201-75572-6 (Student Book)
        0-13-143910-3 (Student Book with Audio CDs) ·

Printed in the United States of America
14 15 16—CRK—12 11 10 09 08
10—CRK—09 08

Contents

Welcome to NorthStar

Second Edition

NorthStar leads the way in integrated skills series. The Second Edition remains an innovative, five-level series written for students with academic as well as personal language goals. Each unit of the thematically linked Reading and Writing strand and Listening and Speaking strand explores intellectually challenging, contemporary themes to stimulate critical thinking skills while building language competence.

Four easy to follow sections—Focus on the Topic, Focus on Reading/Focus on Listening, Focus on Vocabulary, and Focus on Writing/Focus on Speaking—invite students to focus on the process of learning through **NorthStar**.

Thematically Based Units

NorthStar engages students by organizing language study thematically. Themes provide stimulating topics for reading, writing, listening, and speaking.

Extensive Support to Build Skills for Academic Success

Creative activities help students develop language-learning strategies, such as predicting and identifying main ideas and details.

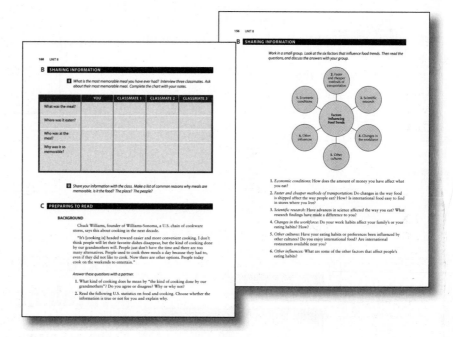

High-Interest Listening and Reading Selections

The two listening or reading selections in each unit present contrasting viewpoints to enrich students' understanding of the content while building language skills.

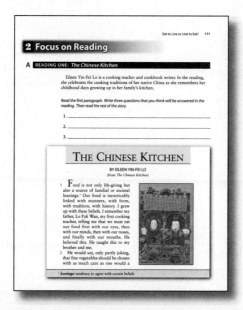

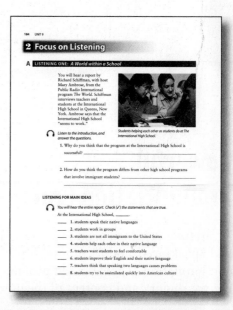

Critical Thinking Skill Development

Critical thinking skills, such as synthesizing information or reacting to the different viewpoints in the two reading or listening selections, are practiced throughout each unit, making language learning meaningful.

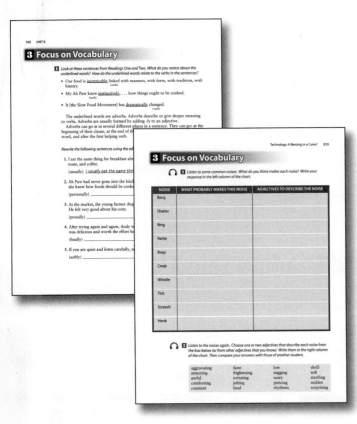

Extensive Vocabulary Practice

Students are introduced to key, contextualized vocabulary to help them comprehend the listening and reading selections. They also learn idioms, collocations, and word forms to help them explore, review, play with, and expand their spoken and written expression.

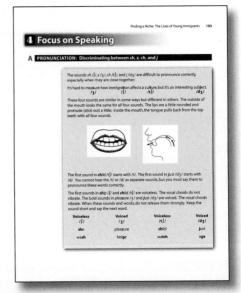

Powerful Pronunciation Practice

A carefully designed pronunciation syllabus in the Listening and Speaking strand focuses on topics such as stress, rhythm, and intonation. Theme-based pronunciation practice reinforces the vocabulary and content of the unit.

Content-Rich Grammar Practice

Each thematic unit integrates the study of grammar with related vocabulary and cultural information. The grammatical structures are drawn from the listening or reading selections and offer an opportunity for students to develop accuracy in speaking or writing about the topic.

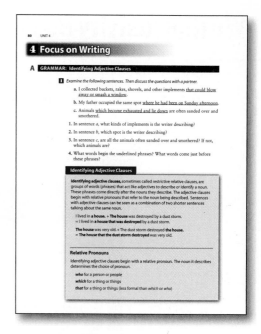

Extensive Opportunity for Discussion and Writing

Challenging and imaginative speaking activities, writing topics, and research assignments allow students to apply the language, grammar, style, and content they've learned.

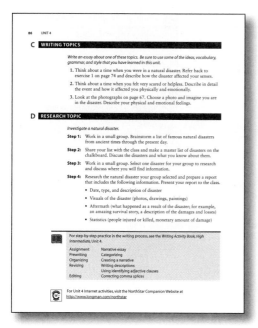

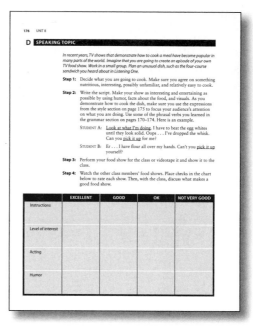

Writing Activity Book

The companion *Writing Activity Book* leads students through the writing process with engaging writing assignments. Skills and vocabulary from **NorthStar: Reading and Writing,** are reviewed and expanded as students learn the process of prewriting, organizing, revising, and editing.

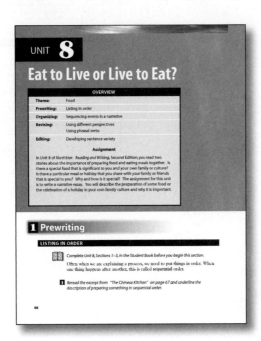
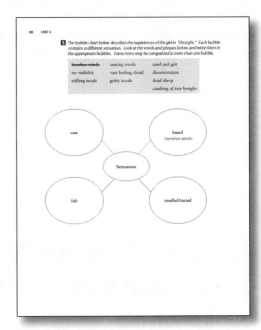

Audio Program

All the pronunciation, listening, and reading selections have been professionally recorded.

Teacher's Manual with Achievement Tests

Each book in the series has an accompanying *Teacher's Manual* with step-by-step teaching suggestions, time guidelines, and expansion activities. Also included in each *Teacher's Manual* are reproducible unit-by-unit tests. The Listening and Speaking strand tests are recorded on CD and included in the *Teacher's Manual*. Packaged with each *Teacher's Manual* for the Reading and Writing strand is a TestGen CD-ROM that allows teachers to create and customize their own **NorthStar** tests. Answer Keys to both the Student Book and the Tests are included, along with a unit-by-unit word list of key vocabulary.

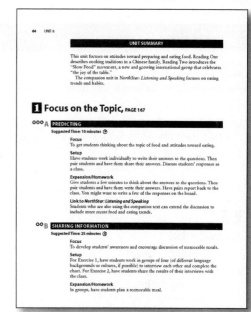

NorthStar Video Series

Engaging, authentic video clips, including cartoons, documentaries, interviews, and biographies correlate to the themes in **NorthStar.** There are four videos, one for each level of **NorthStar,** Second edition, containing 3- to 5- minute segments for each unit. Worksheets for the video can be found on the **NorthStar** Companion Website.

Companion Website

http://www.longman.com/northstar includes resources for students and teachers such as additional vocabulary activities, Web-based links and research, video worksheets, and correlations to state standards.

Scope and Sequence

Unit	Critical Thinking Skills	Listening Tasks

1
For News Resisters, No News Is Good News
Theme: Media
Listening One: *News Resisters*
  A radio news report
Listening Two: *CornCam*
  A report on an unusual Web site
	Compare sources of news
	Recognize assumptions about media
	Interpret graphs
	Infer information not explicit in the interview
	Hypothesize another's point of view
	Analyze goals of news reporting
		Listen for main ideas
		Listen for details
		Provide evidence to support answers
		Relate listenings to personal values
		Synthesize information from both listenings
		Listen to student broadcasts and analyze them
		Evaluate a TV news program

2
The Achilles Heel
Theme: Overcoming Obstacles
Listening One: *Dreams of Flying and Overcoming Obstacles*
  A college application essay
Listening Two: *The Achilles Track Club Climbs Mount Kilimanjaro*
  A television news report
	Identify personal obstacles
	Rank the value of personal qualities
	Analyze narrative techniques in an essay
	Hypothesize another's point of view
	Analyze sensitive language referring to disabilities
	Infer meaning not explicit in the text
	Compare and contrast two life histories
	Frame contrasting points of view on disability issues
		Summarize main ideas
		Listen for details
		Relate listening to knowledge of the world
		Identifying connecting themes between two listenings
		Identify thought groups in speech
		Watch and analyze a movie
		Listen to classmates' reports and pose questions

3
Early to Bed, Early to Rise . . .
Theme: Medicine
Listening One: *Teen Sleep Needs*
  A radio news report
Listening Two: *Get Back in Bed*
  A conversation with a doctor
	Interpret a cartoon
	Interpret a quotation
	Compare and contrast sleep habits
	Hypothesize scenarios
	Draw conclusions about sleep deprivation
	Propose solutions to problems
	Analyze a case of sleep deprivation and its consequences
		Converse with a classmate and take notes
		Summarize main ideas
		Listen for details
		Interpret speaker's tone and emotions
		Relate listening to personal experiences
		Compare information from two listenings
		Identify emphasis in speech and its meaning

4
The Eye of the Storm
Theme: Natural Disasters
Listening One: *Preparing for a Hurricane*
  A radio news report
Listening Two: *Hurricane Hunters*
  A radio news report
	Use context clues to guess meaning
	Analyze a speaker's emotions
	Infer word meaning from context
	Hypothesize another's point of view
	Make judgments
	Support opinions with information from the reports
		Listen to a report with static interference
		Relate previous knowledge to listening
		Identify chronology in a report
		Identify a speaker's emotions
		Summarize main ideas
		Listen for specific information
		Identify intonation patterns in speech
		Listen to student reports and take notes
		Watch a disaster movie and take notes

Speaking Tasks	Pronunciation	Vocabulary	Grammar
Make predictions Summarize points Act out a scripted conversation Give a newscast Express and defend opinions Interview a news specialist	Reducing and contracting auxiliary verbs	Context clues Synonyms Idiomatic expressions Descriptive adjectives Dictionary work Word definitions	Passive voice
Make predictions Construct and perform a dialogue Practice using synonyms, parallelism, and prepositional phrases to enrich a narrative Plan and give a three-minute speech Orally summarize research on overcoming obstacles	Thought groups	Context clues Word definitions Figurative language	Gerunds and infinitives
Make predictions Use new vocabulary in a guided conversation Make contrastive statements using appropriate intonation Act out scripted dialogues Interrupt politely to clarify or confirm information Role-play a meeting Conduct a survey and report results Report survey results to the class	Contrastive stress	Context clues Word definitions	Present unreal conditionals
Make predictions Share personal experiences and fears Construct and perform a dialogue Express surprise, shock, and interest in news Present an emergency weather report Conduct an interview Present a movie review	Listing intonation	Context clues Word definitions Synonyms Word forms	Adjective clauses

Unit	Critical Thinking Skills	Listening Tasks

5
 	
You Will Be This Land
Theme: Conservation
Listening One: *Interview with a Medicine Priest*
    A conversation with a Cherokee spiritual leader
Listening Two: *"Ndakinna"—A Poem*
    An Abenaki poem
	Interpret quotations
	Draw conclusions
	Support generalizations with examples
	Evaluate situations according to criteria set forth in the listening
	Infer information not explicit in the interview
	Hypothesize another's point of view
	Evaluate personal conservation efforts
	Analyze symbolism in a poem
		Summarize main ideas
		Listen for details
		Relate personal experience and values to the listening
		Take dictation
		Compare and contrast viewpoints in the listenings
		Identify sounds
		Listen for specific information
		Listen to and ask questions about student research

6
 	
It's Better to Give Than to Receive
Theme: Philanthropy
Listening One: *Oseola McCarty*
    A report on the life of a philanthropist
Listening Two: *Please Donate or Volunteer*
    Two public service announcements
	Make judgments
	Identify personal assumptions about philanthropy
	Correlate abstract principles with concrete examples
	Hypothesize rationales for philanthropic actions
	Critique public service announcements
	Compare and contrast information
	Rank desirable employee qualities
		Identify main ideas
		Listen for details
		Listen and take notes using a graphic organizer
		Synthesize information from both listenings
		Interpret speakers' intent by analyzing intonation
		Listen to and evaluate student presentations
		Research a charitable organization or philanthropist through telephone inquiries

7
 	
Emotional Intelligence
Theme: Education
Listening One: *Can You Learn EQ?*
    A psychology radio program
Listening Two: *Test Your EQ*
    An emotional intelligence test
	Interpret a cartoon
	Define notions of intelligence
	Identify and evaluate assumptions about intelligence
	Hypothesize another's point of view
	Connect principles of emotional intelligence to specific behaviors
	Interpret quotations
	Analyze past encounters according to principles of emotional intelligence
		Preview a listening
		Take notes while listening using a graphic organizer
		Listen for details
		Provide information from the listening to support answers
		Relate listening to personal experiences
		Integrate information from both listenings
		Listen to classmates' stories and take notes
		Listen to and evaluate student responses
		Watch and analyze student role plays

Speaking Tasks	Pronunciation	Vocabulary	Grammar
Make predictions Express opinions Interview a classmate Read aloud or recite a poem Ask for and give examples Role-play a meeting Use new vocabulary to assess personal conservation habits Report research findings	*th* sounds	Word definitions Synonyms Context clues Word forms	Advisability in the past—past modals
Make predictions Express and support opinions with examples Construct and perform a dialogue Use new vocabulary to discuss examples of charitable efforts Ask for clarification using tag questions Use gambits that indicate priorities Develop and perform a public service announcement Report research findings	Intonation of tag questions	Context clues Word definitions Synonyms	Tag questions
Make predictions Support opinions with examples Compose and perform a dialogue using new vocabulary Recount an emotional experience Use opening gambits to restate information for clarification or emphasis Restate quotations Perform a role play Conduct an interview	Unstressed vowels	Context clues Synonyms Idiomatic expressions	Direct and indirect speech

Unit	Critical Thinking Skills	Listening Tasks

8
 	
Goodbye to the Sit-Down Meal
 	
Theme: Food
 	
Listening One: *French Sandwiches*
    A radio news report
 	
Listening Two: *Food in a Bowl*
    A conversation about food trends
	Identify and analyze food trends
	Relate general factors to specific behaviors
	Interpret meaning from text
	Compare traditional and contemporary food practices
	Infer word meaning from context
	Compare and contrast two restaurants
	Infer situational context
		Summarize main ideas
		Listen for details
		Interpret speaker's tone and attitude
		Relate listening to local food trends
		Classify vowel sounds
		Listen to student food shows and evaluate using a rubric
		Listen to a food show on TV

9
 	
Finding a Niche: The Lives of Young Immigrants
 	
Theme: Immigration
 	
Listening One: *A World within a School*
    A radio news report
 	
Listening Two: *The Words Escape Me*
    A song
	Compare personal experiences
	Recognize personal assumptions
	Hypothesize scenarios
	Infer word meaning from context
	Analyze language usage
	Compare and contrast two immigrant experiences
	Infer meaning not explicit in text
	Propose solutions
		Identify main ideas
		Listen for supporting details
		Interpret speaker's tone and pitch
		Relate listening to personal values and interests
		Take a dictation
		Identify points of view in two listenings
		Classify sounds
		Listen to and comment on student plans

10
 	
Technology: A Blessing or a Curse?
 	
Theme: Technology
 	
Listening One: *Noise in the City*
    A radio news report
 	
Listening Two: *Technology Talk*
    A talk radio show
	Interpret cartoons
	Compare opinions about technology
	Analyze paradox in a poem
	Make judgments
	Hypothesize scenarios
	Draw conclusions
	Define a problem and propose a solution
		Infer situational context
		Listen for main ideas
		Listen for supporting details
		Interpret speaker's tone and word usage
		Take notes while listening
		Listen for specific information in student responses
		Listen for emphasis in speech
		Evaluate student commercials
		Listen to classmates' research findings and ask questions

Speaking Tasks	Pronunciation	Vocabulary	Grammar
Make predictions Share ideas on food trends Use tone of voice to indicate attitude in a role play Use new vocabulary in free conversation Compose and perform a dialogue Practice gambits which call attention to a particular item Explain how to use a tool Develop and perform a food show Report research on food trends	Spelling and sounds: *oo* and *o*	Context clues Synonyms Definitions Figurative meanings of words Vocabulary classification Idiomatic expressions	Phrasal verbs
Make predictions Express opinions using new vocabulary Restate themes of the unit in a guided conversation Practice gambits to hesitate in response to a question Ask and answer questions about a chart Simulate a school board meeting Collaborate to develop an education plan Conduct an interview Compare interview results	Discriminating between *sh, z, ch,* and *j*	Context clues Synonyms Definitions Idiomatic expressions	Present and past—contrasting verb tenses
Discuss opinions Make predictions Act out scripted dialogues Discuss possible future outcomes Practice gambits to express frustration Role-play a conflict between neighbors Develop and present a commercial for a gadget Present findings from research on technology	Stressed adverbial particles	Synonyms Word definitions Context clues Descriptive adjectives	Future perfect and future progressive

Acknowledgments

To all our friends and family, colleagues and collaborators who have supported us throughout this Second Edition of *NorthStar,* our heartfelt thanks. This project would never have come to fruition without you!

The project has been guided and enriched by the contributions of many people. We would like to thank Frances Boyd and Carol Numrich, our dedicated NorthStar series editors. We thank the wonderful editorial staff at Pearson Education, particularly Debbie Sistino and Andrea Bryant. In addition, the many interviewees and commentators heard in the listenings have all left their personal marks on this project. We also extend our thanks to colleagues, students, and friends at Randolph Middle School and Eugenio Maria de Hostos Community College.

And of course, we thank Carlos and Jay, Kelly and Victor, Honor and Ed.

Tess Ferree
Kim Sanabria

For her contribution in developing the NorthStar pronunciation syllabus, the publisher gratefully acknowledges the contribution of **Linda Lane**.

For the comments and insights they graciously offered to help shape the direction of the Second Edition of *NorthStar*, the publisher would like to thank all our **reviewers**. For a complete list of reviewers and institutions, see page 255.

For News Resisters, No News Is Good News

"Meaningless statistics were up one-point-five per cent this month over last month."

1 Focus on the Topic

A PREDICTING

Look at the cartoon and the title of the unit. Then discuss these questions with a partner or small group.

1. What does the cartoon say about the news?

2. "No news is good news" is a common expression in English. What do you think it means? What kind of person do you think a "news resister" might be? In what type of situation would a person "resist" the news?

B   SHARING INFORMATION

1 *There are many different news media—newspapers, television, radio, the Internet, and magazines. On the chart, put a check (✓) under the news medium you use most frequently to obtain different types of information. Then compare your answers in a small group. Discuss the reasons for your choices.*

TYPES OF INFORMATION	NEWS MEDIA					
	Newspapers	Television	Radio	Internet	Magazines	Other People
Local news						
National news						
International news						
Business news						
Weather						
Cultural events						
Movie reviews						
Sports						
Traffic reports						
Technology news						

2 *Check how much time you spend watching, listening to, and reading news. Compare your answers in a small group.*

_____ almost none

_____ fewer than four hours per week

_____ four to seven hours per week

_____ between one and two hours per day

_____ more than two hours per day

C PREPARING TO LISTEN

BACKGROUND

People in the United States have many sources of news, some of which are available 24 hours a day. Some say that Americans have become addicted to the news. In a recent survey, more than 65 percent of American respondents said that they spend from one-half to two hours per day watching, listening to, or reading the news. Twenty percent said they pay attention to the news for more than two hours each day. News comes from every angle, not only from printed sources, but from TV and the Internet as well.

With the increased availability of news, serious questions have emerged about the role of the news media in society. Should the media report every detail about every story, even when the information does not seem timely or relevant? Critics are concerned that by focusing on everything at once, the media increasingly ignore the more important social, political, and economic issues that we face. We become distracted from what's important by reading about what is not. One extreme example of this is the type of information covered by the tabloid media, which focus on negative stories of violence, crime, and scandal.

How can people deal with all the news that is available to them? Some have chosen to turn their backs on news altogether, resisting the urge to turn on the TV and read the paper every day. They argue that this gives them a better perspective on the world and allows them to understand and use information more sensibly. Others have begun to question what "news" actually means. With the rise of the Internet and cable TV, some people have begun to look for stories about everyday life, stories that are often ignored by the traditional news media. Could learning about everyday life be just as interesting as finding out about the latest scandal? Some people think so.

In a national survey, 1,500 American adults were asked their opinions about the news. Work in pairs to find out the results of the survey. Then as a class discuss your reaction to the data.

Take turns reading each other the statements. Student A reads a statement, while Student B looks at the survey question and bar graph. Student B says if the statement is true or false. If the statement is false, Student B gives Student A the correct information. Switch roles after statement 5.

Statements

1. Americans get most of their news from newspapers.

2. Radio is the least common source of news.

3. The Internet is used about as frequently as TV as a source of news.

Survey Questions and Bar Graphs

Overall, where do you get most of your news?

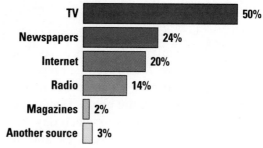

4. Most Americans are very interested in local news.

5. Few Americans are interested in news about crime.

What type of news are you interested in?

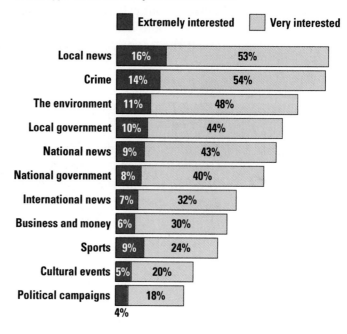

Now switch roles.

Statements

6. More than 40 percent of Americans think that reporting on the national government is good.

7. Almost 50 percent of Americans think that reporting on crime is good.

8. Most people think that reporting on local and national news is not good.

Survey Questions and Bar Graphs

How do you rate the quality of newspaper, TV, Internet, and radio reporting on these topics?

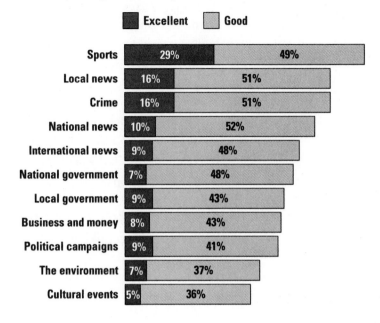

9. Americans trust lawyers more than they trust newspaper reporters.

10. Americans trust corporate executives and medical doctors more than they trust TV reporters.

How much do you trust the following people?

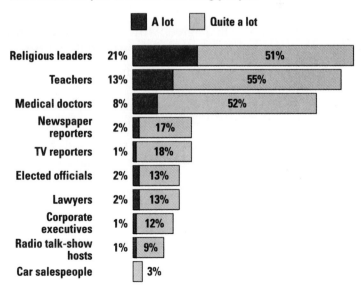

VOCABULARY FOR COMPREHENSION

Read the conversations. Circle the letter of the word or phrase that is closest in meaning to the underlined words.

1. A: Look, it says here that only 20 percent of the people interviewed for this survey get their news from the Internet.

   B: <u>Odds are</u> that'll change soon. I think more and more people are getting their news online.

   a. possibly   **b.** probably

2. A: I've been watching bad news on TV all week, and I just have to turn it off. My news <u>intake</u> is much too high.

   B: Yes, me, too. Let's do something else this evening.

   a. information   **b.** consumption

3. A: What? That politician has been caught stealing money again?

   B: Let's not keep talking about it. Is that story really <u>newsworthy</u>?

   a. unusual   **b.** important

4. A: Sometimes I think the news gets a bit <u>repetitive</u>. I get tired of reading about the same scandal day after day, don't you?

   B: Umm, I'm not sure. We probably need to know all the details.

   a. essential but exhausting   **b.** done many times the same way

5. A: Look at what they are saying on page 1 of the paper. A movie star is getting divorced for the third time, a married politician is seeing another woman. . . . It's all so <u>inconsequential</u>.

   B: I agree. Why do you bother getting a paper? You'd get more important stories if you used the Internet.

   a. unimportant   **b.** deliberate

6. A: I was watching the debate about the elections. Why do those politicians keep saying the same things?

   B: Well, I know this sounds as if I don't care, but I think the <u>underlying</u> reason is that they have run out of things to say!

   a. basic   **b.** untruthful

7. A: Lately, I've been using the Internet to get my news.

   B: You should be careful to check who wrote what you're reading. How do you know what <u>bias</u> the authors may have?

    a. preconceived opinions   **b.** important insights

8. A: I like being able to watch a lot of different news programs. It helps me to <u>get perspective</u> on what is happening.

   B: I'm not sure if I agree with you. The programs all get their news from the same sources, and they all usually say the same thing.

    a. learn to question   **b.** understand the true relation and significance

9. A: You have to keep up with what's happening in the world, <u>regardless of</u> how bad it makes you feel.

   B: I'm not so sure. Sometimes I prefer not to know what is going on. It's too depressing.

    a. in spite of   **b.** in case of

10. A: I've had it with TV! It shows nothing but scandals and murders.

   B: I have the perfect <u>remedy</u>. Switch it off!

    a. reason   **b.** solution

11. A: That's it! I'm finished reading the newspaper forever! It's too depressing.

   B: I agree. There's nothing in the paper but suffering and <u>despair</u>.

    a. hopelessness   **b.** crime

12. A: My mother sits in front of the TV for hours every evening.

   B: Well, television has that effect on a lot of people. It <u>immobilizes</u> you.

    a. makes you want to act   **b.** stops you from doing anything productive

13. A: I was reading about some "news resisters."

   B: Who are they?

   A: People who just <u>disengage from</u> the news.

    a. pay attention to   **b.** avoid becoming affected by

2 Focus on Listening

A   LISTENING ONE: *News Resisters*

You are going to hear the introduction to a news report. The reporter talks to Dr. Andrew Weil, who has written a book about improving our health.

 Listen to the introduction, and answer the questions. Compare your answers with those of a partner.

1. Dr. Weil recommends changing your daily intake of news. What are two possible benefits of doing that?

   _____

   _____

2. The reporter interviews some news resisters, people who avoid taking in too much news. In what professions or occupations do you think she will find them?

   college professor   clergy member
   politician   doctor
   lawyer   business executive
   novelist   computer programmer

LISTENING FOR MAIN IDEAS

 Listen to National Public Radio's Margot Adler interviewing people about how much news we need to know. Circle the letter of the answer that best completes each statement.

1. Andrew Weil, a doctor and author, asked people to _____.
   a. reduce their news intake
   b. stop watching television
   c. give up coffee

2. Mark Harris, an author, believes that _____.
   a. television presents more well-rounded stories than newspapers do
   b. novels allow you to focus on more interesting stories than newspapers do
   c. newspapers are dominated by stories about sports

3. Gabrielle Spiegel, chair of the history department at Johns Hopkins University, argues that the two main things you need in life are _____.
   a. time and money
   b. fantasy and humor
   c. information and repetition

4. John Sommerville, author and professor of history, claims that getting news on a daily basis _____.
   a. makes it harder to understand
   b. increases our understanding of current events
   c. makes it harder to get perspective

5. Tupton Shudrun, a Buddhist nun, teacher, and student of the Dalai Lama, says that news _____.
   a. mobilizes us to do something
   b. can make us more successful
   c. stops us from contributing to society

6. Professor Spiegel adds that we need to spend more time _____.
   a. reading
   b. thinking
   c. watching TV

LISTENING FOR DETAILS

Listen to the interview again. As you listen, circle the letter of the answer that best completes each statement.

1. Mark Harris wrote an essay in the *New York Times* in the early 1970s about newspapers. Since then, he has _____.
   a. changed his opinion
   b. modified his opinion
   c. maintained the same opinion

2. In Harris's opinion, novels get readers to focus on interesting people, such as _____.
   a. sports figures who don't win
   b. teachers at small universities
   c. historical figures who are little known

3. The period in history that Gabrielle Spiegel studies is _____.
   a. the thirteenth and fourteenth centuries
   b. the fifteenth and sixteenth centuries
   c. the nineteenth and twentieth centuries

4. Spiegel doesn't read newspapers because _____.
   a. they are repetitive
   b. she would rather do other things
   c. she wants to spend time with her children

5. In Sommerville's opinion, daily news does not _____.
   a. make us dumb
   b. give us perspective
   c. need to be fixed

6. Sommerville reads the news _____.
   a. every day
   b. every three or four months
   c. never

7. Tupton Shudrun is critical of the media because _____.
   a. they do not present problems well
   b. they create a sense of despair
   c. they do not benefit society

8. Shudrun thinks that people need to _____.
   a. decide how much news to take in
   b. measure the success of newspapers
   c. assume the media know what is important

REACTING TO THE LISTENING

1 *Listen to the excerpts, and answer the questions that follow.*

Excerpt One

1. Speaking of news resisters, Margot Adler gives the example of Gabrielle Spiegel, chair of the history department at Johns Hopkins University. What is her opinion of Spiegel's view?
   a. She is surprised by it.
   b. She disagrees with it.
   c. She understands it.

2. What information does Margot Adler give to support her opinion?

   _____

Excerpt Two

3. Sommerville believes there is a conflict between the daily news and religion. What does Margot Adler think about Sommerville's opinion?
   a. She can't accept it at all.
   b. She has noticed this opinion before.
   c. She was the first person to comment on it.

4. What information does Margot Adler add to Sommerville's idea?

   _____

Excerpt Three

5. Why do you think the news staff at NPR said, "Don't tell anyone"?
   a. They thought they might lose their jobs.
   b. They were shy.
   c. They were angry.

6. What words or phrases did the news staff use? Why?

_____

2 *Work in a small group. Discuss the following questions.*

1. What is a news resister? Are you one of them?

2. Do you think that responsible citizens have to keep up with the news? How much time do you think you should spend keeping up with the news?

3. The reporter interviewed a doctor, a novelist, two professors, and a nun. They are all news resisters. Do you agree with any of their ideas?

B   LISTENING TWO: *CornCam*

Do you think that news is mostly fast-moving action? If you do, you might be surprised to find that not everyone agrees with you. You will now hear a report about CornCam, an unusual local project that has become popular around the world. (You can visit the CornCam website at www.iowafarmer.com and click on CornCam.)

 1 *Listen to the report, and circle the letter of the answer.*

1. Who started CornCam?
   a. a farmer in Iowa   b. editors of an
                                    Iowa publication

2. What does CornCam show?
   a. a field   b. farmers at work

3. How many people tuned in to CornCam last year?
   a. 100,000   b. 600,000

4. What do people see when they visit CornCam?
   a. a digital image   b. a report about corn
      of a cornfield   growing

5. Where do most of the people who tune in to CornCam live?
   a. in cities   b. in Beijing

6. The reporter is not sure that CornCam can really be _____.

   a. relaxing   **b.** riveting

7. What does corn's growth depend on?

   a. weather   **b.** soil type

8. How fast does corn grow?

   a. up to six inches a month   **b.** up to six inches a day

2 *Why do you think so many people have tuned into the site? Choose the most likely reason from the list. Explain your choice to the class.*

- They are very interested in corn.
- They want to feel closer to the earth.
- They find the site by accident.
- They think CornCam is relaxing and soothing.
- They find the site to be educational.
- They are checking on their investments in farm commodities.

C   LINKING LISTENINGS ONE AND TWO

In Listening One, you heard why some people dislike traditional news. Listening Two described how some people are excited by a different type of "news."

Complete the chart. How would the people listed feel about CornCam? Whose opinion do you agree with?

PERSON	LIKE OR DISLIKE CORNCAM?	REASONS WHY
Andrew Weil, doctor and author		
Mark Harris, novelist		
Gabrielle Spiegel, medieval historian		
John Sommerville, professor of religion		
Tupton Shudrun, Buddhist nun		

3 Focus on Vocabulary

1 *Match the words on the left with the definitions on the right. Write the appropriate letter in the blank. Then read the paragraph that follows and fill in the blanks using correct forms of the words on the left.*

_____ 1. to take a break   **a.** to form a relationship

_____ 2. to make a connection   **b.** to stop working in order to relax for a while

_____ 3. to come in second   **c.** deadly

_____ 4. biased   **d.** unfairly influenced by someone's opinion

_____ 5. lethal   **e.** to be after first

Many people complain about the news. Some say most of our news is

_____ and doesn't present an objective viewpoint. Others

complain that most news stories, especially those on TV and radio, don't

provide enough detail or depth for audiences to form thoughtful opinions.

They say that only print media—newspapers and magazines—allow for careful

reflection and make positive contributions to human life. This, they claim, helps

people _____ between their own lives and what's happening

in the world. Electronic news advocates disagree. They argue that the speed of

electronic news and the wide coverage of electronic stories can even save lives.

An example is a story about a product that is recalled because it is harmful or

even _____, such as a defective car seat for babies. When it

comes to getting the news as soon as it happens, the Internet is often people's

first choice. TV news _____, radio news falls third, and print

media come in last. Whatever their media of choice, perhaps the best solution

for people who get annoyed by the news is simply *to take a break*

from it and do something else.

Follow the same procedure: Match the words on the left with the definitions on the right. Write the appropriate letter in the blank. Then read the paragraph that follows and fill in the blanks using correct forms of the words on the left.

_____ **6.** riveting   **f.** to be connected to

_____ **7.** soothing   **g.** the most recent information

_____ **8.** pastime   **h.** extremely interesting

_____ **9.** to tune in   **i.** hobby

_____ **10.** updates   **j.** comforting

One interesting project in the American Midwest is called CornCam. The editor of a farming magazine in Iowa thought that people might like watching corn grow. He pointed a digital camera at a field and fed the image to a site on the Internet every 15 minutes. That way, anyone who is interested can _____ and check the crop's progress. Nobody expected there to be much interest in this unusual project. However, watching the site has become a _____ for a number of people. They like to watch so they won't miss _____ on how fast the corn is growing. CornCam has had more than 600,000 visitors yearly to the site. Since it was started, CornCam has gained a loyal audience of mostly people living in cities. People from Iowa and from as far away as China have tuned in to the site. To some, a cornfield feels dull. To others, it's the opposite; they find it _____. Still others like to log onto the site because watching corn grow is relaxing and _____.

2 *Descriptive words and phrases often have either a positive or a negative meaning. Decide if these words are positive (+) negative (–), or neutral (*). Explain your answers to a partner.*

_____ **1.** newsworthy	_____ **8.** soothing
_____ **2.** immobilized	_____ **9.** inconsequential
_____ **3.** repetitive	_____ **10.** to come in second
_____ **4.** bias	_____ **11.** antagonism
_____ **5.** lethal	_____ **12.** sense of humor
_____ **6.** riveting	_____ **13.** advice
_____ **7.** unappealing	_____ **14.** addicted

3 *Work with a partner.*

Student A: Read Student B the statements. Switch roles after statement 2.

Student B: Cover the left column. Listen and respond in detail using the vocabulary in the right column. Use the words in any order. Then switch roles after statement 2.

Example

A: Some people complain about the news media. Can you explain some of the complaints?

B: bias, have a lock on, repetitive

I think that some people feel the news is **repetitive** because we hear the same stories over and over. News stations also have a **bias** and present only one side of a story. Some people complain that a few companies **have a lock on** most of what we watch and hear.

Student A

1. Mark Harris says he turned from being a journalist to being a novelist because he can now write about things that aren't considered newsworthy. What does he mean? Do you agree with his opinion?

2. The Buddist nun Tupton Shudrun says many people keep themselves "plugged in" to news because they don't like being quiet and alone. What does she mean? Do you agree with her?

Student B

come in second, appeal to, inconsequential

be addicted to, remedy, underlying

Now switch roles.

Student B: Ask Student A the questions.

Student A: Cover the left column. Listen and respond in detail using the vocabulary in the right column. Use the words in any order.

Student B	Student A
3. Professor John Sommerville wrote *How the News Makes Us Dumb*. He thinks that not giving all sides of the picture is something news organizations can fix. However, he thinks that people's need to know the news all the time is not something that can easily be fixed. What does he mean, and do you agree?	newsworthy, bias, remedy
4. Professor Gabrielle Speigel talked about how children are raised "in front of televisions." She also talks about the importance of time spent alone just thinking. Explain what she might mean. Do you agree?	be plugged into, come in second, get perspective on

4 Focus on Speaking

A PRONUNCIATION: Reducing and Contracting Auxiliary Verbs

- Native speakers often use contractions of the verbs **be** and **have** after a pronoun. These contractions sound friendlier and less formal.

  I've been watching the news more and more recently. My husband says I watch too much. He's started reading more instead.

  (Say "Ive" and "Hees.")

- After nouns, auxiliary verbs *are, have,* and *has* have reduced pronunciations. **Are** sounds like an *-er* ending. It is joined with the preceding word.

  Doctors are worried about our health.

  (Say "Doctorser.")

- **Have** is pronounced /əv/ (like the preposition *of*). It is joined with the preceding word.

  Some have chosen to turn off the news.

  (Say "Some of.")

- **Has** is pronounced /əz/ (like the "long plural") after some words.

  My boss has become addicted to the news.

  (Say "bosses.")

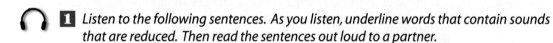

1 *Listen to the following sentences. As you listen, underline words that contain sounds that are reduced. Then read the sentences out loud to a partner.*

1. The United States has become a nation of people addicted to the news.

2. Americans are offered news in many forms.

3. Critics have been concerned about the amount of news we watch.

4. Many viewers have tuned into the CornCam website.

5. Academics are worried about the amount of news we consume.

2 *Listen to the following paragraph about our addiction to the news media. As you listen, fill in the auxiliary verb or contraction that you hear. Then read the paragraph out loud to a partner.*

Americans (**1**) _____ offered many sources of news, some of which (**2**) _____ available 24/7. The country (**3**) _____ become a nation of "news junkies," or people who (**4**) _____ addicted to the news. Some academics (**5**) _____ started to ask serious questions about the role of the news media in society. Some people believe that the media (**6**) _____ focusing on negative stories. Therefore, it focuses less on the important issues that we face. We (**7**) _____ being entertained by gossip about celebrities and politicians, but we (**8**) _____ stopped worrying about serious problems that affect our society.

B   GRAMMAR: Passive Voice

1 *Work with a partner. Read the following sentences, and then answer the questions.*

    a. When you study meditation, you become aware of how your mind <u>is influenced</u> by outside events.

    b. The CornCam website <u>has been visited</u> by people from Beijing, Russia, England, and South Africa.

    c. The way children <u>are raised</u> today, they don't have a lot of time to be by themselves.

  1. Who or what is the focus of the action in these sentences?

  2. How could you rewrite these sentences to change the focus of the action?

Passive Voice

Forming the Passive Voice

To form the **passive,** use the correct form of the verb **be** + the past participle. If the agent of the action is mentioned, use **by** + the agent.

Active	**Passive**
Many people **visit** the CornCam website every day.	The CornCam website **is visited by** many people every day.
The reporter **discussed** the upcoming election.	The upcoming election **was discussed by** the reporter.

Using the Passive Voice

- Use the passive voice to shift focus from the agent of the action to the person or thing being described.

  Tabloid newspapers **are read by** many people.

- Use the passive voice when you do not need to mention the agent of the action, or when the agent is not important.

  The news about the robbery **is being reported** in great detail.

- Use the passive voice when you don't want to mention the agent, particularly to avoid blaming the agent.

  Some factual mistakes **were made** in the article about the murder trial.

2 *News reports often use the passive voice when the agent of the action is unknown or not important, or when the speaker wants to avoid saying who the agent is. Complete the following radio reports with the passive voice, using the verbs in parentheses and the verb tenses indicated.*

"Hi. I'm Douglas O'Brian, reporting today from Iowa, where millions of people ___are being sheltered___ in temporary
1. (shelter/*present progressive*)
accommodations following a severe storm that has left

thousands stranded. Emergency services _____
2. (provide/*past*)
late into the night as water levels rose and houses

_____ . Many people _____ for
3. (flood/*past*)   **4.** (treat/*present perfect*)
shock, and panic _____ as more
5. (report/*present progressive*)
rain _____ ."
6. (predict/*present*)

"Could the actress Kelly McKee _____ as the
7. (regard/*base form*)
new sweetheart of Hollywood? Following the movie

Tales of Passion, which _____ last fall, more
8. (release/*past*)
than 10,000 fan letters _____ by her agent.
9. (count/*present perfect*)
A sequel to the movie _____ for next year.
10. (plan/*present progressive*)
One thing is certain: Ms. McKee _____ by
11. (follow/*future*)
photographers wherever she goes. Good luck, Kelly!"

"Francisco Olloa _____ by his dog, Ted, last
12. (rescue/*past*)
Friday after he fell through the ice into a pond. People

_____ by news reports that the ice was thin
13. (warn/*past perfect*)
and that they should not go near the pond, but Francisco did

not hear the reports. Francisco _____ on
14. (interview/*past*)
Good Morning, Nebraska yesterday. He said that Ted should

_____ a medal for his heroic rescue—and
15. (give/*base form*)
maybe a year's supply of dog bones, too!"

3 *Work with a partner.*

Student A: Read each statement. Switch roles after statement 4.

Student B: Respond to each statement by completing the sentence using a passive form of the verb and the verb tense indicated. Switch roles after statement 4.

Student A

1. Mark Harris found a remedy for his problem: He left his job with the newspaper.

2. There seem to be a lot of news resisters in universities.

3. Professor Spiegel said that reading helps you develop your imagination.

4. Tupton Shudrun seems to think that most news can be immobilizing and depressing.

Student B

1. Yes, it seems that he _____
   (attract / *past*)
   to teaching.

2. That's right. Universities seem

   _____ with people who
   (fill / *infinitive*)
   reject the daily news.

3. Yes, I agree. Your imagination

   _____ when you read.
   (stimulate / *present*)

4. Now, that's definitely true. I remember so

   many times when I _____
   (depress / *present perfect*)
   by bad news on TV.

Now switch roles.

Student B

5. Watching corn grow is definitely soothing!

6. This website seems to be an international success. Who does it appeal to?

7. I don't really understand the interest in watching corn grow. Some people find it riveting.

8. What other information did you learn from CornCam?

Student A

5. That's right. That's why watching corn on the

   Internet _____.
   (promote / *present progressive*)

6. Well, apparently the site

   _____ by people from
   (visit / *present perfect*)
   almost every continent!

7. The interviewer said that when they watched

   the corn, people _____ of
   (remind / *past*)
   their childhoods.

8. Farming information, mainly. For example,

   I heard planting _____ for
   (delay / *past*)
   a month this year.

C STYLE: Stating an Opinion

In any conversation or discussion, it can be important to state your own opinion or viewpoints clearly. Read these excerpts from Listenings One and Two. Notice the phrases that the speakers use to introduce their opinions.

- People keep themselves plugged in because they don't know how to be alone with themselves. Historian Gabrielle Spiegel agrees.

    <u>I have always believed that</u> there are two things you really need to get through life.

- Can CornCam be that riveting, really? What's the appeal?

    <u>I think</u> it's riveting in kind of a quiet sense.

Here are some expressions that can be used to state an opinion.

To express a strong opinion	To express an opinion	If you are unsure what you think
I really think (that) …	In my opinion …	Hmm, I'm not sure, but …
I strongly believe (that) …	I think (that) …	I'm of two minds, but …
I'm sure (that) …	I feel (that) …	Well, I don't know, but …
I have always believed (that) …		I can't make up my mind, but …

Work in a small group. Take turns presenting and responding to these ideas. Use an expression from the box when you give your opinion.

1. A: I think most reporters are just looking for sensational stories. All they want is to sell more newspapers.

   B: <u>I agree. **I really think** newspapers have been influenced too much by</u>

   <u>sensational stories on TV.</u>

2. A: News resisters are crazy!

   B: _____

3. A: I could easily give up reading newspapers every day, couldn't you?

   B: _____

4. A: Do you think that news is always depressing?

   B: _____

5. A: Fantasy and a sense of humor are enough for me.

   B: _____

6. A: Sometimes people on the street are interviewed on TV news. How do you like hearing their opinions on important topics?

   B: _____

7. A: CornCam is ridiculous. I'd never waste my time watching it.

   B: _____

8. A: Newspapers will soon disappear. Everyone will be reading news on the Internet.

   B: _____

9. A: Do you agree that people don't know how to be alone these days?

   B: _____

10. A: Do you think it's better to get your news monthly, not daily?

   B: _____

D   SPEAKING TOPIC

Imagine that you are going to produce a "new" type of news broadcast.

Step 1:   Work in a small group. In Listenings One and Two, you heard some criticisms of the type of news that is common today as well as some ideas about how to improve it. Now, imagine that you are trying to establish a weekly television program that would appeal to news resisters. Read the following suggestions for some new and improved news objectives.

- *Objective:* to present news about those who come in second—news that is not about winners and people who make it to the top, but that concerns ordinary people who have had both successes *and* failures in their lives

- *Objective:* to present news that gives a historical perspective—news that focuses on how historical events are connected to current events, rather than on just the events themselves

- *Objective:* to present news that tries to solve real-life problems— news that is directly targeted not only to learning about problems that face us, but also to taking active steps to solve them

Step 2:   Read the news summaries below and decide how you could present them to reflect one of the objectives on the previous page. As you discuss them, use the expressions from the box on page 21 to explain your ideas.

- Candidates battle to be the party's nominee in an upcoming mayoral election.

- An elderly woman helps out regularly in her local hospital.

- A new device has been invented to help blind people get around.

- A young man has been arrested in your town for speeding.

- A major fire is burning out of control in a rural area.

- A new weight-loss product has been approved for sale.

Step 3:   Choose one story from the list above. Use your imagination to fill in the details. Then record a two- to three-minute news broadcast about it. Use passives from the grammar box on page 18 to explain your ideas. Here is an example.

"Good evening, everybody. Tonight, I want to tell you an inspiring story about a youth baseball team from the rural town of Oxville that has made it to the national finals. This team was first discovered last year by a business executive who was vacationing nearby. He recognized the team's potential and made a generous financial contribution to them so that they could buy uniforms. This is a beautiful story, because even though the team has been eliminated from the competition for several years, the team members haven't given up. The pitcher says that he has always dreamed of reaching the finals. He read a book when he was only a small boy about overcoming difficulties, and he thought, 'I can do something great in my life!' Let's talk to him now. . . ."

Step 4:   Take turns presenting your news broadcasts to the class. Ask the class to guess which objective your news presentation demonstrates.

E   RESEARCH TOPICS

Report on one of these topics related to the media.

1. What do TV and radio programs try to accomplish? Watch a TV news program or listen to a radio news report. Make a list of the stories that are reported. Place a check (✓) under the goals that apply to each news story. Discuss your results with the class.

NEWS STORY	SOLVES PROBLEMS	MAKES A HISTORICAL CONNECTION	IS SOOTHING	SHOWS DESPAIR

2. Visit a local newspaper, TV station, or radio station, or invite a speaker from one of these organizations to visit your class. Ask questions about the business, including some on the following topics. Then discuss with the class what you found most interesting or surprising about what you learned.

readership/audience   strategies to boost circulation
content   advertising
editorial decisions   influence of the Internet and/or cable TV

For Unit 1 Internet activities, visit the NorthStar Companion Website at http://www.longman.com/northstar.

The Achilles Heel

1 Focus on the Topic

A PREDICTING

Look at the photograph and the title of the unit. Then discuss these questions with a partner or small group.

1. The people in the photograph are members of the Achilles* Track Club, an international organization for athletes with disabilities. What obstacles do you think the athletes have to overcome?

2. What do you think the unit will be about?

---

* Achilles was a figure in Greek mythology whose one weakness was a weak or vulnerable spot in his heel. His name and the term *Achilles heel* have become synonymous with the problems and obstacles that people face in their lives.

B   SHARING INFORMATION

Many people believe that each of us has an "Achilles heel" to overcome. Look at this list of common obstacles. Have you, or has someone you know, ever faced one of them?

illness	discrimination	learning disability
injury	lack of money	lack of self-confidence
shyness	physical disability	low grades in school

Work with a partner or small group. Discuss how you or the person you know faced the obstacle.

- What happened? Did you, or the person who faced the obstacle, finally overcome it? How?

- What were the most difficult aspects of facing this challenge?

- What lessons did this experience teach you or the person you have described?

C   PREPARING TO LISTEN

BACKGROUND

The ability to overcome obstacles is a highly regarded value in American culture. Many believe it shows that a person is strong and willing to work hard to achieve goals. Yet some people are shy about discussing personal challenges. In some cultures, it may even be seen as a sign of weakness to admit difficulties.

One place where you may be asked to describe a personal obstacle is on a college application essay. On one part of the application, students list the facts: academic grades, awards, and participation in sports, teams, clubs, and organizations. In the essay section, students have an opportunity to present their personalities. This gives an admissions committee a chance to know what makes students unique: what drives their passions, fires their intellect, and makes them special and different from everyone else. According to the *Chronicle of Higher Education,* reading applicants' essays is the main way colleges have of understanding students' personalities.

When students write their college essays, they usually have to respond to a general question in a personal way. Successful essays often tell about experiences—such as overcoming obstacles—that have inspired the writers or made them grow in some important way. Applicants are encouraged to discuss the topic clearly and concisely, in their own style. This could include using stories, dialogue, humor, or images.

Work in a small group. What personal qualities of college applicants do you think are most important? Look at the list below. Add two more qualities to the list. Then pick the top three qualities that you would look for in a college applicant if you were a member of an admissions committee. Discuss your selections with your group.

curiosity	tolerance	flexibility
perseverance	ambition	_____
independent thinking	sense of humor	_____
compassion		

VOCABULARY FOR COMPREHENSION

Read the words and phrases and their definitions. Then complete the sentences using the correct word or phrase.

- **had in store for:** had planned for
- **revelation:** insight, discovery
- **landscape:** a view across an area of land
- **soared:** flew very high or fast
- **mangled:** damaged badly
- **collapsed:** fell down suddenly
- **crushed:** pressed something so hard it broke
- **crutches:** special sticks used under the arm to help a person walk
- **perseverance:** determination to keep trying
- **compassion:** a strong feeling of sympathy for a creature who is suffering
- **overcome:** succeed in controlling a problem
- **proof:** facts that prove that something is true
- **limitations:** things that keep you from going beyond certain boundaries
- **scars:** marks left on skin from a cut or wound

1. Sometimes an important event can cause us to have a _____, leading us to see something in a new way.

2. The mountain _____ was dotted with tiny cottages and trees.

3. An eagle _____ over our heads, inspiring us with its powerful beauty.

4. We _____ the dried flowers into a powder and boiled them to make tea.

5. Luckily no one was inside the old barn when it _____ under the weight of the snow.

6. As a result of the accident, the car was _____ beyond repair. It looked like a twisted pile of metal and nothing more.

7. He is the kind of person who doesn't accept the idea of _____. Even if you tell him he can't do something, he will always try.

8. She had a bad accident when she was a child. The _____ have never completely healed.

9. The girl used _____ to help her walk until her broken leg got better.

10. I admire Anna's _____. She never gives up once she starts to do something.

11. Howard tried to _____ his fear of flying by forcing himself to fly as often as possible.

12. Carolina has enormous _____ for animals and seems to understand them very well.

13. For my friend who is blind, graduating with honors was _____ that he could overcome great obstacles if he had the determination.

14. We didn't know in advance what the mountain-climbing adventure _____ us, but we decided to go ahead and try it.

2 Focus on Listening

A   LISTENING ONE: *Dreams of Flying and Overcoming Obstacles*

You will hear the introduction to a radio broadcast. Bob Edwards, of National Public Radio's *Morning Edition,* talks about a special college application essay.

🎧 *Listen to the introduction, and answer the questions.*

1. More than 150 essays were sent to the radio station. Thinking about the theme of the unit, how do you think the radio station chose which essays to broadcast?

   _____

2. Many people write about overcoming obstacles, but Richard Van Ornum wrote about it in a very creative way. What are some ways a person could describe obstacles creatively?

   _____

LISTENING FOR MAIN IDEAS

🎧 *You will hear Richard Van Ornum describe his dreams and his reality. Listen to the essay and answer the questions.*

1. What did Richard dream about when he was a young boy?

   _____

2. What happened to Richard when he was a young boy?

   _____

3. What was the revelation that Richard had?

   _____

4. What lessons has Richard learned from his experiences?

   _____

LISTENING FOR DETAILS

🎧 *Listen to the essay again. As you listen, write whether each statement is true (T) or false (F).*

_____ 1. As a child, Richard used to dream about falling down.

_____ 2. As a child, Richard always dreamed about the same landscape.

_____ 3. Richard had an accident when he was six.

_____ 4. He was forced to get around in a wheelchair.

_____ 5. Richard was in Britain when he had a revelation.

_____ 6. He was sitting in San Marco Square.

_____ 7. Richard can now walk.

_____ 8. He dreamed he was flying over the Red Sea.

REACTING TO THE LISTENING

1 *Listen to the excerpts and answer the questions that follow.*

Excerpt One

1. To tell his story, Richard uses a variety of related words. What two other verbs are similar to *flying*? What do these words mean? _____

_____

2. What one other word is similar to *collapse*? What does it mean? _____

_____

3. How does Richard's use of a variety of related words improve his story? ____

_____

Excerpt Two

4. To tell his story, Richard also repeats some structures (parallel structure). What phrases does he repeat with forms of the word *could*? _____

_____

5. How does this repetition improve his story? _____

_____

Excerpt Three

6. Here Richard repeats structures with *knew*. What three phrases does he use?

_____

7. How does this repetition improve his story? _____

_____

Excerpt Four

8. Richard also uses many related prepositional phrases about physical location. Complete the phrases in the list below by adding the correct prepositions.

   a. _____ the rooftop   c. _____ the left

   b. _____ a ledge   d. _____ me

9. How does this repetition improve his story? _____

_____

2 *Work in a small group. Discuss the following questions.*

1. Richard suffered physical hardships after a truck hit him. He could have become angry and resentful and blamed the truck driver. Yet in his essay, he never mentioned the driver, only the truck itself. What does this show about him?

2. Richard's essay was selected for broadcast throughout the United States. What qualities might make this essay appeal to many people? What parts of the essay appeal to you? Why?

3. How do you believe Richard's mother helped him to become stronger? When we are facing difficult challenges, how do the attitudes of the people around us help or hurt us?

B ▐ **LISTENING TWO:** *The Achilles Track Club Climbs Mount Kilimanjaro*

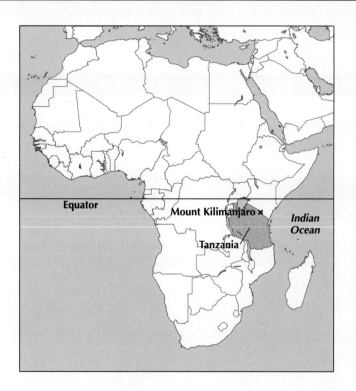

Mount Kilimanjaro is a mountain in Tanzania, East Africa. Its peak is the highest point in Africa at 19,340 feet (5,895 meters). Because it is approximately 200 miles south of the equator, Kilimanjaro's climate is extreme, with tropical weather at the base and arctic-like temperatures and strong winds closer to the peak.

You will hear a television news report about a group of athletes from the Achilles Track Club who climbed Mount Kilimanjaro. Before you listen, think about what would be difficult about climbing this mountain. Then think about what might make it difficult for a person with a disability. Discuss your ideas with the class.

🎧 **1** *Listen to the report, and answer the questions. Share your answers with the class.*

1. How many climbers were there? _____

2. What disabilities did the climbers have? _____

3. What record did the group set? _____

4. Who gave the climbers their inspiration? _____

2 *Work with a partner. Discuss your reaction to the story of the Achilles Track Club project. What makes it special and inspirational to other people?*

3 *Many people dislike the term* disabled. *They would rather use terms such as* differently abled *or* physically challenged. *With a partner, analyze the words and explain why people have different reactions to them. What term do you think the Achilles Track Club athletes would choose to describe themselves? Why?*

C   LINKING LISTENINGS ONE AND TWO

Complete the chart comparing Richard Van Ornum and the Achilles Track Club. Then discuss the questions with the class.

QUESTIONS	RICHARD VAN ORNUM	ACHILLES TRACK CLUB
1. What physical obstacles were these people trying to overcome?		
2. What were their goals? What were their difficulties in achieving these goals?		
3. What personal qualities helped them to achieve their goals?		
4. Was their achievement strictly personal? Did it also have a wider meaning or lesson for others?		

1. What do you think is the main similarity between these two stories?

2. What is the main difference between what these people achieved?

3 Focus on Vocabulary

1 *During their ascent of Mount Kilimanjaro, one of the members of the Achilles Track Club kept an online journal similar to the one below. Fill in the blanks with the words that are listed above each paragraph.*

landscape	inspiration	scattered
challenging	determined	swooping

Ascent of Mt. Kilimanjaro

To: All my friends   **Subject:** Day One

Dear Friends in New York,

Hi, everyone! We're at the foot of this amazing mountain. It's over 5,895 meters high. That's 19,340 feet. This will be the most **(1)** _____ thing I've ever done, but I'm really **(2)** _____ to succeed. I think we're carrying a message of **(3)** _____ and hope. I'm not in good shape, but I've set a high goal for myself anyway. If I reach it, maybe others will try to do the same.

From up here, the **(4)** _____ is spectacular. There are some houses **(5)** _____ around the base of the hill. Birds are **(6)** _____ down all around me. This is beautiful!

---

recognize	recognition	collapsed	inspirational

Ascent of Mt. Kilimanjaro

To: All my friends   **Subject:** Day Three

Dear all,

We have spent the last two days getting used to the altitude. The air is kind of thin up here! After a day of climbing, I **(7)** _____ into bed last night. When I opened the tent this morning, I saw a small figure in the distance. At first I didn't **(8)** _____ her, but when I called out, "Hello," she responded by waving. It was one of the other athletes. She was admiring the beauty of the sunrise. It was a very **(9)** _____ moment. Now I can't wait to get going!

I am getting a lot of **(10)** _____ from the others. They're always commenting on the things I do well and telling me how strong I am, both physically and emotionally. The guides are very strong climbers and they give us the physical support we need, and of course I need that.

| courageous | judging | perseverance |
| empowerment | limitations | |

Ascent of Mt. Kilimanjaro

To: All my friends   **Subject:** Day Five

Hi, everyone,

   I can't believe I am writing this, but the summit is very close. This is such a spectacular and imposing place. I am so glad I decided to take part in this project. And now our **(11)** _____ is finally paying off. I will be able to say that as a cancer survivor, I have scaled one of the highest mountains in the world! Sometimes people seem to look at disabled people with sympathy. Other people almost seem annoyed that we try to do things they think are impossible. It's as if they are **(12)** _____ us negatively for not acting helpless or something. They probably don't mean to hurt us, but it's sometimes hard to ignore them.

   But now, I think that despite all our **(13)** _____, we have done something really special—something that hardly anybody manages to do. I feel so proud that my teammates have been so **(14)** _____. I think that we are bringing a message of **(15)** _____ to everyone who wants to overcome a difficult challenge.

| altitude | peak | soaring |
| had in store for | proof | tough |

Ascent of Mt. Kilimanjaro

To: All my friends   **Subject:** Day Seven

Hello, everyone,

   Get ready to hear the good news . . . We're here! We're at the **(16)** _____! When we got to the top, we took a photo of the group as **(17)** _____ that we made it! ☺ Then we released a bag of feathers into the air, to symbolize our story going out to other people. This has been an amazing experience, but you can't believe how **(18)** _____ it was. I can't believe we made it. Last week we were standing at the bottom of the mountain and we didn't know what it **(19)** _____ us. The **(20)** _____ was really hard to deal with, but we didn't give up!

   There are birds **(21)** _____ below us, and the air is clear. I want to remember this day forever.

2 *Read this information, and do the exercise that follows.*

In Listening One, Richard Van Ornum uses certain words and phrases to mean something different from what they most commonly mean. For example, look at the way the word *weight* is used in the first sentence. Compare it to the way Van Ornum uses it in the second sentence:

- The <u>weight</u> of most cars is over 1,000 pounds.

- "I would realize that no real person could fly, and I'd collapse on the floor, crushed by the <u>weight</u> of my own limitations."

In the first sentence, *weight* means the heaviness of something in pounds or kilograms. It is concrete and physical. This meaning is called the *literal meaning*. In the second sentence, *weight* means mental burden or pressure. This meaning is called the *figurative meaning*. It creates a picture or image in the mind.

*Work with a partner. Read the sentences, and focus on the underlined phrases. Write **L** (literal) or **F** (figurative) for each sentence. Discuss your choices with each other. Then explain them to the class.*

1. _____ **a.** Andrea <u>got to the top of</u> the class by working hard.

 _____ **b.** The Achilles Track Club finally <u>got to the top of</u> the mountain.

2. _____ **a.** While Charlotte was working late every night, she couldn't prepare dinner for her children. They had to <u>make it</u> for themselves.

 _____ **b.** Charlotte decided to enter the marathon to support cancer research. She knew she was going to <u>make it</u> when she got close to the final stretch of the race.

3. _____ **a.** After several film failures at the box office, the movie director knew he had to <u>turn</u> his career <u>around</u> by doing something very different.

 _____ **b.** When the runner realized he was going in the wrong direction, he <u>turned around</u> and headed the other way.

4. _____ **a.** Jackie dropped his keys in the lake and had to <u>reach deep down</u> into the mud to find them.

 _____ **b.** When the mountain climber thought she was too weak to take another step, she <u>reached deep down</u> inside herself and found the determination to make it back to the camp.

5. _____ **a.** The Achilles athletes <u>reached a high point</u> in their climb and stopped to admire the view.

 _____ **b.** I <u>reached a high point</u> in my career when I finally got the recognition I felt I deserved.

3 *Work with a partner. Take turns asking each other these questions. Use the underlined words in your answers. Before you begin, look at the questions and jot down a few notes to help you when it's your turn to speak.*

1. Did you ever manage to <u>get to the top of</u> your class in a particular subject?

2. The Achilles athletes really wanted to <u>make it</u> to the top. What do you think helped them succeed?

3. After Richard had that experience in Italy, he was able to really <u>turn</u> his life <u>around</u>. Has anything like that happened to you?

4. When have you had to <u>reach deep down</u> inside yourself to find unusual strength or courage?

5. Have you ever felt that you had <u>reached a high point</u> in your academic or work career, or in a sport or hobby?

4 Focus on Speaking

A   PRONUNCIATION: Thought Groups

- When we speak, we group words together and join the groups into sentences. The groups are called thought groups. They help the listener organize the meaning of the sentence. Look at the thought groups in the following sentence.

  My Achilles heel was shyness.

- Thought groups are often grammatical phrases or structures, like prepositional phrases or short clauses.

  When I was little, I dreamed I was flying.

- Words can be combined into thought groups in different ways. Look at the two ways to group the words in the following sentence.

  I was on the roof of the Cathedral of San Marcos.

  I was on the roof of the Cathedral of San Marcos.

- Pronounce the words in a thought group together smoothly. Join thought groups together by holding the end of a thought group briefly before you start the next group.

  My Achilles heel was shyness.

1 *Listen to the following sentences. As you listen, mark the thought groups. With a partner, compare thought groups, and practice reading the sentences to each other.*

1. When Richard was little, he dreamed he was flying.

2. He looked at his scar and imagined it was an eagle.

3. When he visited Venice, he realized that he had great gifts.

4. He suddenly realized that he could overcome his obstacles.

5. The essay he wrote about his experience was chosen for broadcast.

2 *Look at the following two charts. They contain three sentences each. Read the first thought group from column 1, and find the best way to complete the sentence by choosing one thought group from each of columns 2, 3, and 4. Then do the same with the next two thought groups in column 1. Read the completed sentences to a partner.*

1	2	3	4
Richard's scar	hit Richard Van Ornum	that was flying	after the accident
A runaway truck	was mangled	and he couldn't walk	in preschool
Richard's leg	looked like an eagle	when he was on a field trip	on his leg

1	2	3	4
The Achilles Track Club	showed photos	that decided to undertake	as they climbed the mountain
The athletes	who participated in the climb	of the athletes	about their achievement
Many newspapers	is the organization	talked emotionally	this remarkable project

3 *Work with a partner. Write a short conversation beginning with one of the sentences below. Mark your sentences for thought groups. Then read your conversations out loud.*

- I also remember a dream I had a long time ago . . .

- I also have an Achilles heel . . .

- I had an experience that was a revelation to me . . .

A: _____

B: _____

A: _____

B: _____

A: _____

B: _____

B GRAMMAR: Gerunds and Infinitives

1 *Work with a partner. Read the sentences below, and then answer the questions.*

a. It is a story of <u>reaching</u> new heights and <u>overcoming</u> great odds.

b. Of course, I always hit the ground, but not before <u>remembering</u> that I'd been dreaming.

c. <u>Getting</u> to the top was definitely the high point.

d. I'd leap off my bed, expecting <u>to soar</u> out of the window.

e. I just wanted <u>to reach</u> deep down and grab all the energy I had.

1. In sentences a, b, and c, what do the underlined verbs have in common?

2. In sentences d and e, what do the underlined verbs have in common?

Gerunds and Infinitives

Gerunds

To form the gerund, add *-ing* to the base form of the verb:

Use of the Gerund

Use the gerund as the subject of a sentence.

Use the gerund as the object of a sentence after certain verbs, such as *avoid, stop, continue,* and *recommend.*

Use the gerund after a preposition, such as *for, in, of,* and *about.*

Examples

It's a story of **reaching** new heights and **overcoming** great odds.

Getting to the top of the mountain was a great achievement for the athletes.

Richard Van Ornum almost **stopped dreaming** completely.

Throughout his childhood, Richard thought **about walking** again.

Infinitives

To form the infinitive, use *to* and the base form of the verb:

Use of the Infinitive

Use the infinitive after a *be* + **adjective** combination such as *happy, willing, ready, prepared,* and *reluctant.*

Use the infinitive after certain verbs, including *agree, decide, expect, hope, learn, manage, need, try,* and *want.*

Use the infinitive after certain nouns, such as *ability* and *freedom.*

Examples

I'd leap off my bed expecting **to soar** out of the window.

The athletes **were ready to do** whatever they had to do so that they could carry their message of inspiration to the top of the mountain.

One of the Achilles athletes did not **expect to reach** the summit and almost turned back several times.

He had the **ability to accomplish** anything he wanted.

2 *Look at the following flyer. It contains a list of devices that can help the disabled. With a partner, discuss how these devices might improve the everyday lives of disabled people. Use the expressions in the box below the flyer and gerunds and infinitives.*

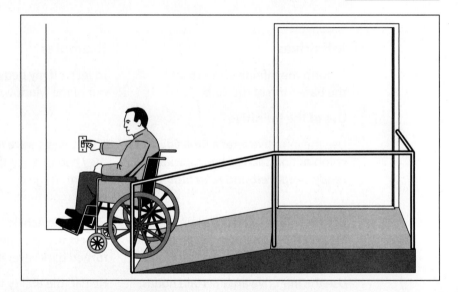

Tips to Make Your Home or Community Accessible for the Disabled

- Ramps at the entrances to buildings
- Braille signs in public elevators
- Wide doorways and hallways
- Baths/showers with grip bars
- Low light switches
- Mechanical lifts

- Contrasting colors on ledges, counter edges, and steps
- Strobe lights on smoke and burglar alarms
- Raised buttons on appliances
- New ideas? _____

Makes it easier …	People can try …
Allows people …	This device is good for …
Stops people from …	It will make people aware of …
When people are ready …	It gives people freedom …
People need …	

3 *Read this information, and do the exercise that follows.*

Since the Americans with Disabilities Act was passed in the United States in 1990, more people have become aware of the changes that must be made in public places to allow disabled individuals to deal with their challenges. Government and city officials have more responsibility to provide access to services for people with disabilities.

Work with a partner. Think about the difficulties that a person with a disability has doing everyday tasks. Complete the chart so that each statement indicates the view of an advocate for the disabled or the view of a government or city official. Use verbs in either the infinitive or the gerund form. Add as much information as you can.

Discuss other innovations that might help the disabled. Then discuss whether your town or city has implemented such ideas.

ADVOCATE FOR DISABLED INDIVIDUALS	GOVERNMENT OR CITY OFFICIAL
Getting around the city is very hard.	The city has agreed
presents a real challenge.	We need
must be extremely difficult.	We will try
Disabled people are forced to learn	We should be prepared
They often can't manage	We should be ready
They must be reluctant	We should avoid
I'm sure they would be happy	We are willing

C STYLE: Using Narrative Techniques

Richard Van Ornum tells his story vividly. Read these excerpts from Listening One.

- When I was little, I dreamed I was <u>flying</u>. . . . I would wake up thinking it was true and I'd <u>leap</u> off my bed, expecting to <u>soar</u> out the window.
- <u>I knew</u> what my gifts were. . . . <u>And I also knew</u> what my first obstacles had been. . . . <u>But I knew</u> that the obstacles weren't impossible.

- Sitting <u>on the rooftop</u> of the Cathedral of San Marco, I wasn't sure what life had in store for me. . . . <u>To the left</u>, the Grand Canal snaked off into the sea. . . . <u>Below me</u> in the square, pigeons swirled away from the children.

Notice the narrative techniques he uses.

• Synonyms or closely related words	"flying … leap … soar"
• Parallelism, which repeats a grammatical structure again and again	"I knew … And I also knew … But I knew"
• Several prepositional phrases about physical location	"on the rooftop … to the left … below me"

1 *Work with a partner. Read the newspaper clipping about the Achilles Track Club's climb. Underline synonyms or closely related words, draw a circle around parallelism, and draw a box around prepositional phrases about physical location.*

Members of the Achilles Track Club, an organization for people with disabilities, have just managed to climb Kilimanjaro, one of the highest mountain peaks in the world. On their backs they carried their equipment, but in their hearts they also carried the hopes and dreams of everyone who at some point in their lives has felt afraid, fearful, or intimidated. As they reached the summit, with the mist below them, the peaks all around them, and the sun above them, their hearts were full of pride and joy. They showed us the truth in the words of American writer Ralph Waldo Emerson: "What lies behind us and what lies before us are tiny matters compared to what lies within us."

2 *Work with a partner. Use the narrative techniques above to describe the climbing experience from the point of view of a member of the Achilles Track Club. Use the steps on page 43 as a guide.*

Step 1
Imagine the challenge ahead of you. Describe the scenery.

Step 2
Imagine that you are cold and exhausted from the climb. Describe your progress so far.

Step 3
Imagine that you have reached the peak. Describe the spectacular view and your feelings.

D SPEAKING TOPICS

1 *Plan a two- to three-minute speech about an important event or period in your life or about an obstacle you have overcome.*

Step 1: As you plan, keep in mind the deeper meaning the event had for you. Use the following guidelines to strengthen the impact of your account.

1. Enrich your narrative with the three narrative techniques from the style section on pages 41–42: related words, related structures, and related prepositional phrases about physical location.

2. Use the information in the left column of the chart below to plan your speech. Take notes in the right column.

The Beginning A description of the challenge or obstacle you faced	
The Hard Part What you did to address the problem or face the challenge; the personal qualities this required	
The Success How you felt when you finally managed to overcome your difficulties	

Step 2:   Present your speech to the class or record it to play for the class.

2 *Work in a small group. Imagine that you need to write a college application essay.*

1. What topic would you choose? What personal strengths would you want to reveal? What example or experience would you recount? Discuss your ideas with your group, and prepare an oral version of the essay. Present it to the class.

2. After your presentation, go back to your group, and discuss what each presentation revealed about the person's personality. Would the presentations work well as written essays on college applications? Explain why or why not.

E   RESEARCH TOPICS

Report on one of these topics related to overcoming obstacles.

1. Many movies have been made about the heroism and achievements of people who have overcome obstacles. Some examples are *Forrest Gump* (developmental disability), *My Left Foot* (physical disability), *Rain Man* (autism), *Philadelphia* (AIDS), and *A Beautiful Mind* (mental illness). In a small group, research movies that are available on video and DVD, and choose one to watch. Describe the movie to the rest of the class. Focus on how it shows someone overcoming obstacles.

2. Visit the library or do research online to find recent newspaper and magazine articles about disabilities. You can focus on the need to improve workplace or public access for disabled individuals, the educational needs of disabled students, or other topics that interest you.
   • Read the article and take notes.
   • Prepare a short oral summary of the article.
   • Present your summary to the class. Explain what was interesting about your research, and answer questions from the class.

For Unit 2 Internet activities, visit the NorthStar Companion Website at http://www.longman.com/northstar.

Early to Bed, Early to Rise . . .

"I couldn't sleep."

1 Focus on the Topic

A PREDICTING

Look at the cartoon and the title of the unit. Then discuss these questions with a partner or small group.

1. Describe the cartoon. What is the man doing? Why?

2. The title of this unit comes from a fifteenth-century proverb about the importance of sleep. The complete proverb is, "Early to bed, early to rise, makes you healthy, wealthy, and wise." What does it mean? Do you agree with it?

B SHARING INFORMATION

Work with a partner. Exchange information about each other's sleep habits. Take notes on what your partner says. Report your findings to the class. Be sure to mention anything interesting or unusual that you find out.

	YOU	YOUR PARTNER
Before going to bed • Do you usually eat or drink anything? If so, what? • Do you watch TV or read a book? If so, what? • Do you spend time thinking or planning the next day? • What else do you do?		
During the night • Do you often get up during the night? If so, how many times? • Do you have dreams or nightmares? • Do you snore, kick, or walk in your sleep? • What else do you do?		
In the morning • Are you in a good mood? • Do you need an alarm clock to wake up? • Do you need to drink tea or coffee to feel alert? • What else do you do?		

C   PREPARING TO LISTEN

BACKGROUND

We spend nearly a third of our lives asleep. For centuries, people have talked about how much we need a good night's rest. Lately, doctors have begun to consider this an area of human behavior that should be seriously studied. Are Americans getting enough sleep?

Recent research by the National Sleep Foundation showed that millions of people in the United States are sleep deprived, meaning that they just do not get enough sleep. Most people need eight hours of sleep per night, but 33 percent of adult Americans sleep for less than seven. And when people shortchange themselves of sleep night after night, they develop a "sleep debt," meaning that they "owe" their body many hours of sleep, which they may never repay.

The following shows some startling results of various sleep research studies done in the United States. Match the category on the left with the percentages (%) on the right. Then check your answers below. Did any of the results surprise you?

Category   **Percentage**

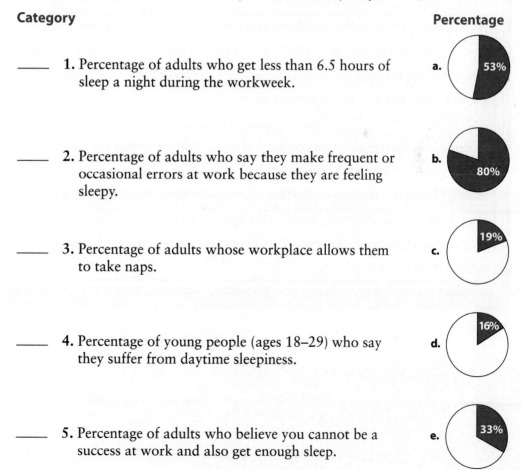

_____ 1. Percentage of adults who get less than 6.5 hours of sleep a night during the workweek.   a. 53%

_____ 2. Percentage of adults who say they make frequent or occasional errors at work because they are feeling sleepy.   b. 80%

_____ 3. Percentage of adults whose workplace allows them to take naps.   c. 19%

_____ 4. Percentage of young people (ages 18–29) who say they suffer from daytime sleepiness.   d. 16%

_____ 5. Percentage of adults who believe you cannot be a success at work and also get enough sleep.   e. 33%

Answers: 1. e   2. c   3. d   4. a   5. b

VOCABULARY FOR COMPREHENSION

Read this correspondence between an 18-year-old college student and the staff of an online health hotline at his university. Match the underlined words with the definitions that follow. Write the correct numbers in the blanks on page 49.

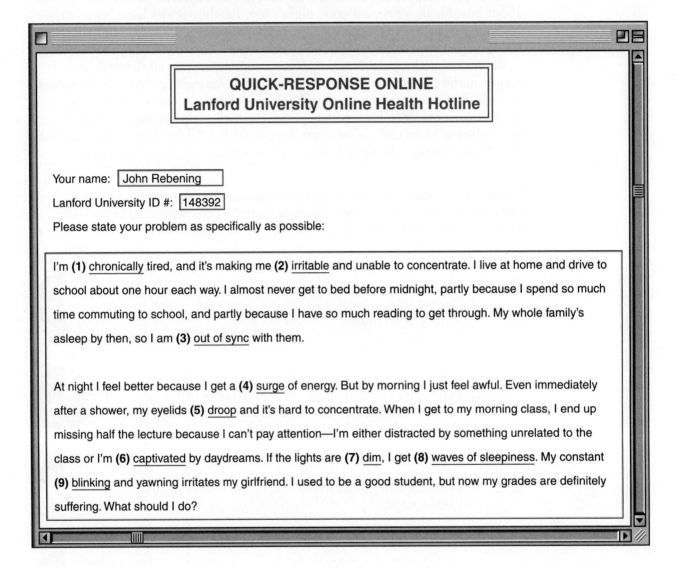

QUICK-RESPONSE ONLINE
Lanford University Online Health Hotline

Your name: John Rebening

Lanford University ID #: 148392

Please state your problem as specifically as possible:

I'm **(1)** chronically tired, and it's making me **(2)** irritable and unable to concentrate. I live at home and drive to school about one hour each way. I almost never get to bed before midnight, partly because I spend so much time commuting to school, and partly because I have so much reading to get through. My whole family's asleep by then, so I am **(3)** out of sync with them.

At night I feel better because I get a **(4)** surge of energy. But by morning I just feel awful. Even immediately after a shower, my eyelids **(5)** droop and it's hard to concentrate. When I get to my morning class, I end up missing half the lecture because I can't pay attention—I'm either distracted by something unrelated to the class or I'm **(6)** captivated by daydreams. If the lights are **(7)** dim, I get **(8)** waves of sleepiness. My constant **(9)** blinking and yawning irritates my girlfriend. I used to be a good student, but now my grades are definitely suffering. What should I do?

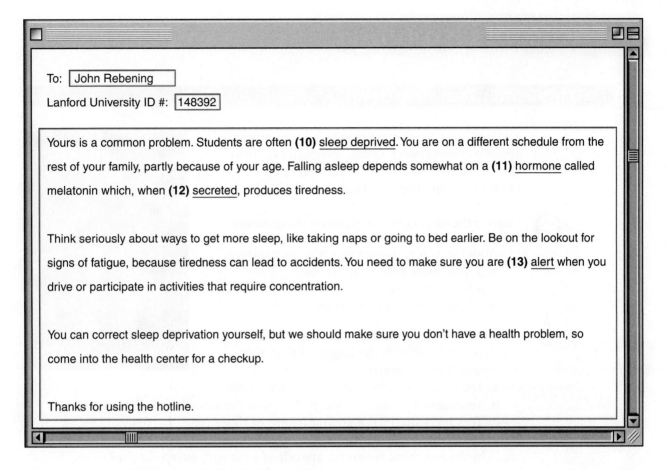

To: John Rebening

Lanford University ID #: 148392

Yours is a common problem. Students are often **(10)** <u>sleep deprived</u>. You are on a different schedule from the rest of your family, partly because of your age. Falling asleep depends somewhat on a **(11)** <u>hormone</u> called melatonin which, when **(12)** <u>secreted</u>, produces tiredness.

Think seriously about ways to get more sleep, like taking naps or going to bed earlier. Be on the lookout for signs of fatigue, because tiredness can lead to accidents. You need to make sure you are **(13)** <u>alert</u> when you drive or participate in activities that require concentration.

You can correct sleep deprivation yourself, but we should make sure you don't have a health problem, so come into the health center for a checkup.

Thanks for using the hotline.

_____ **a.** a chemical substance in the body

_____ **b.** produced and released

_____ **c.** closing and opening the eyes quickly

_____ **d.** able to think clearly

_____ **e.** permanently, constantly

_____ **f.** a boost, increase

_____ **g.** on a completely different schedule

_____ **h.** easily and quickly annoyed

_____ **i.** sag, or hang

_____ **j.** low, not bright

_____ **k.** strong feelings of fatigue

_____ **l.** short of sleep

_____ **m.** attracted by; interested in

2 Focus on Listening

A LISTENING ONE: *Teen Sleep Needs*

You will hear an introduction to a radio report about teenagers' sleep needs, in which National Public Radio's Michelle Trudeau interviews a number of experts in the field.

 Listen to the introduction, and answer the questions.

1. About how long do teenagers want to sleep?
   a. a little more than eight hours
   b. a little more than nine hours
   c. a little more than ten hours

2. How does the length of time that teenagers sleep compare with the length of time that young children sleep?
   a. Teenagers sleep for a shorter length of time.
   b. Teenagers and children sleep for about the same length of time.
   c. Teenagers sleep for a greater length of time.

3. Why do you think teenagers are out of sync with everyone else?

   _____

4. What do you think you might learn from this report?

   _____

LISTENING FOR MAIN IDEAS

 You will now hear comments by several authorities on sleep, including Dr. William Dement, Dr. Mary Carskadon, and researcher Ronald Dahl. Listen to the report and answer the questions.

1. Why do teenagers tend to stay up so late at night?

   Teenagers are "night owls" because they have a lot to do. Also, . . .

   _____

2. How does sleep deprivation affect teenagers' school experience?

   _____

   _____

3. What dangers can adolescents face as a result of their sleep deprivation?

_____

_____

4. How does sleepiness affect teenagers' emotional state?

_____

_____

LISTENING FOR DETAILS

 Listen to the interview again. As you listen, circle the letter of the correct answer to each of the following questions.

1. When is melatonin secreted in adolescents?
   a. before 10:00 P.M.
   b. around 11:00 P.M.
   c. after midnight

2. Which of the following statements about melatonin is *not* true?
   a. It is secreted in the morning.
   b. It is a hormone.
   c. It "turns on" in the evening.

3. What time do most high schools begin?
   a. 7:30 A.M.
   b. 8:00 A.M.
   c. 9:00 A.M.

4. In Dement's lab experiments conducted during the morning in a quiet environment, how many minutes did it take for the teenagers to fall asleep?
   a. less than two and a half
   b. less than three and a half
   c. less than eight and a half

5. Most teenagers need to sleep more than they do. About how many more hours per night do they need on average?
   a. one
   b. two
   c. three

6. How many high school students in the United States are chronically sleep deprived?
   a. 97 percent
   b. 85 percent
   c. 35 percent

7. About how far does a car travel during the time it takes for a person's eyelids to blink?
   a. 6 feet
   b. 16 feet
   c. 60 feet

8. About how many traffic accidents are caused by teenagers?
   a. fewer than half
   b. more than half
   c. 89 percent

9. Which of the following effects of sleep deprivation is *not* mentioned in the interview?
   a. reaction time
   b. sadness and frustration
   c. poor family relationships

REACTING TO THE LISTENING

 1 *Listen to the excerpts from the interview and answer the two questions that follow the chart. For question 1, use the chart to choose one or two adjectives describing the feeling. For question 2, use the chart to decide how the feeling is expressed in the voice.*

Adjectives Describing the Feeling		How the Feeling Is Expressed in the Voice
playful	enthusiastic	changes in intonation (a rise or fall in tone)
aggressive	amused	exaggerated word stress (a word is pronounced particularly loudly)
shocked	unhappy	
respectful	confused	elongated word length (a word is "stretched out")

Excerpt One

You will hear Dr. Mary Carskadon's explanation of the effect of melatonin and then a comment by the interviewer.

1. What feeling does the interviewer express? _____

2. How is the feeling expressed in the voice? _____

Excerpt Two

You will hear a comment by Dr. Dement and then a comment by the interviewer.

3. What feeling does the interviewer express? _____

4. How is this feeling expressed in the voice? _____

Excerpt Three

You will hear a student comment about feeling tired.

5. What feeling does the student express? _____

6. How is this feeling expressed in the voice? _____

Excerpt Four

You will hear Dr. Dement comment on teenagers' behavior.

7. What feeling does Dr. Dement express? _____

8. How is this feeling expressed in the voice? _____

2 *Work with a partner. Discuss the following questions.*

1. Recent findings have shown that teenagers are on a different schedule from adults because of biological reasons. Do you think schools should change their schedules to make it easier for adolescents to remain more alert during school hours? How would teachers and students respond? How would teachers and parents respond?

2. Listening One focused on sleep deprivation among young people in school, but other groups of people are also vulnerable to this problem. How might sleep deprivation affect the following people? Can you think of any other professions where sleep deprivation could cause problems?

   truck drivers
   medical students
   factory workers
   other professions: _____

3. Why is sleep deprivation such a growing problem in today's world? Do you think most people agree that they need more sleep? Do you agree?

B   LISTENING TWO: *Get Back in Bed*

You will hear part of an interview from *Satellite Sisters,* a radio show featuring a conversation among five sisters who live on five continents. Lian, one of the sisters, is talking with Dr. Joyce Walsleben, director of New York University's Sleep Disorder Center.

 Listen to the interview, and circle the letter of the answer.

1. Lian complains about being constantly tired. What reason does she give for her exhaustion?
   a. She can't fall asleep at night.
   b. She has small children.
   c. She wakes up in the middle of the night.

2. According to Dr. Walsleben, what do we need to do to combat sleep deprivation?
   a. We should make sleep a priority.
   b. We should not try to combine careers and motherhood.
   c. We should make sure our days are active.

3. Dr. Walsleben mentions the accident that happened to the *Exxon Valdez* oil tanker. What do some people suspect about the causes of the accident?
   a. The captain was not paying attention.
   b. The mate had been working for too many hours.
   c. The papers had not prepared the crew for the weather conditions.

4. How does sleep deprivation affect Lian?
   a. She's too tired to see her parents.
   b. She makes bad parenting decisions.
   c. She can't decide what to eat.

5. How do most people feel about the effects of sleep deprivation?
   a. They think they don't have them.
   b. They accept them.
   c. They think they are uncommon.

6. What happens to many workers by the end of the workweek?
   a. They accumulate a large sleep debt.
   b. They often need to take Fridays off work.
   c. They can no longer get things done at work.

7. According to Dr. Walsleben, about how many hours of sleep are many people missing by Friday?
   a. four
   b. five
   c. seven

C LINKING LISTENINGS ONE AND TWO

Work in a small group. Complete the chart with information from Listening One and Listening Two. The first answers have been started for you.

QUESTIONS ABOUT THE LISTENINGS	LISTENING ONE	LISTENING TWO
What are some of the causes of sleep deprivation?	*Teenagers have a biological need to go to sleep late.*	*Parents of young children can't get the sleep they need.*
What are some of the symptoms of not getting enough sleep?		
What are the dangers of sleep deprivation?		
What recommendations did the doctors and researchers make about our sleep habits?		

Now respond to the questions below. Share your answers with the class.

1. Do you suffer from any of the causes of sleep deprivation described in the listenings?

2. Have you experienced any of the symptoms described in the listenings?

3. Which of the dangers of sleep deprivation seem the most serious to you?

4. Would you follow any of the recommendations from the listenings?

3 Focus on Vocabulary

1 *Read the information about sleep disorders. Match the underlined words with the synonyms that follow. Write the correct numbers in the blanks on page 57.*

Sleep Disorders: *Are You a Victim?*

Many Americans are absolutely exhausted a lot of the time. Tiredness can leave you feeling frustrated and **(1)** miserable. The solution is simple: Get more sleep!

However, if your tiredness **(2)** accumulates and you can't seem to get enough sleep over a long period of time, you may be suffering from a sleep disorder.

Sleep disorders are more common than you might think. Here is some information about common sleep disorders and their effects. If you **(3)** suspect you have a sleep disorder, see a doctor. **(4)** Chronic lack of sleep can lead to some very serious problems.

Insomnia
If you have insomnia, you have difficulty falling asleep or you wake up in the middle of the night. Studies show that at least 50 percent of people have this problem. Here are some possible symptoms of insomnia:
- You have a **(5)** surge of energy in the middle of the night and can't sleep.
- You lack **(6)** alertness during the day.

Apnea
Apnea is a blocking of normal breathing during sleep. Here are some symptoms of apnea:
- You **(7)** snore very loudly in your sleep and sometimes wake yourself up.
- You are very **(8)** cranky in the morning.

Restless Legs Syndrome
Restless Legs Syndrome (RLS) is an uncomfortable, painful feeling in your legs that makes you kick your legs while asleep. If you suspect you have RLS, make it a **(9)** priority to

visit your doctor. Here is some important information about RLS:
- It can lead to **(10)** fatigue. This can be dangerous if you operate machinery or drive.

Sleepwalking
The lights are **(11)** dim. Everything is peaceful. But sleepwalkers have an unusual, **(12)** spontaneous reaction: They get out of bed while they are still asleep and walk around. If you see somebody sleepwalking, rest assured: This behavior is probably nothing to worry about. Here is some advice:
- Let the person continue to sleep.
- Talk quietly and gently. In a **(13)** subtle way, try to get the person back to bed.
- Suggest that the person get a physical checkup, just to be safe.

Daydreaming
It's the middle of the day. You begin to yawn and **(14)** blink a lot, and your mind wanders. Here's how to tell if you have a tendency to daydream:
- People often tell you "you're in another world."
- You become distracted and you lose concentration on what is going on around you.

Nightmares
Everyone has bad dreams from time to time. Unless you often have serious nightmares, don't worry if you experience the occasional scare in the middle of the night! Here is some advice:
- It is safe to go back to sleep. You probably won't have the same nightmare again.
- Try to **(15)** do without caffeine in the afternoon and evening. You might sleep more peacefully.

_____1____ **a.** very unhappy

___10___ **b.** extreme tiredness

____3___ **c.** believe to be true

___4____ **d.** always present

____2___ **e.** adds up

____7___ **f.** breathe noisily while
sleeping

____9___ **g.** sudden increase

___12___ **h.** happening without planning

____8___ **i.** easily irritated or annoyed

___11___ **j.** low, not bright

___13___ **k.** indirect

____9___ **l.** most important thing to do

___14___ **m.** open and close your eyes
quickly

___15___ **n.** not have

____6___ **o.** focus and concentration

2 *Work with a partner.*

Student A: Read question 1 aloud. Listen to Student B's response and make comments of your own. Switch roles after question 3.

Student B: Cover the left column. Listen and respond to your partner. Speak in detail, using the vocabulary words in the right column. Use the words in any order.

Example

A: Does reading in bed keep you awake or help you fall asleep?

B: blink, suspect

I <u>suspect</u> that reading keeps me awake if the book is too good. On the other hand, when a book is a little dull, I start to <u>blink</u> and yawn right away, and pretty soon, it's morning.

Student A	**Student B**
1. Does exercising before going to bed at night keep you awake?	do without, alertness
2. Does drinking coffee, tea, or cola keep you from sleeping?	surge, cranky
3. Do you feel better or worse after a nap?	spontaneous, dim

Now switch roles.

Student B	**Student A**
4. The research says that most of us need a lot more sleep than we're getting. What do you think?	accumulates, priority
5. Do you ever try to sleep late on weekends?	chronic, miserable
6. Do you think it is a good idea to sleep while on a bus or train?	snore, subtle

4 Focus on Speaking

A PRONUNCIATION: Contrastive Stress

- In some sentences, you might want to emphasize and contrast certain words. Native speakers contrast these words by using heavy stress and high pitch. In the following example, the speaker wants to contrast *body* with *brain* and *classroom* with *pillow*:

  My BODY's in the CLASSROOM, but my BRAIN's still on the PILLOW.

- Sometimes, speakers need to emphasize a particular word or thought. This can be very important when asking and answering a question. Notice how different questions can produce the same answer, but with different words stressed:

  WHAT has Dr. Dement done? Dr. Dement has done a lot of RESEARCH.

  WHO did a lot of research on sleep deprivation? DR. DEMENT has done a lot of research.

  HOW much research did Dr. Dement do? Dr. Dement has done A LOT of research.

 1 *Listen to the following sentences. As you listen, underline the contrasted words. Then repeat the sentences with a partner.*

    1. I need to go to bed, but I'm feeling energetic.

    2. Adolescents wake up late, but children wake up early.

    3. Lian is fast asleep, but her children are awake.

    4. My husband has insomnia, but I need to sleep.

    5. I'm sleepy in the morning, but I'm wide awake at night.

2 *Take the following quiz, and compare your answers with those of a partner. Then report your findings back to the class using sentences that contrast your partner's response and your own. Be sure to use contrastive stress to indicate your comparisons. The stress will depend on the information you have found.*

Example

I OFTEN wake up at night, but X NEVER does.

OR

I DON'T wake up at night, and NEITHER does X.

	YOU	YOUR PARTNER
1. Do you often wake up at night?		
2. Do you snore?		
3. Do you daydream?		
4. Do you ever take a nap?		
5. Do you use an alarm clock?		

3 *Work in pairs. Look at the following chart with contrasting information. Using contrastive stress, make up sentences that contrast the information you have found.*

Example	**Example**
What are some obvious effects of sleep deprivation? (absenteeism) *ABSENTEEISM is an OBVIOUS effect of sleep deprivation.*	What are some subtle effects of sleep deprivation? (emotional problems) *EMOTIONAL problems are a more SUBTLE effect.*
1. When is melatonin secreted in adults? (evening)	**1.** When is melatonin secreted in adolescents? (late at night)
2. When does melatonin "turn on"? (evening)	**2.** When does melatonin "turn off"? (morning)
3. Why do adults think that teenagers stay up late? (because they are having fun)	**3.** Why do teenagers say they stay up late? (because they are night owls)
4. How do many parents feel on Monday morning? (tired)	**4.** How do many parents feel by Friday night? (absolutely exhausted)

4 *Read the following sentences. Then work in pairs. Take turns asking and answering questions about the information. Make sure you emphasize the word(s) you want to stress in each question you ask and each answer you give.*

Example

The Department of Transportation estimates that teenage drivers cause more than half of all fall-asleep crashes.

STUDENT A: WHO estimates that teenage drivers cause more than half of all fall-asleep crashes?

STUDENT B: The DEPARTMENT OF TRANSPORTATION.

STUDENT B: Do ADULT drivers cause more than half of all fall-asleep crashes?

STUDENT A: No, TEENAGE drivers do.

1. Dr. Dement suggests that teenagers skip about two hours of sleep every school night.
   - Who estimates that teenagers skip about two hours of sleep every school night?
   - How many hours of sleep are teenagers skipping every school night?
   - When do teenagers usually skip two hours of sleep?

2. A researcher explained that teenagers can fall asleep at the wheel and travel 60 feet in one second.
   - Who explained that teenagers can fall asleep at the wheel?
   - How far can people travel in one second?
   - Where can teenagers fall asleep?

B   GRAMMAR: Present Unreal Conditionals

1 *Work with a partner. Read this advice that a doctor gave to a sleep-deprived patient and answer the questions.*

PATIENT: I'm exhausted. I just can't keep my eyes open during the day.

DOCTOR: It seems that you are quite sleep deprived. You should try to go to bed earlier. If you went to sleep earlier, you would feel a lot better.

PATIENT: There's only one problem, doctor: I can't go to bed early. I work the night shift, and I don't get home until 10:00 or 11:00 P.M.

DOCTOR: Well, perhaps you could take naps instead. If you took regular naps, you'd feel less sleepy.

1. What two suggestions does the doctor make?

2. Does the woman go to bed early? Does she take naps?

3. What words helped you answer questions 1 and 2?

Present Unreal Conditionals

A **present unreal conditional** sentence has two clauses: the *if-clause,* which states the condition, and the **result clause,** which states the result. Use the present unreal conditional to talk about something that is untrue, impossible, or imagined.

To form the present unreal conditional, use the past form of the verb in the *if*-clause.	If I **didn't work** at night, I **could go** to bed early. (I work at night, so I can't go to bed early.)

Use *would* + **base form** of the verb in the main clause to describe a definite result.

If Lian **didn't have** such a hectic lifestyle, she **would spend** more time asleep.

If more people **paid attention** to their sleep habits, the problem **would not be** so serious.

Use *might* or *could* to describe a possible result.

If people **knew** more about the dangers of sleep deprivation, they **might treat** their sleep habits more seriously.

To make a question, use question order in the main clause.

If you were sleep deprived, **would you be** able to tell?

The *if*-clause is not needed if the condition is understood by the listener.

How **would you be** able to tell?

For the verb *be,* use *were* for all subjects.

If I **were** a doctor, I would tell my patients about sleep debt.

You can begin the sentence with either the *if*-clause or the main clause. When writing, put a comma between the clauses in sentences that start with the *if*-clause.

If I went to bed earlier, I would feel better. (comma)

I would feel better **if I went to bed earlier.** (no comma)

2 *Read the following interviews. Complete the sentences using present unreal conditionals. Then, with a partner, read the conversations aloud with feeling in your voice.*

Interview between a Sleep Researcher and a Medical Worker

SLEEP RESEARCHER: Thank you for taking the time to share your experience with me. Can you tell me about the sleep problems that medical workers have?

MEDICAL WORKER: Well, one of the problems is that medical residents and interns can work up to 100 hours a week. They can get really overtired. If they

_____*worked*_____ less, they _____ so tired.
    1. (work)   **2.** (not / get)

SLEEP RESEARCHER: And does this fatigue cause serious problems in the health profession?

MEDICAL WORKER: Sure. Just think about your own work. How well

_____ your job if you _____ only five or six
    3. (do)   4. (sleep)

hours a night?

SLEEP RESEARCHER: Aren't there any rules about how much you can work?

MEDICAL WORKER: Yes, but they are not strict enough. For example, if interns

_____ for work for six days and _____ for 16
    5. (show up)   6. (work)

hours, they _____ following the regulations, as long as they
                    7. (be)

worked less the following week.

SLEEP RESEARCHER: That's terrible! What can be done to make getting sleep a

priority?

MEDICAL WORKER: We need to raise public awareness. For example, surgeons

and anesthesiologists can be on call for many nights every week. If they

_____ to do that, there _____ fewer problems.
    8. (not/be allowed)   9. (be)

Interview between a Sleep Researcher and a Pilots' Association Official

SLEEP RESEARCHER: Hello there. I'd like to ask you about sleep regulations in the

airline industry.

PILOTS' ASSOCIATION OFFICIAL: Well, luckily there have been several studies about

the importance of having pilots sleep adequate amounts. Sleep is important

for everyone, but pilots, in particular, cannot be tired or distracted. Can you

imagine what _____ if a pilot _____ asleep on
                    10. (happen)   11. (fall)

the job?

SLEEP RESEARCHER: Fell asleep? I can't imagine that!

PILOTS' ASSOCIATION OFFICIAL: Well, many people take what we call "microsleeps,"

which last from 5 to 10 seconds. But if a pilot _____ one of
                                                        12. (take)

these little naps during takeoff or landing, the results _____
                                                                13. (be)

disastrous.

SLEEP RESEARCHER: I see. So you need to make sure pilots are awake and alert.

PILOTS' ASSOCIATION OFFICIAL: Yes, alert is the right word. For example, if you

yourself _____ adequate sleep, your reaction time
               14. (not/get)

_____ affected. The same thing _____ to a
       15. (be)   16. (happen)

pilot who _____ enough.
              17. (not/sleep)

SLEEP RESEARCHER: Are all pilots made aware of the dangers of sleep deprivation?

PILOTS' ASSOCIATION OFFICIAL: Certainly. The number of accidents

_____ significantly if we _____ some serious
       18. (increase)   19. (not/institute)

regulations about sufficient sleep.

3 *Work in a small group. Imagine that some high school students have called the Satellite Sisters to get advice about sleep problems. Divide your group into students and Satellite Sisters. Take turns describing the problems and giving advice. Use the vocabulary from the unit and the unreal conditionals from the grammar box on pages 60–61.*

Example

STUDENT: I have an erratic schedule. Sometimes I go to bed early,
                     sometimes late, depending on my workload. When I finally
                     do go to bed, I can't sleep.

SATELLITE SISTERS: Why don't you take a bath before going to bed? If you took
                     a warm bath, you would find it easier to go to sleep.

1. I have trouble sleeping in warm weather. I often wake up feeling really hot and have a headache.

2. My father gets home from work at nine o'clock every evening. I have dinner very late.

3. I am a coffee addict. I make a big pot of coffee after dinner and drink it throughout the evening.

4. I fall asleep with the TV on. I usually wake up at two or three o'clock in the morning, go to bed, and can't fall asleep again.

5. I get home from club meetings at 9:00 P.M. Then I go online and answer email to keep in touch with friends. I don't usually get to bed until after midnight.

6. I get a surge of energy late at night. I keep remembering things I need to do for the next day, so I stay up until two or three o'clock in the morning taking care of them.

C STYLE: Interrupting Politely to Ask Questions

At times, you may need to interrupt a speaker to ask a question to make sure you understand what the person said. This is particularly important when you need to clarify factual information. You may not have heard the information clearly because it was spoken too fast, or because of background noise or poor pronunciation. Here is an example.

STUDENT A: Joelle, I heard some horrifying statistics—over 30 percent of traffic accidents are caused by sleepiness! People should be more careful!

STUDENT B: What was that you said? Thirteen percent?

STUDENT A: No, I said over 30 percent. That's a lot, don't you think?

STUDENT B: Thirty percent! I see what you mean! Wow! That's a very high figure.

Here are some expressions that can be used to interrupt a speaker when you do not understand something. Remember to use rising intonation for the questions.

Questions to Clarify Information	Requests to Confirm Information
Excuse me? What was that you said?	I'm sorry, I didn't catch that. Could you say that again?
Pardon me?	
What? (informal)	I wonder if you could repeat that.
Sorry?	Sorry, I didn't hear you. What was that?

Work with a partner.

Student A: Read statement 1 out loud. Deliberately make mistakes so Student B will have to interrupt to ask a question. Speak too softly or too quickly, or pronounce an important word incorrectly so that Student B won't understand what you say. Switch roles after statement 3.

Student B: Listen to your partner. Interrupt to ask a question or to ask your partner to repeat any information you didn't understand. Use one of the expressions in the box above when you interrupt.

Example

A: I read that 17 percent of Americans are insomniacs!

B: Sorry, could you repeat that?

Student A

1. There are about 1,500 sleep-disorder clinics in the United States.

2. Almost 20 percent of Americans are shift workers, meaning that they often have changes in their work schedules.

3. During the winter, there can be 14½ hours of darkness in some parts of the United States. There's no excuse for not sleeping!

Now switch roles.

Student B

4. Even if a person is seriously sleep deprived, he or she can get back on a regular pattern of sleep after only three weeks.

5. If rats are deprived of sleep completely for 2½ weeks, they die.

6. Sleeping pills first became popular in the United States in the 1970s.

D SPEAKING TOPIC

Read the situation, roles, and the task that follows. Then follow the procedure for the role play. The situation describes a problem at Hilldale General Hospital. This problem is increasingly common in the United States.

Situation

Two weeks ago, a boy of ten was admitted to a private hospital in Colorado for some routine surgery. In preparation for the operation, he was accidentally given an overdose of his medication. He became very ill for several days, but fortunately he recovered. Investigations revealed that the intern who ordered the medication that night, as well as the nurse who administered it, were both seriously sleep deprived. They had both been on duty for 15 hours when the boy received his medicine. The intern had worked ten hours per day for the past eight days, while the nurse had worked the same shifts for six days in a row. Just before checking on the boy and ordering his medicine, both the intern and the nurse had spent five hours in the operating room working on victims of a car accident emergency. The story appeared in the local newspaper, and the hospital received a general review. Although the nurse and intern were negligent, fortunately the boy was not seriously affected by the overdose.

In addition to this latest case, Hilldale General Hospital is having serious financial problems. The only other hospital in the community of Hilldale closed down two years ago due to lack of funding, leaving Hilldale General to cope with too many patients and too little money.

Roles

Hospital Administrators: You are worried. There is so little money on which to operate the hospital that you are seriously understaffed. Your staff works long hours to cover all the shifts and keep the emergency room open 24 hours a day. Doctors' shifts cannot last longer than 16 hours a day, with one continuous 24-hour period off every week. You do what you can for your staff, but you know it's not enough. Hilldale General is in serious financial trouble.

Interns: You are worried. You are dedicated professionals. You work long, hard hours for very little pay, but you are committed to helping the community of Hilldale. You know that sometimes you don't perform well because you are sleep deprived, but you don't feel you have a choice. There is no one else to take your place.

Patients' Rights Group: You are concerned about the patients. You fear that someone will be hurt because the hospital staff is overworked and sleep deprived.

Task

There will be a meeting to establish hospital policies on how long medical personnel can work until rest is required. Represented at this meeting are hospital administrators, interns, and a patients' rights group.

Procedure

Step 1:   Divide the class into three groups: hospital administrators, interns, and patients' rights group. Work together to clarify your viewpoint on the issue. Make a list of points you want to discuss.

Step 2:   Discuss the role. Brainstorm ideas about what you will say in the role play. Use information from the unit, and think of new ways to solve the problem. As you prepare, use the present unreal conditionals from the grammar box on pages 60–61, and interrupt to ask questions when you need to, as shown in the style box on page 64. Here is an example.

HOSPITAL ADMINISTRATORS: We are seriously understaffed. If we <u>had</u> more staff members, we <u>would not be</u> so concerned about sleep deprivation among the interns.

INTERNS: Yes, that's true. For example, there are only two of us on the ward at night. If my partner and I <u>didn't show up</u> for work one evening, there <u>would be</u> no one available to help incoming patients.

PATIENTS' RIGHTS GROUP: <u>Excuse me?</u> Did you say there were only *two* people on the ward?

Step 3: Now divide into new groups of three, with each student playing one of the roles. Role-play a meeting to discuss the situation. Each person should discuss his or her point of view. Try to reach a compromise that will satisfy everyone.

Step 4: Meet as a class. Talk about what should be done. Does this problem exist in other places? What can be learned? Answer the following questions:

- What are the causes of the crisis at Hilldale General Hospital?
- What are some possible solutions?
- Who should be responsible for addressing the problems?

Step 5: Summarize the meeting. Each group reviews its notes and writes up a short report on the meeting, giving their recommendations. As a class, read all the reports and make a master list of suggestions for the hospital.

E RESEARCH TOPIC

Report on sleep deprivation.

A sleep deprivation center is an establishment, often associated with a hospital, where people who are having trouble sleeping are studied by medical professionals. Sleep deprivation centers usually begin to assess their patients' problems by giving them a questionnaire. Use the questionnaire on page 68 to gather information about your sleep behavior and that of two other people. Before you interview them, make sure they are willing to respond to questions about their sleep habits. For example, you could say: "I'm sorry to bother you, but I'm doing some research about sleep deprivation. Would you be willing to answer a few questions about your sleep habits? It shouldn't take more than five or ten minutes."

1. Take the survey yourself. The more *yes* answers you have, the more likely it is that you have a sleep problem.

2. Give the survey to the two people you have chosen. Before you begin, ask for some basic information: age (are they teenagers? young adults?), family status (do they have small children? live alone?), and type of job (do they follow a similar daily schedule? do night work?)

3. Report your findings to the class. Make a class tally of the *yes* and *no* answers on the board or an overhead. Which behaviors are most common? Do factors such as the respondents' age, family status, and type of job affect their responses?

4. Present your conclusions about the sleep behavior of the group of people studied by your class, based on the information you gathered.

	YOU		PERSON A		PERSON B	
Age: **Family Status:** **Type of Job:**			**Age:** **Family Status:** **Type of Job:**		**Age:** **Family Status:** **Type of Job:**	
	Yes	No	Yes	No	Yes	No
1. Do you have trouble falling asleep when you first get into bed?	❑	❑	❑	❑	❑	❑
2. Do you wake up during the night after falling asleep?	❑	❑	❑	❑	❑	❑
3. Do you snore a lot?	❑	❑	❑	❑	❑	❑
4. Do you ever feel that you could fall asleep while driving?	❑	❑	❑	❑	❑	❑
5. Do you often have nightmares?	❑	❑	❑	❑	❑	❑
6. Do you ever fall asleep in front of the TV?	❑	❑	❑	❑	❑	❑
7. Do you ever fall asleep in class or at work?	❑	❑	❑	❑	❑	❑
8. Do you wake up feeling tired?	❑	❑	❑	❑	❑	❑
9. Do you ever not hear your alarm clock?	❑	❑	❑	❑	❑	❑
10. Do you ever have difficulty breathing at night?	❑	❑	❑	❑	❑	❑
11. Do you need to take naps on weekends?	❑	❑	❑	❑	❑	❑
12. Do you often yawn during the day?	❑	❑	❑	❑	❑	❑

For Unit 3 Internet activities, visit the NorthStar Companion Website at
http://www.longman.com/northstar.

The Eye of the Storm

1 Focus on the Topic

A PREDICTING

Look at the photograph and the title of the unit. Then answer these questions, first with a partner and then with the class.

1. What do you think is happening in this scene?

2. What do you think "the eye of the storm" means? What do you think this unit will be about?

B   SHARING INFORMATION

Work in a small group. Discuss the following questions.

1. According to the *World Disasters Report* published by the International Federation of Red Cross and Red Crescent Societies, floods and high winds are the most frequently occurring natural disasters. Have you ever experienced a flood, very high winds, an earthquake, or other natural disaster? If not, do you know anyone who has? Describe the experience.

2. What type of natural disaster would be the most difficult for you to deal with? Why?

3. How do you react in a disaster or crisis? Do you panic or remain calm?

C   PREPARING TO LISTEN

BACKGROUND

Hurricanes (also known as tropical cyclones) are severe tropical storms that form in the southern Atlantic Ocean, Caribbean Sea, Gulf of Mexico, and the eastern Pacific Ocean. They are caused by a combination of water vapor and heat energy, which together cause the air to begin rotating. Hurricanes have wind speeds of over 75 miles (121 kilometers) per hour. Sometimes the wind can reach up to 190 mph (289 kph).

Hurricanes are most violent just around the central "eye," an area that is normally very calm. Hurricanes' strong winds and heavy rain can cause severe flooding, which can be fatal for anyone in their path. One of the deadliest hurricanes ever to hit the United States occurred in 1900 in Galveston, Texas. More than 6,000 people were killed. Hurricanes can also cause billions of dollars in damage.

Hurricanes have a life span of one to thirty days. Although they form over the water, they can cause extensive flooding inland. However, once hurricanes touch land, they tend to lose strength quickly.

Look at the drawing on page 71. It shows the parts of a hurricane. Then read the descriptions of the different parts of a hurricane.

Match each description with its part of the hurricane. Write the correct letter in the blank.

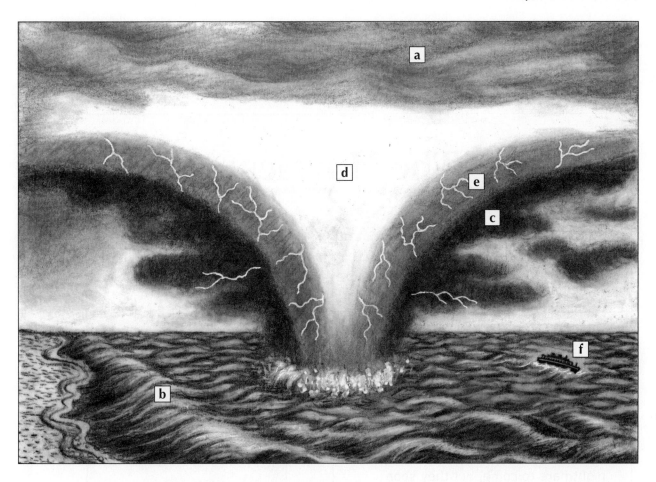

_____ **1.** The <u>eye of the storm</u> is a calm area about 20 miles (30 kilometers) in diameter with extremely low atmospheric pressure, which causes the outside air to rush in.

_____ **2.** The <u>eye wall</u> is the area where the wind moves at speeds of between 75 and 190 miles per hour (121–289 kilometers per hour), and contains the ring of thunderstorms that surround the eye.

_____ **3.** The <u>storm surge</u> is a large mass of water that can reach up to 40 feet (12 meters) high, sweeping along the coast and causing severe flooding.

_____ **4.** An <u>object</u> in the hurricane's path can be destroyed if the hurricane passes over it.

_____ **5.** <u>Spiral rain bands</u> are bands of thunderstorms that wrap around a hurricane.

_____ **6.** <u>Atmospheric conditions</u>, such as low pressure and warm air, contribute to the formation of hurricanes between May and September.

VOCABULARY FOR COMPREHENSION

Read the following story about a major hurricane. Match each underlined word with a definition that follows. Write the correct number in the blank.

The Hurricane of 1938

Part One

The great hurricane of September 1938 began in the Atlantic Ocean, southeast of the (1) <u>coast</u> of Florida. (2) <u>Jittery</u> at first about bad weather warnings, residents of the area relaxed when the storm turned north and (3) <u>inland</u>, away from the water. No one realized that the storm would soon pick up great speed and head toward the Northeast. In 1938, meteorologists did not have the (4) <u>sophisticated</u> technology they do today. Residents of the Northeast had no idea of the nightmare to come, but they soon learned just how (5) <u>vulnerable</u> they were.

The morning of the hurricane, the weather was (6) <u>deceptively</u> pleasant, though a bit windy, on Long Island, New York. Some beachside residents telephoned friends who lived inland and invited them to come and watch the huge waves that were beginning to roll in from the Atlantic. People sat outside on their porches and enjoyed the view. However, by mid-afternoon the sky had grown dark, and violent winds began to blow with such (7) <u>intensity</u> that garden furniture sailed through the air and pieces of houses began to break off and fly away. People watched in shock as a thick wall of clouds came in from the sea toward the shore. As it came closer, they realized they weren't looking clouds at all: It was a wall of water!

_____ **a.** strength

_____ **b.** easily hurt

_____ **c.** technologically advanced

_____ **d.** land next to the ocean; the seashore

_____ **e.** nervous

_____ **f.** away from the seashore

_____ **g.** making something seem true when it isn't

Part Two

Because there was little or no warning of the hurricane, people expected only some (8) <u>foul weather</u> and didn't (9) <u>panic</u>. They remained calm and stayed in the area until disaster struck. Then they were (10) <u>caught off guard</u>. When the hurricane hit the shore, some houses were suddenly under 30 feet of water. According to surviving witnesses, some of the houses blew up when the water hit, as if from a bomb; others flew up into the air and crashed back into the water. In the city of Providence, Rhode Island, office workers later reported looking outside at the street, which was suddenly flooded. They saw desks, cars, and children's toys floating down the street, and they watched helplessly as people floated by, too.

The storm knocked over telephone and electricity poles, creating a power (11) <u>outage</u> that cut off communication. Because many people had not received warnings to (12) <u>evacuate</u>, they stayed in their homes, thinking that this would be just another storm. Unfortunately they were wrong. Even those who had prepared for possible emergencies by (13) <u>stocking up</u> on food, water, and other (14) <u>provisions</u> couldn't save their homes or, in some cases, their lives. By the time its terrible work was finished, the hurricane of 1938 had left 600 people dead and 60,000 more (15) <u>dislocated</u>.

_____ **h.** move from a dangerous place

_____ **i.** saving or buying extra amounts to use later

_____ **j.** wet and stormy conditions

_____ **k.** moved from one's normal place or situation

_____ **l.** supplies

_____ **m.** feel a sudden fear or anxiety

_____ **n.** surprised

_____ **o.** failure of a service, such as electricity

2 Focus on Listening

A   LISTENING ONE: *Preparing for a Hurricane*

You are going to hear the first part of a radio report about preparing for a hurricane in Florida. Listen carefully. The radio's reception is poor, so you can't hear all of the information.

🎧 *Listen to the first part of the report. Use the information you can hear, as well as your own ideas about what a hurricane report includes, to complete the following sentences.*

1. The sky is clear blue, and the ocean is deceptively calm here in southern Florida. It's the kind of day when you would expect

   _____

   _____

2. But the beaches are _____

   _____

3. Traveling inland, though, you'll find a totally different mood. Parking spaces

   _____

4. . . . and there are long lines at _____

5. You see, despite the calm weather now, people here are _____

   _____

LISTENING FOR MAIN IDEAS

🎧 *You will hear reporter Allison Sasso's account of the Florida hurricane. Read the list of topics below. Then listen to the radio report. Number the topics in the order she mentions them.*

_____ a resident who lost her house

_____ a resident who is not evacuating

_____ a tourist who is scared

_____ advice for tourists

_____ how hurricane forecasts are made

_____ supplies that people should buy

__1__ the mood in Homestead, Florida

_____ the weather report

LISTENING FOR DETAILS

Listen to the report again. As you listen, circle the letter of the answer that best completes each statement.

1. The beaches are _____.
   a. packed with tourists   **b.** closed to the public   **c.** silent and empty

2. Inland, it is hard to find _____.
   a. a parking space   **b.** supplies   **c.** food and water

3. The hurricane has already caused damage in _____.
   a. the shopping center   **b.** Central America   **c.** the Caribbean

4. Authorities are stressing that people should _____.
   a. use their judgment   **b.** leave town immediately   **c.** follow the advice of officials

5. Sophisticated equipment helps hurricane forecasters to predict _____.
   a. the potential damage   **b.** the hurricane's possible path   **c.** unexpected changes in temperature

6. Hurricanes often change _____.
   a. direction or intensity   **b.** into rainstorms   **c.** size

7. People should have ready a couple of gallons of water (approximately seven liters) per _____.
   a. day   **b.** family   **c.** person

8. When returning home after a hurricane hits an area, residents should _____.
   a. wear boots   **b.** not use electricity   **c.** take medication

9. According to the reporter, _____ may enter the house during a hurricane.
   a. rats   **b.** snakes   **c.** fish

10. Tourists going to a coastal spot should _____.
    a. ask for their money back if there's a hurricane   **b.** plan for a possible hurricane   **c.** choose another place for a vacation

11. Tourists may need access to _____.
    a. extra money   **b.** an additional car   **c.** alternative hotels

12. Barbara Swanson, a resident for 50 years, says that she is _____.
    a. definitely leaving   **b.** definitely staying   **c.** trying to decide whether to stay or leave

REACTING TO THE LISTENING

Speakers communicate meaning in many ways. The literal words are important, but features such as the speed, pitch, pausing, and other effects (such as laughter) are also very important.

1 *Work in pairs. Listen to each speaker as he or she reacts to predictions about the upcoming storm. Look at the confidence scale below. Discuss what each term means. Discuss where to place each speaker on the scale. Then discuss what features in each person's speech helped you make your choice.*

CONFIDENCE SCALE
Fearful . . . . . . Guarded . . . . . . Confident . . . . . Overconfident

Excerpt One

1. Where would you place Adam on the confidence scale? _____

2. What features of his speech (beyond the words) helped you decide?

_____

Excerpt Two

3. Where would you place Kyle on the confidence scale? _____

4. What features of his speech (beyond the words) helped you decide?

_____

Excerpt Three

5. Where would you place Dale on the confidence scale? _____

6. What features of her speech (beyond the words) helped you decide?

_____

Excerpt Four

7. Where would you place Mrs. Swanson on the confidence scale? _____

8. What features of her speech (beyond the words) helped you decide?

_____

Work in a small group. *Discuss the following questions.*

1. The three people in the radio report had different reactions and plans for dealing with the hurricane. What would you do if a hurricane were approaching? Discuss how you would react if you were:

a police officer	a grocery store owner
a hospital administrator	a lifeguard
a home owner with children	a vacationer

2. The media have to make difficult decisions during an emergency situation such as an approaching hurricane. Do you think it is better for them to talk about the possibility of evacuation (and risk panicking people), even when they are not 100 percent sure that it is necessary, or is it more important for the media to give people information only when sure of the facts?

B   LISTENING TWO: *Hurricane Hunters*

You will now hear a radio report by the Hurricane Hunters, a division of the U.S. Air Force. This report talks about their unique job responsibilities.

Listen to the report and take notes. Discuss your answers with a partner.

1. What do the Hurricane Hunters do? Why?

_____

_____

2. What are weather conditions like on the trip?

_____

3. What can humans do that computers cannot?

_____

4. Why would anyone want to be a Hurricane Hunter?

_____

C   LINKING LISTENINGS ONE AND TWO

1 *Work in pairs. Imagine that a hurricane will reach the coast of Florida in two days. The Hurricane Hunters have flown into the area to investigate. They are going to relay information about the hurricane to local authorities, who will then decide how best to advise the public. Before the Hurricane Hunters begin, the two groups need to exchange information.*

Step 1:   Complete the chart with questions the Hurricane Hunters and the local authorities might ask each other.

HURRICANE HUNTERS	LOCAL AUTHORITIES (MAYOR, POLICE, FIREFIGHTERS)
What questions might you ask the local authorities?	What questions might you ask the Hurricane Hunters?

Step 2:   Student A, you are a Hurricane Hunter. Student B, you are a representative for one of the local authorities.

Plan a short dialogue, asking each other questions and sharing information. Use questions from the chart you just completed, and make up answers. Perform your dialogue for the class.

2 *Discuss your answers to the following questions with your partner.*

1. If you had to choose, would you rather be a hurricane forecaster, who works in an office, or a Hurricane Hunter, who flies into hurricanes in an airplane? What aspects of each job appeal to you, and what aspects do not?

2. Have you made any plan that you would follow in case of a natural disaster or emergency? If your home were threatened, would you evacuate or stay there to protect it? Compare your reactions to those of the people you heard in Listening One.

3 Focus on Vocabulary

1 *The past participle and present participle can be used as adjectives. The **-ed** form often describes how a person feels, while the **-ing** form refers to the cause of the feeling.*

Complete each sentence with the correct form of the adjectives given. Write the answer in the blank.

1. exciting, excited

   a. A severe snowstorm can be an _____ experience for someone from a warm climate.

   b. My Mexican friend Andrés, who was visiting me in Vermont one Christmas, was _____ when he heard that a blizzard was forecast.

2. amazing, amazed

   a. At first, he was _____ that the snow could get so deep that we couldn't open the front door.

   b. The amount of snow we received was _____ to him.

3. interesting, interested

   a. We told Andrés that it snowed a lot in Vermont. He thought our stories about snowstorms were very _____.

   b. We went upstairs and looked out at the beautiful scene. He was _____ in taking some photographs to send home to his family.

4. frightening, frightened

   a. Later, when the power outage made our lights go out, Andrés started to feel _____. I think he felt very vulnerable.

   b. I admit, it was also a little _____ when our electric heat went off and the temperature outside was below 0° Fahrenheit. But we didn't panic.

5. heartening, heartened

a. At about midnight, it was _____ to hear the sounds of snowplows clearing the road and the power company trucks repairing the electric lines.

b. We were also _____ when the power came back on a few hours later.

6. comforting, comforted

a. Having lights and heat again was _____. We all started to feel relieved.

b. Fortunately, we had stocked up on provisions. We were _____ by hot coffee and a good breakfast.

7. encouraging, encouraged

a. It was _____ to see how well the local authorities had dealt with the situation.

b. Andrés said he was _____ by our reactions, too. He was pleased to see us tough it out as bravely as we did.

8. surprising, surprised

a. Andrés found our reactions quite _____. We were in good spirits most of the night.

b. I was _____ when my Mexican friend said later that the blizzard had been the best experience of his U.S. visit.

2 *Work with a partner. Imagine you and your partner are discussing the radio report about the Hurricane Hunters. Student A, read the directions below. Student B, read the directions at the top of page 225.*

Student A, complete each sentence on the next page with the correct word from the box. Then read each statement to Student B. Listen to the response. As you listen to Student B, listen for the words in parentheses. Ask Student B to repeat if you do not hear the correct word. Tell Student B the word you are listening for if you still don't hear the word.

| deceptively | scared stiff | sophisticated | vital | vulnerable |

1. The people who fly into hurricanes are really brave. I would feel so

_____ in that plane. (panic)

2. I know the technology on that plane is very _____, but I think

being a Hurricane Hunter is frightening work. (power outage)

3. Yes, and what would you do if the equipment broke down? Those machines

are absolutely _____. (evacuate)

Work with the same partner. Imagine you are friends on vacation together. You have learned that a severe storm is approaching, and you are preparing to wait out the storm in a small beach house.

Student A, read the directions below. Student B, read the directions at the bottom of page 225.

Student A, complete each sentence with the correct word from the box. Then read each statement to Student B. Listen to the response. As you listen to Student B, listen for the words in parentheses. Ask Student B to repeat if you do not hear the correct word. Tell Student B the word you are listening for if you still don't hear the word.

| forecast | flooded | route | jittery | provisions |

1. OK. Let's see. I guess we have enough _____ to last for a few
days. We've got plenty of canned food . . . Oh, what about a can opener?
This electric one may not work if there's a power outage! (manual)

2. Wow! It looks like the road is already _____. That means the
sewers might back up and contaminate the water supply. (stock up on)

3. I guess we're in for quite an experience. As long as we keep our heads, we'll

be fine. But I sure wish we had believed the weather _____
when we first heard about this storm. (second-guess)

4 Focus on Speaking

A PRONUNCIATION: Listing Intonation

- When you are listing items in a sentence, your voice rises on the first items in the list and falls on the last. Read the following example:

  There is a big storm approaching. You can expect rain, wind, and flooding.

- The rise tells the listener that the speaker has more to say, and the fall tells the listener that the speaker has finished. Sometimes the speaker's voice stays high on the last word of the list, showing that the speaker is uncertain or wants to continue:

  We don't know how many inches of rain to expect: one, two, three . . .

  Note: The items in a list can be single words, phrases, or clauses.

1 *Listen to the following sentences. As you listen, underline the words or ideas that are being listed. Then draw an arrow to show the rising or falling intonation.*

1. People are buying batteries, water bottles, and flashlights.

2. The sky is blue, the ocean is calm, and the beaches are empty.

3. My house was flooded, my furniture was ruined, and my car is gone.

4. The hurricane has passed by Cuba, Puerto Rico, and southern Florida.

5. There were big hurricanes in 1938, 1965, and 1997.

2 *Look at the category for each item. Write complete sentences listing the things that belong in each category. Then circle the thought groups or items, and draw arrows to show rising or falling intonation. Practice reading your sentences with a partner.*

Example

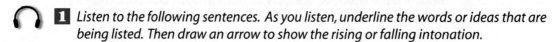

Things that Hurricane Hunters do: *Hurricane Hunters* (fly into the eye of the storm,)
(collect data,) and (send the data back) to the mainland.

1. Ways that you can prepare for a hurricane: _____

_____

2. Types of natural disasters: _____

_____

3. States that are often affected by hurricanes: _____

_____

4. Feelings experienced during a natural disaster: _____

_____

5. Ways friends can help each other during a disaster: _____

_____

3 *Work with a partner. Take turns asking the following questions. Answer with an unfinished list, using rising intonation to show that you are unsure or might continue.*

Example

STUDENT A: How wide is the eye of a hurricane?

STUDENT B: I'm not sure. Is it ten miles, twenty miles, a hundred miles . . . ?

1. During what months can hurricanes form?

2. What dangers are people exposed to during a hurricane?

3. How much can it cost to repair the damage after a big storm?

4. How many people were evacuated during natural disasters last year?

B GRAMMAR: Adjective Clauses

1 *Work with a partner. Read the sentences below, and then answer the questions.*

a. The Hurricane Hunters gather vital information <u>that</u> is needed to predict the path of a hurricane.

b. The eye wall, <u>which</u> is the thick layer of clouds around the hurricane's eye, can be several miles wide.

1. The underlined words refer to other words in the sentences. Which words do they refer to?

2. What information is added to the sentences after the underlined words?

Adjective Clauses

Adjective clauses (also called relative clauses) are used to identify or add information about nouns. Usually, the adjective clause directly follows the noun it refers to. These clauses are introduced by a relative pronoun, such as *who, that, which, whose, where,* or *when.*

Using Relative Pronouns in Adjective Clauses	Examples
Use *who* to refer to people. It can be used as a subject or object of the adjective clause. In spoken English, *who* is usually used instead of the more formal *whom,* even when it is the object of the adjective clause.	The people **who** *[subject]* spoke to me were worried about the forecast of a hurricane. The people **who (or whom)** *[object]* I spoke to were on vacation in Florida during the hurricane.
Use *that* and *which* to refer to places and things. They can be used as subject or object of the adjective clause.	Homestead is the town **that/which** was hit by the hurricane.
That cannot be used in a non-identifying adjective clause or after a preposition.	Homestead, **which** is in Florida, was hit by the hurricane.
Use *whose* to refer to people's possessions. It can be used as a subject or object of the adjective clause.	The residents **whose** houses were destroyed are staying at a temporary shelter.
Use *where* to refer to a place or *when* to refer to a time. They are used as the object of the adjective clause.	Homestead is the town **where** my friends live. May to September is the period **when** most hurricanes occur.

Identifying and Nonidentifying Adjective Clauses	Examples
An **identifying adjective clause,** sometimes called a restrictive clause, gives essential information about the noun it refers to.	Homestead is the town **where my friends live.**

In identifying adjective clauses, English speakers often delete the relative pronoun in speaking when it is the object of the verb.

He was the meteorologist (who) **the radio reporter interviewed.**

A **nonidentifying adjective clause,** sometimes called a nonrestrictive clause, gives additional information about the noun it refers to. In writing, the nonidentifying adjective clause is separated from the rest of the sentence by commas.

I live in Florida, **which is often hit by hurricanes.**

In speaking, people often pause before the clause, or they use a lower tone of voice to say the words in the clause.

Homestead, **which is in Florida,** was hit by the hurricane.

2 *Work with a partner. Fill in the blanks with the relative pronouns **who, that, which, whose, when,** or **where.** Then take turns reading the warning announcements with feeling.*

Enter Your "City, State" [_____] Go

WARNING 1

People **(1)** ____who____ are in poor health or over 65 years of age are being advised to stay indoors as the weather reaches record temperatures. A temperature of 105°F, **(2)** _____ is a record for this time of year, was reported in Chicago yesterday, and in some areas it climbed even higher. If the apartment **(3)** _____ you live is not air-conditioned, you might consider staying for a few days with a neighbor **(4)** _____ home is cooler. There are certain basic things **(5)** _____ you can do to stay safe: Drink plenty of liquids, don't panic, try to remain patient, and stay indoors! You will be able to go out later **(6)** _____ the heat wave is over.

Enter Your "City, State" [＿＿＿＿＿] [Go]

WARNING 2

If you're one of the many people **(7)** _____ cars have been washed away or flooded by recent storms in the area, do not attempt to leave your house. Wait for the help of the official rescue teams, **(8)** _____ will be circulating throughout the flooded area in special vehicles. You'll be able to recover your car in several days, **(9)** _____ the flood subsides. A special warning to children **(10)** _____ might be tempted to play outside in the lakes and rivers that have formed in their streets: Don't! Water **(11)** _____ has been contaminated by sewers and broken pipelines can make you sick! You are advised to stay inside. That is **(12)** _____ you will be safest.

Enter Your "City, State" [＿＿＿＿＿] [Go]

WARNING 3

The snowy conditions **(13)** _____ exist throughout the Northeast have forced many people to stay indoors, and transportation is extremely limited. If you're one of the many people **(14)** _____ driveways and paths are under four feet of snow, relax, stay at home, and tough it out. There will be plenty of time to dig out your car **(15)** _____ the snow stops. Those **(16)** _____ are in good health might be tempted to start now, but don't forget that people **(17)** _____ are not fit can give themselves a heart attack if they do such heavy work. Instead, take out the book **(18)** _____ you have been planning to read lately, and don't do heavy work for **(19)** _____ you are not prepared!

Enter Your "City, State" [＿＿＿＿＿＿] [Go]

WARNING 4

If you've stepped outside today, you already know this: It's *hot!* Our data,

(20) _____ go back over 100 years, show that today will be one of the

hottest days on record. Activities **(21)** _____ you should avoid are:

exercising, heavy lifting, or anything tiring. People **(22)** _____ air-

conditioners are broken: Go visit a neighbor! And seriously, if you're the type

(23) _____ can't sit still, at least make sure you drink plenty of liquids or

step inside from time to time, **(24)** _____ it's likely to be cooler. If you

decide to take the day off work and go to the beach—**(25)** _____ is not

such a bad idea—use plenty of sunscreen. And wear loose, light-colored

clothes, **(26)** _____ will help to protect you against the sun.

3 *Guessing Game. Divide the class into two Groups, Group A and Group B.*

Group A: read the instructions below.

Group B: read the instructions on page 226.

Group A, complete each sentence on the next page with the correct adjective clause. Take turns reading the sentences to Group B. Group B must identify the item or person you've described. (The words in parentheses on the next page are suggested answers.) If Group B answers correctly, they receive one point. If they answer incorrectly, Group A receives one point.

Then play again. Listen to Group B's sentences and identify the item or person they describe.

The team with the most points wins.

Example

GROUP A: They're the people <u>who</u> fly into the eye of a hurricane.

GROUP B: Hurricane Hunters.

Group B is correct and gets one point.

1. It's the state _____ the report takes place. (answer: Florida)

2. Give me the name of an item _____ you need for an emergency. (answer: flashlight, radio, etc.)

3. It's the area _____ includes countries like Cuba, Jamaica, and Haiti. (answer: the Caribbean)

4. They're the people _____ are often unprepared for hurricanes because they don't live in the area. (answer: tourists)

5. They're the machines _____ won't work without power. (answer: ATMs, etc.)

6. Name a country _____ there are many earthquakes. (answer: Japan, etc.)

7. Name a time of year _____ a hurricane is likely to form. (answer: summer, autumn)

C   STYLE: Expressing Surprise and Shock

There are many ways of expressing surprise or shock. English uses a wide range of words and intonation, along with exaggerated stressed syllables, in order to communicate stronger reactions. Here are some phrases that can be used to express surprise or shock:

Mild surprise/Interest	Strong surprise/Disbelief	Shock/Dismay
Really?	Wow, that's amazing!	Oh, no!
That's interesting.	That's unbelievable!	Oh, my goodness!
I didn't know that.	That's incredible!	That's terrible!
Huh!	You're joking!	That's awful!
Oh, yeah?	I can't believe it!	That's horrible!
Oh, come on!	You're pulling my leg!	

Here are some reactions that often follow expressions of surprise or shock:

Where did you hear that?	I wonder why that is.
I'm surprised that's possible.	Then what happened?

Work with a partner.

Student A: Read each statement to your partner.

Student B: Listen to your partner. Respond with mild surprise, disbelief, or shock. Use a range of intonation, along with exaggerated stressed syllables, to communicate your reaction. Then add a question or comment that continues the conversation.

Student A: Listen to your partner's intonation. Answer with a question or comment that indicates whether he or she is expressing mild surprise, strong surprise, or total shock. Switch roles after statement 5.

Example

STUDENT A: The summer population of coastal areas can be up to 100 times the size of the winter population.

STUDENT B: (mildly surprised) Really? Where did you read that?

STUDENT A: It's shocking, isn't it?

STUDENT B: Not really. I'm just a little bit surprised.

1. A man was found clinging to a metal pipe after a hurricane. He was wearing shoes and socks, but his clothes had been ripped off by the wind.

2. In April 1974, there were 148 tornadoes in the American Southwest within a period of 28 hours.

3. Near the eye of a hurricane, winds can reach up to 200 miles per hour.

4. There were 830,000 deaths from an earthquake in China in 1556, which is the highest earthquake death toll in history.

5. In 1958, a tsunami that was 1,720 feet high hit Alaska at 100 miles per hour.

Now switch roles.

6. The intense winds in one hurricane sent a drinking straw through a sign.

7. In a hurricane, coastal areas can get hit with waves over 40 feet high.

8. Hurricane Hunters don't carry parachutes.

9. The Krakatoa volcano eruption of 1883 was 26 times as powerful as the largest hydrogen bomb test. It was heard over 8 percent of the earth's surface.

10. In the past, U.S. officials used only women's names for hurricanes, but now they use men's names, too.

D   SPEAKING TOPIC

Imagine that you have just heard an emergency weather announcement on the radio and have been asked to make a public report in your school or workplace.

Step 1:   Work in pairs. Write a short report on the natural disaster. Use the information you have learned in this unit. Then add details of your own, including specific information about your town or city.

Step 2:   Present your report to the class, or record it and then play it for the class. The announcement should provide your classmates with:

- details about the disaster, such as what it is and where it is happening

- clear instructions about what to do or not to do

Use the adjective clauses you learned about in the grammar section on pages 83–88 and the expressions of surprise or shock from the style section on pages 88–89.

Example

STUDENT A: We have just been informed that because of the severe storm and the winds, <u>which</u> are reaching over 50 miles an hour, part of the school roof has just broken loose.

STUDENT B: <u>That's unbelievable!</u> I hope nobody has been hurt!

STUDENT A: No, but we need to evacuate in an organized way, so listen to the information <u>that</u> we have just been given.

Step 3:   Listen to the announcements of other class members. Take notes. Then discuss which reports are the most effective, and talk about why.

E   RESEARCH TOPICS

Report on one of these topics related to disasters.

1. Interview someone who has experienced a natural disaster. Ask what it was like before, during, and after the disaster. Take notes, and tell the story.

2. Watch a movie about a disaster, such as *The Perfect Storm* (disaster at sea), *Dante's Peak* (a volcano), *Twister* (a tornado), or *Deep Impact* (a collision with a meteor). Take notes about how people were warned, how they prepared, and how the movie made you feel. Discuss which parts of the film seemed realistic and which didn't. Discuss why these movies are popular.

For Unit 4 Internet activities, visit the NorthStar Companion Website at http://www.longman.com/northstar.

You Will Be This Land

It's everyone's home.

1 Focus on the Topic

A PREDICTING

Work with a partner. Look at the illustration and the title of the unit. Then discuss the following questions.

1. This illustration is a reprint of a postcard. It was first published by Co-op America, an organization that promotes a clean, healthy environment. What messages does the picture communicate?

2. The title comes from a poem by a Native American writer. What do you think "you will be this land" means? What do you think this unit will be about?

B   SHARING INFORMATION

1 *Work in a small group. Discuss the following quotations. Match each quotation with its meaning, and write the correct letter in the blank.*

_____ **1.** "We cannot command Nature except by obeying her."

—Francis Bacon (1561–1626)

English philosopher

_____ **2.** "The greatest joy in nature is the absence of man."

—Bliss Carman (1861–1929)

Canadian poet

_____ **3.** "Nature is not human-hearted."

—Lao-tzu (sixth century B.C.)

Chinese philosopher

_____ **4.** "We are nature. We are nature seeing nature."

—Susan Griffin (b. 1943)

U.S. poet, writer, educator

_____ **5.** "It is far from easy to determine whether [nature] has proved a kind parent to man or a merciless stepmother."

—Pliny the Elder (A.D. 23–79)

Roman scholar

a. People and nature are equal.

b. People must listen to and respect nature.

c. Nature sometimes causes problems for people.

d. People have a negative effect on nature.

e. Nature and people are very different from each other.

2 *Do you agree with any of the quotations? Do you disagree with any of them? Share your opinions with your group.*

C   PREPARING TO LISTEN

BACKGROUND

There are hundreds of Native American Indian tribes in North America today. Each tribe has its own religious beliefs, yet most tribes share some beliefs and practices. For example, religious ceremonies about the relationship between people and the earth are common. One of these is a ceremony performed before an animal is killed. People give thanks to the animal for giving its life so that people can be fed.

Because of their feeling for the earth, many Native Americans are interested in conservation and ecology. They have both a religious and a practical interest in protecting the land. To many Native Americans, destruction of the environment means destruction of their religious values and of their way of life.

Eagles are a symbol of the Native American attitude toward nature. These large, soaring birds are admired for their beauty and excellent hunting abilities. One type of eagle, the bald eagle, is a symbol of the United States and is found on coins and postage stamps. Eagles were once common in the United States, but

The bald eagle

they have become endangered because of the effects of pollution and loss of their natural habitat. Many Americans respect these birds for their beauty and majesty. To Native Americans, however, eagles also have a religious meaning. The Pawnee Indians, for example, believe that the eagle exists to remind people of the lessons of the Creator. The Pawnee story "The Teachings of the Eagle" illustrates these beliefs:

> Look at the Eagle and you will see [the Creator's] teachings. The Eagle has two wings, and those wings are balanced in strength when it flies. In the same way, a man and a woman are balanced in strength and are two. . . .
>
> Look upon the Great Eagle's feathers. You will see that half of the feather is dark and half of it is white. Just so, we have day and night, winter and summer, sunshine and clouds. . . .
>
> As the Eagle flies, it looks in two directions. Just so, we human beings may look in two directions. We may look in the direction of good or we may look in the direction of that which is bad. We may see happiness or we may see sorrow.[1]

Thus, to the Pawnee, if people harm the eagle, they are harming a symbol sent by the Creator to teach them about life.

---

[1] Michael J. Caduto and Joseph Bruchac, *Keepers of the Animals: Native American Stories and Wildlife Activities for Children* (Golden, CO: Fulcrum Publishing, 1991), p. 54.

Discuss the following questions with a partner.

1. Based on what you have read, how do you think traditional Native Americans would feel about the following activities? Support your answer with information from the reading. Then discuss how *you* feel about these things:
   - raising animals for food
   - hunting animals for food
   - hunting animals for sport

2. What else do you know about the Native Americans of North America? What do you know about other indigenous groups? How are they similar to or different from Native Americans?

VOCABULARY FOR COMPREHENSION

Read the statements. From the list on page 95, match a word or phrase that is similar in meaning to the underlined word. Write the correct letter in the blank.

_____ 1. As the human population grows, animals must <u>compete with</u> humans for land, water, and food. Unfortunately, people usually win the contest for natural resources.

_____ 2. Many vegetarians don't eat meat because they don't want to <u>take the life of</u> an animal.

_____ 3. Each religion has <u>sacred</u> places where people go to worship. For example, the city of Jerusalem is sacred to Christians, Jews, and Muslims.

_____ 4. Until recently, people <u>gathered</u> mushrooms in the wild. Now, instead of collecting wild mushrooms, people have discovered ways to grow them on farms.

_____ 5. Ideally, political leaders should <u>serve the interests of</u> their people, but in reality they sometimes do things that do not benefit the people they represent.

_____ 6. Some religions believe that a <u>spirit</u> occupies the body of a person until that person dies. Then the spirit is released from the body to travel to another place.

_____ 7. Each person may not pollute very much, but the <u>sum</u> of all the pollution from all the people on earth is a serious problem.

_____ 8. Technology has added to the problem of pollution. For example, <u>manual</u> tasks (like shoveling snow or washing dishes) are now performed by machines that use gas or electricity.

_____ 9. When we throw garbage away, we think that it is gone forever. Actually, all our trash <u>winds up</u> in the environment. Our trash is buried in the earth, dumped in the water, or burned, with the smoke going into the air.

_____ 10. Some farmers are trying to reduce the amount of pesticides, or poisons, they use to kill insects on their crops. They are trying <u>organic</u> methods to grow fruits and vegetables.

a. work for the benefit of
b. done by hand
c. ends up; ends
d. collected, harvested
e. holy

f. kill
g. non-chemical
h. living thing without a physical body
i. total amount
j. try to be more successful than

2 Focus on Listening

A LISTENING ONE: *Interview with a Medicine Priest*

You will hear the introduction to an interview with David Winston, a Cherokee medicine priest, or spiritual leader. The Cherokee are a Native American tribe from the southeastern United States. David Winston talks about Cherokee beliefs regarding the environment and conservation.

Listen to the introduction, and answer the questions. Compare your answers.

1. What is the Great Life? _____

_____

2. What do you think the three Laws of Nature might be?

_____

_____

_____

_____

LISTENING FOR MAIN IDEAS

Listen to the interview. Write the three Laws of Nature. David Winston gives examples to illustrate each law. Take notes. Compare your notes with those of another student.

1. First Law of Nature _____

   Example _____

   _____

2. Second Law of Nature _____

   Example _____

   _____

3. Third Law of Nature _____

   Example _____

   _____

LISTENING FOR DETAILS

Listen to the interview again. Circle the answer that best completes each statement.

1. The Cherokee people believe that we should try to _____ nature.
   a. understand   b. live with   c. compete with

2. The needs of people are _____ the needs of animals and plants.
   a. less important than   b. just as important as   c. more important than

3. The great Laws of Nature tell people how to live in relationship with
   _____.
   a. other people   b. animals and plants   c. everything in the world

4. Following the First Law of Nature, one good reason for taking life is to
   _____.
   a. make money   b. hunt for sport   c. protect yourself

5. The Cherokee people believe that stones are _____.
   a. alive   b. magical   c. important

6. Taking the life of a plant is _____ taking the life of an animal.
   a. less serious than   b. the same as   c. more serious than

7. According to the Second Law, one spirit fills _____.
   a. all things   b. only humans   c. only plants and rocks

8. "Don't pollute where we live" means don't pollute _____.

   a. our houses   **b.** our countries   **c.** the planet Earth

9. The three Laws of Nature _____.

   a. are difficult to   **b.** don't apply to   **c.** are not important
   follow today   today's world   today

REACTING TO THE LISTENING

 1 *Listen to three excerpts from the interview. Look at the chart. How acceptable do you think each action would be under the Laws of Nature? Rate their acceptability from **1** (Very Acceptable) to **4** (Not Acceptable). Circle your answer. Then discuss your answers.*

EXCERPT ONE: FIRST LAW	VERY ACCEPTABLE			NOT ACCEPTABLE
Hunt an animal for sport	1	2	3	4
Pick flowers growing wild in a forest	1	2	3	4
Pick tomatoes on a farm	1	2	3	4
EXCERPT TWO: SECOND LAW				
Clean up a polluted beach	1	2	3	4
Put endangered animals in a zoo	1	2	3	4
Cut down trees to build a house	1	2	3	4
EXCERPT THREE: THIRD LAW				
Dump garbage in the ocean	1	2	3	4
Start a neighborhood recycling program	1	2	3	4
Send garbage into outer space	1	2	3	4

2 *Work in a small group. Discuss the following questions.*

1. David Winston describes a special relationship to nature. How are your personal beliefs similar to or different from his? Give some examples.

2. David Winston described Native American beliefs about nature. Are there native people in your country who hold similar beliefs? If so, does the government in your country respect their views and incorporate them into national policy? Explain.

B LISTENING TWO: *"Ndakinna"—A Poem*

You will hear the poem "Ndakinna" (Our Land) by poet and storyteller Joseph Bruchac of the Abenaki tribe from the northeastern United States.

The Hudson River Valley, New York State. Many Native American tribes hunted and fished along the river's banks.

1 Listen to the poem. Check (✓) whether Bruchac would agree or disagree with each of the following statements. Discuss your answers with a partner.

According to Bruchac, we should understand the land _____.

	Agree	Disagree
1. with maps	❏	❏
2. with eyes like birds	❏	❏
3. by walking on roads	❏	❏
4. by walking where deer walk	❏	❏
5. by using all five senses	❏	❏

2 Listen to the poem again. Check (✓) whether Bruchac would agree or disagree with the following statements. Discuss your answers with a partner.

	Agree	Disagree
1. The earth is like a dead animal.	❏	❏
2. People are sometimes wasteful.	❏	❏
3. Rivers divide the earth.	❏	❏
4. Human beings are a part of nature.	❏	❏
5. We can learn from other animals.	❏	❏
6. The Earth is essential to us.	❏	❏

3 *"Ndakinna" is reprinted below with some words missing. Fill in the words you remember. Then listen to the poem again. Fill in the missing words. Compare your answers with those of your classmates.*

Ndakinna

BY JOSEPH BRUCHAC

You cannot understand
this land with _____,
lines drawn as if earth
were an _____ carcass[1]
cut into pieces, skinned,
though always _____ _____
than thrown away.

_____ this land instead
with a wind-eagle's eyes,
linked with _____ and _____
like sinews[2] through leather,
sewed strong to hold the _____
to the _____.

Do not try to know the land by _____.
Let your _____ instead
caress[3] the soil in the way of deer,
whose trails _____
the ways of least resistance.

When you feel this land
when you _____ this land.
when you hold this land as lungs hold breath
when your songs _____ this land,
when your ears sing this land,
_____ _____ _____ this land.
_____ _____ _____ this land.

---

[1] *carcass:* the body of a dead animal.
[2] *sinews:* cords or threads made of leather.
[3] *caress:* to gently touch.

C   LINKING LISTENINGS ONE AND TWO

Work in a small group. Complete the chart. Compare the views of David Winston and Joseph Bruchac. Would they agree or disagree with these quotations? Support your opinion with examples from the interview and the poem.

	DAVID WINSTON	JOSEPH BRUCHAC
	Agree/Disagree	Agree/Disagree
"We cannot command Nature except by obeying her."		
"The greatest joy in nature is the absence of man."		
"Nature is not human-hearted."		
"We are nature. We are nature seeing nature."		
"It is far from easy to determine whether [nature] has proved a kind parent to man or a merciless stepmother."		

3 Focus on Vocabulary

1 *Work with a partner. You and your partner each choose five different words from the chart on page 101. Look up the missing forms for your words in the dictionary. Share your information and complete the chart. An **X** means there is no common form for this category.*

Noun	Verb	Adjective	Adverb
1. benefit			
2.	compete		
3.		electric, electrical	
4.		industrial, industrialized	X
5. nature	X		
6.	pollute		X
7. protection			
8.	recycle		X
9. spirit	X		
10. waste			

2 *Complete the paragraphs. Use the correct word forms of the words from the chart above. (Not all word forms will be used.) Compare your answers with a partner's. Then discuss whether you agree or disagree with the statements.*

1. benefit

In modern life, we generally think of nature as existing for the

(a) _____ of people. However, the relationship is usually not

(b) _____ to nature. We (c) _____ from all that

nature offers us, without thinking about what we are giving back.

2. competition

Today's development forces us to have a (a) _____

relationship with animals. We (b) _____ for many natural

resources. This (c) _____ is harmful for both people and

animals.

3. electricity

Since the invention of (a) _____, people have tried to

(b) _____ everything. These days, almost anything can be

(c) _____ run. This has greatly increased our demand for

(d) _____ power.

4. industrialization

With the growth of **(a)** _____, pollution has increased. In addition, people in **(b)** _____ societies don't feel connected to the earth, so they don't see the impact of the pollution. As society continues to **(c)** _____, the problem will get worse.

5. nature

People who live in cities are not in touch with **(a)** _____, and they lose their **(b)** _____ connection to the earth. People should try to live more **(c)** _____ by moving out of cities, giving up technology, and living a simpler life.

6. pollution

Factories **(a)** _____ the rivers by dumping their waste into the water. The **(b)** _____ rivers run into the sea, contributing to the **(c)** _____ in the ocean.

7. protection

We must do more to **(a)** _____ endangered animals. We need more **(b)** _____ laws to save their natural habitats. With our **(c)** _____, endangered animals may be able to survive for many more years.

8. recycling

(a) _____ can be good for business as well as for the environment. Companies can increase their profits when they **(b)** _____. Many consumers want to buy products that are made from **(c)** _____ materials.

9. spirit

Conservation is a topic that is **(a)** _____ important to many Native Americans. They believe that people have a **(b)** _____ connection to the earth and that animals, plants, rivers, and mountains all contain **(c)** _____. They are right.

10. **waste**

It is easy to live less (**a**) _____ in modern society. For example, don't buy anything that uses (**b**) _____ packaging. Then you won't have to throw away so much (**c**) _____ each day.

3 *Many items we commonly use or throw away can be harmful for the environment. Work with a partner. Answer the questions in the chart. Use the words from the box below in your answers. Be sure to use the correct form of the words.*

waste	recycle	pollute	benefit	industrial	protect
benefit	wind up	manual	compete	Earth	natural

ITEMS	DO YOU USE THEM?	DO THEY HARM THE EARTH? EXPLAIN.	ARE THERE GOOD ALTERNATIVES?
Electric appliances such as toothbrushes, shavers, or hair dryers	*I use an electric toothbrush.*	*Yes, I think they waste electricity.*	*A manual toothbrush would probably work just as well.*
Disposable batteries			
Styrofoam cups			
Air-conditioners			
Garden pesticides			
Household cleaning products			
Plastic bags and food wrap			
Large cars, such as SUVs			

4 Focus on Speaking

A   PRONUNCIATION: *th* Sounds

> For people learning English as a second language, the **th** sounds are among the most difficult sounds to pronounce.
>
> Put the tip of your tongue between your teeth to say the beginning sounds in **th**is /ð/ and **th**ing /θ/.
>
> - The sound in **this** is voiced. The vocal chords vibrate.
>
> - The sound in **thing** is voiceless. The vocal chords do not vibrate.
>
> Be careful. Some students substitute /s/, /z/, /t/, or /d/ for the **th** sounds. All of these substitutions are incorrect.

1 *Listen to the following words. You will hear one word from each pair below. Circle the word you hear.*

1. three	tree	8. though	dough
2. say	they	9. soothe	sued
3. there	tear	10. day	they
4. sink	think	11. bathe	bays
5. though	so	12. udder	other
6. ladder	lather	13. breeze	breathe
7. worthy	wordy	14. Zen	then

2 *Pronounce the words from Exercise 1 with a partner. Check your partner's pronunciation of the **th** sounds.*

3 *Work with a partner. Practice reading the words below.*

breath	Earth	father	gather
north	south	strength	thanks
that	theirs	there	things
think	third	this	those
though	thread	three	throw
toothbrush	within		

4 *Work with a partner. Student A, read the directions below. Student B, read the directions on page 227.*

Student A: Ask Student B each question below. Listen to Student B's response, and check for both the answer in parentheses and the pronunciation. Then listen to and answer Student B's questions.

1. What do you call air in our lungs? (breath)

2. What is another way to say "not here"? (there)

3. What's another word for "believe"? (think)

4. How else can we say "nevertheless"? (though)

5. Which is it if it's not "that"? (this)

6. What's another word for "objects"? (things)

7. What's the name of our planet? (Earth)

8. How else can we say, "I appreciate it"? (thanks)

5 *Listen to Joseph Bruchac's poem again while looking at the text on page 99. Underline all the words with **th** sounds. Then read the poem to another student. Pay careful attention to the correct pronunciation of **th**.*

B　**GRAMMAR: Advisability in the Past—Past Modals**

1 *Work with a partner. Read this excerpt from a pamphlet written by the Nature Club of Randolph Middle School of Randolph, New Jersey. Pay attention to the underlined words and answer the questions.*

"People have a responsibility to protect the Earth, but in the past we did not live up to that responsibility. We <u>should have protected</u> the Earth. We <u>shouldn't have allowed</u> the environment to become so polluted. We <u>could have kept</u> the water and air cleaner. If we had been more careful, we <u>could've avoided</u> a lot of the environmental problems that we have today."

1. Is the paragraph about actions in the past or present?

2. Which sentences focus on things that were done? Which focus on things that were not done?

3. What feeling is communicated in the paragraph?

Advisability in the Past—Past Modals

Past Modals	Examples
To form a past modal, use the **modal** + *have* + **past participle.**	I **should have recycled** this can.
	I **should've recycled** this can. (spoken form)
To express regret or blame and to talk about actions that were possible or advisable in the past, use:	
should have / (should've)	We **should've protected** the river from pollution. (We didn't protect the river, and now we are sorry.)
could have / (could've)	We **could've kept** the water cleaner. (It was possible for us to keep the water cleaner, but we did not.)
ought to have (contracted form is not used)	We **ought to have been** at that meeting. (We didn't go to the meeting.)
To make a negative statement or question, use:	
should not have / shouldn't have	**Shouldn't** the town **have closed** the factory?
	Yes, it should have. It **should not have** allowed the factory to pollute the river.
could not have / couldn't have	Town officials **couldn't have known** about the health risks.

GRAMMAR TIP: *Couldn't have* expresses past assumption, not blame or regret.

In short answers, use the **modal** + *have.*	**Should** the government **have passed** laws against pollution?
	Yes, it **should've.**
With the verb *to be,* use the **modal** + *have* + *been.*	Were you at the meeting?
	No, but I **should have been.**

GRAMMAR TIP: In speech, the word *have* in past modals is often pronounced like the word *of:* /əv/.

2 *Complete the sentences. Use the past modals of the verbs in parentheses. Then, work with a partner. Take turns reading the story aloud using contractions and correct pronunciation.*

Love Canal is a small community in the state of New York. More than 20 years ago, a nearby manufacturing company disposed of its waste by pouring chemicals into the ground. At the time, this was the normal way to dispose of waste.

1. At the time, the company officials _____ that the
   (could / not / know)
   chemicals would have terrible effects many years later.

2. Workers at the company _____ the chemicals into the
   (should / not / pour)
   ground, but they did.

Long after the company closed down, developers, working with the city, bought the land and built new houses on it, despite the pollution. A school and playground were also constructed for children in the area. The development resulted in disaster.

3. Developers _____ houses on a chemical dump, but they did.
   (should / not / build)

4. City officials _____ very careful about selecting a place
   (ought to / be)
   for the school and playground, but they weren't.

The town developed a strange chemical smell. The yards and gardens of some of the houses bubbled and produced strange liquids.

5. Finally, officials realized that chemical waste in the ground

   _____ in the ground, even after 20 years. All the families
   (could / stay)
   of Love Canal had to leave their town and find new places to live.

6. People throughout the United States heard about Love Canal. They thought

   that it was a tragedy that _____ .
   (should / not / happen)

3 *Work with a partner.*

Step 1:   In his interview, David Winston suggested several things that people can do to take care of the earth and live by the three Laws of Nature, even in industrialized societies. Discuss what you have done (or not done) recently to conserve energy and natural resources and to reduce pollution. Are you satisfied with your own behavior regarding the environment? Explain.

Step 2: Think about your actions last year and evaluate their effect on the earth. Look at the Personal Environmental Report. Then look at the categories and the examples of things people can do. Rank your actions from **1** (did a lot to protect the environment) to **5** (did not do anything to protect the environment). Discuss your ranks with a partner. Do you feel proud of doing something? What could you have done differently or better? Use *should've, could've,* or *ought to have.*

Example

STUDENT A: I gave myself a 4 for conserving gasoline and oil. I drove to school every day when I <u>could've</u> walked. I <u>shouldn't have</u> been so lazy. But I <u>could've</u> done worse—I did walk to the grocery store! What did you give yourself?

STUDENT B: I gave myself a 1. I took the train or bus whenever possible and used my car very little. I <u>couldn't have</u> done much better than that.

Personal Environmental Report

RANK

CONSERVING ENERGY AND NATURAL RESOURCES

	1	2	3	4	5
Gasoline and oil					
• avoid using car when possible	☐	☐	☐	☐	☐
• keep heat/air-conditioning low in home	☐	☐	☐	☐	☐
Water					
• don't run faucet when brushing teeth or doing dishes	☐	☐	☐	☐	☐
• conserve water when showering	☐	☐	☐	☐	☐
Electricity					
• turn off lights when you're not in the room	☐	☐	☐	☐	☐
• run power appliances only when necessary	☐	☐	☐	☐	☐
Animal / plant life					
• avoid wasting food	☐	☐	☐	☐	☐
Reducing Pollution					
In the air					
• keep car in good condition	☐	☐	☐	☐	☐
• avoid using aerosol products	☐	☐	☐	☐	☐
On land					
• follow recycling rules	☐	☐	☐	☐	☐
• make efforts to buy recycled products	☐	☐	☐	☐	☐
• avoid littering	☐	☐	☐	☐	☐
In the water					
• don't pour chemicals and chlorine cleaners down drains	☐	☐	☐	☐	☐

C STYLE: Asking For and Giving Examples

It is often easier to understand a speaker's ideas when he or she gives examples to illustrate a point. In addition, the listener can request examples if an idea needs clarification. In the interview with David Winston, Barbara Cassin asked him to give examples of the ideas he was explaining. Here is what he said about killing plants:

> "All of those things should be done in a sacred way and in a good way. <u>For instance</u>, when you go to gather a plant, you don't want to go and say, 'Wow, here is a whole bunch of plants,' and gather them all. You gather a few, leaving the majority of the plants so they grow and continue to flourish."

Often when a speaker makes a general statement, the listener will ask for examples to illustrate the speaker's point. Here is an example.

STUDENT A: My government is getting more and more concerned about protecting the environment.

STUDENT B: <u>Could you tell me what you mean?</u>

STUDENT A: Well, there are a lot of new recycling programs.

STUDENT B: <u>Such as?</u>

STUDENT A: <u>For example</u>, a factory that recycles tires has just opened in my city. They should have opened the factory sooner, but I'm glad it is finally open.

Here are some expressions that can be used to ask for and give examples.

To ask for examples	To give examples
Could you explain in more detail?	For example,...
Could you give me an example?	For instance,...
Such as?	Such as ...
Could you tell me what you mean?	One example is ...

Work in a small group. Take turns telling each other about environmental programs or policies that your government or community has initiated or should have initiated. As each student describes the program, the rest of the group should ask for specific examples. Use expressions from the box above.

D SPEAKING TOPICS

1 *Read the situation, the roles, and the task below. Then follow the procedure for the role-play. You will play a role in a meeting about building a factory on Native American land.*

Situation

The Acme Paper Company wants to build a paper-making factory on Native American land in Washington state. However, the company does not have a good history with the Native Americans. In the past, the paper company built a similar factory near Native American land in another part of the country. The factory caused a lot of environmental problems. Trees were cut, and the river and land were polluted. The factory also failed to respect the culture of the Native American tribe. Sacred animals and plants were destroyed, so the tribe members could not follow their traditional religious practices. In addition, the company hired workers from other parts of the country to work in the factory, instead of hiring people from the tribe. The tribe members were unemployed, and many new people moved into the area and built houses and stores. In the end, many members of the tribe moved away from the area.

Roles

Factory Representative: You believe this land is the best place to build the company's factory. It is close to the forest where the company will cut down the trees to make paper. It is also near a river that can provide water for the factory. However, this time the company does not want to repeat its mistakes. It wants to work with the tribe to build a factory that will not destroy the environment or harm the tribal culture.

Medicine Priest: You are opposed to the factory. You don't trust the paper company. You feel that the land, trees, and river are sacred and should not be harmed. You feel that the factory representative doesn't understand your tribe's religious beliefs. You are also worried that some members of your tribe are forgetting their traditional ways and care more about earning money than about protecting the earth.

Unemployed Tribe Member: You are in favor of the factory, but only if it is built in an environmentally safe way and if it employs tribe members. You feel that if the factory is not built, many people will move away because they don't have jobs. You think that the factory can be built in a way that will protect the environment.

Task

The factory representative, the medicine priest, and the unemployed tribe member meet. They discuss what was wrong with the way the factory was built before, and how the company and the tribe can compromise to build a new factory.

Procedure

Step 1: Divide the class into three groups: factory representatives, medicine priests, and unemployed tribe members.

Step 2: Meet with other students who will be playing your role. Discuss the role. Brainstorm to come up with ideas about what you will say in the role play. Use information from the unit, and think of new ways to solve the problem. As you prepare, use the past modals from the grammar section on pages 105–108 to discuss past mistakes, and give and request examples to make your points clear, as in the style section on page 109.

Step 3: Now, divide into new groups of three, with each student playing one of the roles. Role-play a meeting to discuss the proposal for the paper factory. Each person should discuss his or her point of view. Try to reach a compromise that will satisfy everyone. Here is an example:

TRIBE MEMBER: The factory polluted the river. The paper company should have been more responsible.

FACTORY REPRESENTATIVE: We are taking steps to protect the environment.

MEDICINE PRIEST: Such as?

Step 4: Meet as a class. Discuss how each person felt playing his or her role. Compare the different solutions each group came up with.

2 *Work with a partner. Find a picture or photograph that shows the beauty of the earth, or use the photograph on page 98.*

1. List the images you see in the picture.

2. Describe the way the picture makes you feel, or explain the memories it helps you recall.

3. Write a poem about the picture. If you wish, use a line from *"Ndakinna"* to begin your poem (for example, "You cannot understand this land . . ." or "See this land . . .").

4. Read or recite your poem to the class, and show them the picture.

3 *Find a short poem about nature. Read the poem and analyze it. Decide what message the author is giving about nature. Then recite the poem for the class, and explain the meaning.*

E   RESEARCH TOPIC

Report on Native American ideas about nature.

Step 1: Use a dictionary of quotations, or use the Internet and search for
"Native Americans," "American Indians," or "Indigenous People."
Find a quote you like and copy down the name of the author, the text
from which the quote is taken, and the date of publication. Make a list
of quotations that you find interesting. For example:

> "We are the land. To the best of my understanding, that is the
> fundamental idea that permeates American Indian life."
> —Paula Gunn Allen, *The Sacred Hoop* (1986)

> "The most common trait of all primitive peoples is a reverence for
> the life-giving earth, and the Native American shared this elemental
> ethic: the land was alive to his loving touch, and he, its son, was
> brother to all creatures."
> —Stewart Lee Udall, *The Quiet Crisis* (1963)

> "Not even anthropologists or intellectuals, no matter how many
> books they have, can find out all our secrets."
> —Rigoberta Menchu, *I, Rigoberta Menchu* (1983)

> "It is only a matter of time, Indian / You can't sleep with the river
> forever."
> —Leslie Marmon Silko, *Storyteller* (1981)

Step 2: Read your quotations to the class. Explain why you chose them and
what you have learned about indigenous people from your research.
Answer questions the class has about the quotations.

For Unit 5 Internet activities, visit the NorthStar Companion Website at
http://www.longman.com/northstar.

It's Better to Give Than to Receive

Former U.S. President Jimmy Carter (center) working for Habitat for Humanity International, an organization that builds houses for people in need. Volunteers build the houses for no pay, and local businesses donate the construction materials.

1 Focus on the Topic

A PREDICTING

Look at the photograph, its caption, and the title of the unit. Then discuss these questions with a partner.

1. Why do you think a former president of the United States does construction work to help build houses for people in need? Do you think this is an appropriate activity for a former president? Why or why not?

2. What do you think "it's better to give than to receive" means? Do you agree with this statement?

B   SHARING INFORMATION

Work in a small group. Read the definition of philanthropy, and answer the questions.

Philanthropy is a way that people and organizations show concern for others or work to improve the world. Some people and organizations give money to individuals or to charities (groups that help people), while others volunteer their time (work without getting paid).

1. Do you know of any famous philanthropists? Do they give money, time, or another kind of help? Describe their philanthropy.

2. Have you ever volunteered your time to help other people (for example, in a school or a community organization)? If you have, describe what you did and how you felt about it.

3. Is giving money to charity common in your culture?

4. If you had a substantial amount of money to donate, who do you think you would give it to? Read the following choices, and write *1*, *2*, and *3* next to your top three choices. If there is another type of organization you would donate to, add it to the list. Explain the reasons for your decisions to your classmates.

_____ a museum, theater, or performing arts group

_____ a university, college, or school

_____ an environmental group

_____ a hospital, mobile health clinic, or homeless shelter

_____ a church, synagogue, mosque, temple, or other religious organization

_____ a library, community center, or park

_____ an animal rescue center

_____ (your own idea) _____

C   PREPARING TO LISTEN

BACKGROUND

Philanthropy has always had an important role in American history and is an accepted American custom. In fact, in 1999, charitable giving in the United States reached a total of $190 billion—its highest level in 28 years! Approximately 72 percent of Americans donate to charity, and 51 percent do volunteer work. About 2 million not-for-profit organizations and charities in the United States today receive this help. These not-for-profit organizations include universities, hospitals, religious groups and their charities, social service agencies, museums, and scientific research organizations.

There are three types of philanthropists: individuals, foundations, and private corporations. Individuals give money or volunteer their time to support causes that are important to them. Foundations are organizations started by very wealthy individuals. Their "business" is not to make a profit but to give money away to not-for-profits. Private corporations may also use a portion of their business profits to make donations, or they may give away their products or services free of charge. However, foundations and corporations are responsible for only 20 percent of charitable donations; 80 percent comes from individuals.

What makes people and institutions give away their time and money? One reason is altruism, the unselfish desire to help other people and make the world a better place. Other reasons involve personal interest. Under U.S. tax law, an individual or business does not have to pay income tax on money that is donated to charity. For extremely wealthy individuals and corporations, this can mean millions of dollars they do not have to pay in taxes to the government. In addition to tax benefits, donors (people and companies who give) often receive favorable publicity for making donations, and they have an opportunity to influence the world around them.

Work in a small group. Read the reasons for donating that are listed below, and add some other reasons why you think people give time and money. Then read the newspaper clippings on page 116. Next to each clipping, write the number(s) of the reason or reasons you think the donors gave. Discuss your choices.

Some Reasons People Donate Money

1. so others can do something the donor felt fortunate to be able to do

2. so others can do something the donor never had a chance to do

3. so others will feel grateful to the donor

4. to change society / to change the world

5. to say "thank you" for help in the past

6. to encourage others to give

7. so the donor will feel good about himself or herself

8. so the donor can receive publicity for his or her company

9. because the donor feels guilty about having a lot of money

10. because the donor doesn't have anyone else to give the money to after he or she dies

11. to become famous

12. to pay less income tax

13. to satisfy religious beliefs

14. _____

_____

15. _____

_____

16. _____

_____

_____ a.

G. J. Ford Donates $20 Million to Southern Methodist University

As the chairman, CEO, and principal stockholder of a bank worth $30 billion, G. J. Ford says he owes his success to the education and preparation for life he received as a Southern Methodist University student in the 1960s. In return, he has made a $20 million payment on his "debt of gratitude" to SMU, to help the Dallas school build a 32,000-seat football stadium and all-sports facility.

_____ b.

Gates Foundation Offers Minnesota School a $4.3 Million Grant

The Gates Foundation has offered a huge amount of money to a small public school to help the school replicate its success at 15 other schools. This will make the Gates Foundation the largest single donor to public education in the history of U.S. education. The grant will cover the cost of scholarships and will also support curricular innovations such as project-based learning and "hands-on" ventures. It will help to make the newest technology available to more students, and it will favor school government by a teachers' cooperative.

_____ c.

Oracle Corporation Donates $100 Million

Oracle Corporation and its chairman and CEO, Larry Ellison, will give $100 million in support of America's Promise—Alliance for Youth. The donation by the world's second-largest computer software company will go to Oracle's Promise, a non-profit foundation whose goal is to put a computer on every student's desk. "We need a computer that is affordable and easy to use, so that every child can have [one]," said Ellison. "Today's personal computer is creating a society of haves and have-nots."

VOCABULARY FOR COMPREHENSION

Read the following pamphlet encouraging people to give money to a charity. Match each underlined word with a definition. Write the number of the definition in the blank.

People in Need . . .

- A (**1**) <u>stunned</u> family standing in front of their house after it was destroyed by fire.

- Children who go to school in dirty clothes because their house has no water and they have no place to do (**2**) <u>laundry</u>.

- Parents who have lost their jobs and have to spend their (**3**) <u>nest egg</u>, money that was (**4**) <u>tucked away</u> over many years, on food and shelter.

A Helping Hand . . .

These are stories that (**5**) <u>touch us</u> and make us feel like we want to help. Well, you can help. It's easy. Just fill out the enclosed card to (**6**) <u>pledge</u> a small amount of money to help those who could use it. The money will (**7**) <u>fund</u> a variety of programs to help people in need. We also have a special (**8**) <u>scholarship</u> to pay for needy children to go to college.

Your Reward . . .

You won't (**9**) <u>regret</u> your decision to give because in addition to helping others, giving will make you feel better about yourself. As a (**10**) <u>benefactor</u>, you will feel the rewards of helping people. The money you donate will surely change someone's life!

The (**11**) <u>recipients</u> of your gift will always remember that when life was at its worst, someone reached out to help them.

Thousands of generous people have already helped. Don't let them (**12**) <u>show you up</u>. You can make a difference too!

_____ **a.** a person who helps someone by giving money

_____ **b.** embarrass you by doing something better than you can

_____ **c.** clothes that need to be washed

_____ **d.** feel sorry about

_____ **e.** make us feel an emotion

_____ **f.** money given to pay for a student's education

_____ **g.** money saved to use for something special later

_____ **h.** pay for

_____ **i.** people who receive something

_____ **j.** promise to give

_____ **k.** saved in a safe place

_____ **l.** very surprised; shocked

2 Focus on Listening

A   LISTENING ONE: *Oseola McCarty—An Unusual Philanthropist*

You will hear a television report by Barbara Walters. Ms. Walters interviews Oseola McCarty, who was selected as one of the most fascinating people of 1995. She died in 1999 at the age of 91. She was an inspiring woman who is greatly missed by all those who have been touched by her story.

 Listen to the introduction, and answer the questions.

1. What do you think Oseola McCarty did that made her famous?

    _____

    _____

2. Why do you think she saved so much money?

    _____

    _____

LISTENING FOR MAIN IDEAS

 *Listen to the entire report, and write **T** (true) or **F** (false) next to each phrase below. Correct the statements that are wrong.*

Oseola McCarty _____.

_____ 1. worked most of her life doing laundry

_____ 2. saved almost $250

_____ 3. had very little education

_____ 4. pledged her money to start scholarships at a university

_____ 5. regretted giving away her money

_____ 6. inspired local business people to contribute money

LISTENING FOR DETAILS

 Listen to the report again. As you listen, circle the letter of the answer that best completes each statement.

1. Oseola McCarty was _____ by many people before she gave away her money.

   a. well known   **b.** visited   **c.** not noticed

2. Ms. McCarty _____ high school.

   a. finished   **b.** dropped out of   **c.** never attended

3. Ms. McCarty's scholarship is for promising _____ students.

   a. female   **b.** black   **c.** poor

4. Ms. McCarty left school to _____.

   a. work for a doctor **b.** teach sixth grade   **c.** take care of her grandmother

5. The president said if more people were like Ms. McCarty, there would be

   _____.

   a. more scholarships at universities   **b.** very few problems in the United States   **c.** few poor people

6. The trip to the White House was the first time Ms. McCarty had _____.

   a. left the South in 50 years   **b.** traveled away from home   **c.** been to Washington, D.C.

7. Stephanie Bullock is _____.

   a. a member of Ms. McCarty's family   **b.** the first recipient of the Oseola McCarty scholarship   **c.** a friend of Ms. McCarty's

8. At the time of the interview, Stephanie Bullock _____.

   a. hadn't started college yet   **b.** was in college   **c.** had already graduated from college

9. At the time of the interview, Ms. McCarty _____.

   a. had a new job   **b.** still did laundry for people   **c.** wasn't working anymore

10. Local business people _____.

    a. are contributing to the Oseola McCarty scholarship fund   **b.** are starting a new scholarship fund   **c.** don't remember Ms. McCarty

REACTING TO THE LISTENING

1 Listen to the excerpts from the interview. List all possible reasons Oseola McCarty might have had for giving her money to the university. Use reasons from the list below, or think of your own. Compare your answers with those of another student.

- change society

- make people admire her

- show other people up

- help people who can't afford to go to college

- help people do something she couldn't do

- get an income tax break

- be more powerful

- meet the president

- feel better about herself

- encourage local businesses to give money

- become famous

- get interviewed on TV

- show that giving is important

- (your own ideas) _____

_____

Excerpt One

1. Reasons: _____

_____

_____

Excerpt Two

2. Reasons: _____

_____

_____

Excerpt Three

3. Reasons: _____

_____

_____

2 Work in a small group. Discuss the following questions, and share your opinions with the class.

1. In what ways do you think Ms. McCarty was an unusual human being? Were you inspired by her story? What do you find remarkable about it?

2. Besides providing financial help, what effect do you think Ms. McCarty's generosity might have on students like Stephanie Bullock?

3. What other examples of unexpected or unusual generosity have you witnessed or experienced?

B   **LISTENING TWO:** *Please Donate or Volunteer—*
                      Public Service Announcements

Public service announcements (PSAs) are advertisements on television or radio that educate people about important issues or encourage people to do things for the good of society.

   You will hear two public service announcements that encourage people to give money or volunteer to help others.

 1 *Listen to each announcement, and write down what it is asking people to do and why they should do it. Compare your answers with those of another student.*

	WHAT IS THE ANNOUNCEMENT ASKING PEOPLE TO DO?	ACCORDING TO THE ANNOUNCEMENT, WHY SHOULD PEOPLE DO IT?
PSA 1		
PSA 2		

2 *Work in a small group, and share your answers with the class.*

   1. Which PSA do you think is more effective? Why?

   2. What other information would you like to know?

C   LINKING LISTENINGS ONE AND TWO

A Venn diagram is a useful way to compare and contrast information. Compare the reasons Oseola McCarty gave money (Listening One) with the reasons people are encouraged to give money or volunteer time (Listening Two). Fill in the Venn diagram below with ideas and information from the two listenings. In the shaded area, write reasons that are similar or the same for both.

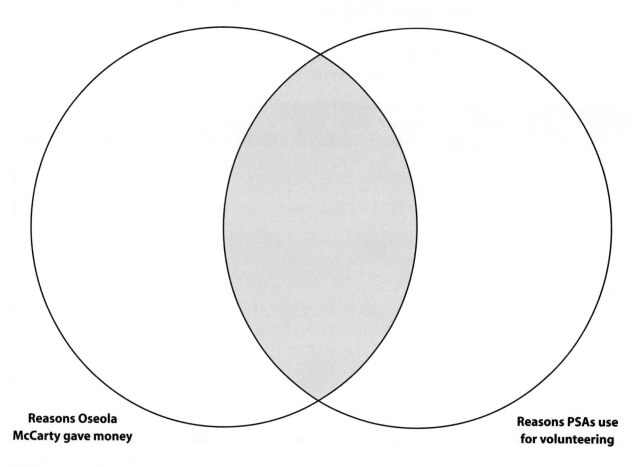

**Reasons Oseola
McCarty gave money**

**Reasons PSAs use
for volunteering**

3 Focus on Vocabulary

1 *Pronounce the words in the box on page 123 with your teacher. Then complete the following newspaper article using the correct words from the list. Each word is marked as a noun (n), verb (v), or adjective (adj).*

benefactor (n)	nest egg (n)	retired (adj)	tucked away (v)
donation (n)	recipient (n)	stunned (adj)	volunteer (n)
fund (v)	regretted (v)	touched (v)	

"TEDDY BEAR LADY"
SURPRISES HOSPITAL WITH GIFT

Chicago's Children's Memorial Hospital is the lucky
(1) _____ of a surprise $18 million gift.
Gladys Holm was a (2) _____ secretary who
never earned more than $15,000 a year and never married. She lived
alone in a tiny apartment in Evanston, Illinois, and was a
(3) _____ at Children's Memorial Hospital in
Chicago. She was called the "Teddy Bear Lady" because she brought
stuffed animals to sick children on her regular visits. But Miss Holm,
who died in 1996 at the age of 86, was also a long-time buyer of
stocks. Over the years, she (4) _____ money
that grew into an impressive (5) _____ of
$18 million, which she left to Children's Memorial. It was the
largest single (6) _____ in the hospital's
115-year history. The hospital president, Jan Jennings, was
(7) _____ when she heard the news. "When
[Miss Holm's attorney] called to tell me the amount, I asked him to
repeat it, since I was certain I had misheard."

Why did Gladys Holm feel so strongly about Children's Memorial?
Jennings says the hospital first (8) _____ Miss
Holm's heart nearly 50 years ago, when doctors there saved the life of her
friend's daughter. She never forgot the relief she felt all those years ago.

Holm's gift will (9) _____ heart
disease research. People at the hospital said they
(10) _____ that they couldn't thank their
(11) _____ for the generous gift.

2 *Work with a partner. Read the following article. Write a dialogue between two of the adult Burton children as they discuss how best to use their father's money. Use at least ten of the words and phrases given in the box below the article. (You may use the words in any form.) Then practice your dialogue out loud, and perform it for the class.*

Peter Burton Leaves $7 Billion to Charity

Peter Burton, former chairman of electronics giant Davis-Burton, died recently, leaving approximately $7 billion to his foundation. This gift makes the Peter and Leslie Burton Foundation one of the wealthiest foundations in the world. Burton established the foundation to "help people through the improvement of scientific knowledge, education, health, employment, and the environmental quality of life." Burton's four children must decide how the foundation will use the money.

benefactor (n)	nest egg (n)	scholarship (n)
charity (n)	philanthropy (n)	show someone up (v)
donate (v)	pledge (n, v)	stun (v)
donor (n)	provide (v)	stunned (adj)
feed the hungry (v)	recipient (n)	touch someone (v)
foundation (n)	regret (n, v)	tuck away (v)
fund (n, v)	retired (adj)	volunteer (n, v)

3 *Work with a partner. Read about the following charitable organizations, and discuss how you feel about them. Use vocabulary from the list below.*

benefactor	feed the hungry	show up
charity	fund	stunned
donate	pledge	touch someone
donation	provide	volunteer
donor	recipient	

1. *Penny Harvesters:* This group works with local schoolchildren across the United States. Children ask adults whom they know to donate any pennies they might have lying around the house, gathering dust. They take the pennies to school. Members of the Penny Harvesters drive from school to school and collect the pennies. The money is donated to various causes.

2. *New York Cares:* It can get quite cold on New York City streets in the winter, so this coat drive is very important. New York Cares collects coats that are no longer used, perhaps because they have gone out of fashion or are now the wrong size. It collects the coats, cleans them, and distributes them to people who are cold and do not have proper winter clothing.

3. *City Harvest:* This organization collects food and distributes it to people who are hungry. The food can be in cans and packages, or it can be cooked food that is left over from restaurants and parties. Businesses contribute, as do schoolchildren, whose classes sometimes compete to contribute the most food. City Harvest makes sure that nothing gets thrown away, that it is given instead to people who do not have enough food.

4. *Dress for Success:* This organization helps low-income women enter the work force by providing them with free clothing. It gives each woman a suit to wear when she goes for a job interview, plus an additional suit if she gets the job and begins working. Proper clothes are not all that people need to be successful at work, though. The group also has a network of support to help women with their professional careers.

4 Focus on Speaking

A PRONUNCIATION: Intonation of Tag Questions

In spoken English, people commonly use tag questions. Tag questions have two parts: a statement and a tag, an added question. Intonation on the tag part of the tag question can rise or fall.

... didn't they?   ... isn't it?

- Rising intonation on the tag indicates that speakers are not sure about the comment before the tag:

  Bill Gates donates money to a lot of schools, **doesn't he?**
  (This is a real question: The speaker is not sure of the answer.)

- Falling intonation on the tag indicates that the speaker is sure about the comment before the tag and is just seeking confirmation or agreement.

  Oseola McCarty is a remarkable woman, **isn't she?**
  (The speaker is not asking a question, just making a comment.)

1 *Listen, and draw intonation lines on the tag questions. Decide whether the speaker is asking a question or making a comment. Write **C** (comment) or **Q** (question) next to each question.*

_____ 1. Oseola McCarty saved her money for about 50 years, didn't she?

_____ 2. Wealthy philanthropists save a lot of money on taxes, don't they?

_____ 3. A lot of Americans donate to charity, don't they?

_____ 4. People give more today than they used to, don't they?

_____ 5. Children in your country are encouraged to volunteer, aren't they?

2 *Work with a partner. Read the dialogue. Mr. and Mrs. X. Tremely Generous want to donate $5 million to charity. They are discussing which organization should receive their money. Decide whether the tag questions should have rising or falling intonation. Draw intonation lines over the tag questions, and practice the dialogue.*

MRS. GENEROUS: Dear, we have a good life. People with much less money often give money to charity, so I think we should, too. I've got some brochures here for various organizations. Let's pick one.

MR. GENEROUS: That's a good idea. Let's see . . . I admire the work of the Dinosaur Egg Association, don't you? They're trying to find out how to re-create dinosaurs from ancient DNA samples.

MRS. GENEROUS: Well, that's interesting, yes, but I'm more impressed by Save the Rain Forests, or the Clean Ocean Fund. It helps clean up the oceans. I think we should encourage more ecological programs, don't you?

MR. GENEROUS: Well, I guess so. Look at this one! How about the Space Alien Research Institute? It would be great to make contact with some aliens from outer space, wouldn't it?

MRS. GENEROUS: Now that's silly, isn't it? Here's something serious. How about Options for Independence? It's an organization that helps elderly people live on their own. I think that's important, don't you?

MR. GENEROUS: You know, honey, maybe we should split up the money, and each give to different organizations.

MRS. GENEROUS: Terrific idea!

B   GRAMMAR: Tag Questions

1 *Work with a partner. Read the following conversation, paying attention to the underlined words. Then answer the questions.*

A: I didn't read that story about Oseola McCarty, <u>did you</u>?

B: Yes, I did. She's a poor woman who saved $250,000 and gave most of it to a university.

A: Wow. That's amazing!

B: Yes, it is, <u>isn't it</u>?

1. How are the underlined phrases similar?
2. How are they different?

Tag Questions

In spoken English, people commonly use **tag questions**. Tag questions have two parts: a **statement** and the **tag**, an added question.

- If the verb in the statement is affirmative, the tag is negative:

  Oseola McCarty **is** amazing, **isn't** she?

- If the verb in the statement is negative, the tag is affirmative:

  Oseola McCarty **wasn't** highly educated, **was** she?

- Tags always use a form of **be;** or the auxiliary verbs **do, have,** or **will;** or a modal verb such as **can, could, should,** or **would.** Like a verb, the tag must agree with the subject:

  You're late for the meeting, ~~isn't you?~~ **aren't** you?

There are two types of tag questions: the question type and the comment type.

Question Type	Examples
Use a tag question to get information. Use rising intonation to show that a question is being asked.	A: Oseola McCarty didn't have any education, **did she**?
	B: Yes, she did. She finished sixth grade.
	A: My appointment for the volunteer interview is at 6:00 P.M., **isn't it**?
	B: No, it's at 7:30.

(continued)

Comment Type

Use a tag question to make a comment that is not really a question. An answer is not necessarily expected, but confirmation is. In this case, the tag question means "Isn't that true?" For comment-type tag questions, use falling intonation.

Examples

A: Oseola McCarty is a wonderful woman, **isn't she?**

B: Yes, she is.

A: Oseola McCarty gave a lot of her money away, **didn't she?**

B: Yes, she did.

Answering Tag Questions

Answer tag questions the same way you answer *yes/no* questions. You can agree with a tag question (comment type), or you can answer a tag question (question type) by giving information.

Examples

A: Gladys Holm was a very caring person, wasn't she? (comment type)

B: **Yes, she certainly was.**

A: Gladys Holm did volunteer work at the hospital, didn't she? (question type)

B: **Yes, she did. She visited sick children regularly.**

---

2 *Work with a partner.*

Step 1: Complete the conversation using the appropriate tags. (Note that most conversations do not use as many tag questions.)

A: You've heard about Oseola McCarty's gift to the university,

(1) ___*haven't you*___ ?

B: Yes, I have. It's an amazing story, (2) _____?

A: Uh-huh. Some people are more generous than others,

(3) _____?

B: That's the truth. Most people wouldn't give away all their money,

(4) _____?

A: Of course not. Even very wealthy people don't give a very high

percentage of their money away, (5) _____?

B: Right. I remember reading that low-income people give an average of 3.6 percent of their income and wealthy people only 1.6 percent. That's surprising, (6) _____?

A: But it's not true for everyone. Look at media tycoon Ted Turner. He gave $1 billion to the United Nations, (7) _____?

B: That's right. It's hard to imagine having that much money to give, (8) _____?

A: It sure is. But more wealthy people should give away more of their money, (9) _____?

B: I agree, but I wonder how I'd feel if I were rich!

Step 2: Now listen to the conversation. Go back to the dialogue in Step 1, and mark the rising and falling intonation. Then compare your work with that of your partner.

Step 3: Practice the dialogue with your partner. Be sure to use the correct intonation with each tag.

3 *Work with a partner.*

Step 1: Read the statements about Oseola McCarty below. Work alone and underline the parts of the statements that are *not* true.

1. Oseola McCarty was a hardworking woman who spent her life cleaning houses.

2. After finishing high school, she began to invest her money.

3. She was careful about watching over her nest egg as it grew.

4. When her three children grew up and moved away, Oseola lived alone in her later years.

5. Then she decided to make a contribution to help college professors.

6. She donated $100,000 to a university.

7. The first recipient of her scholarship didn't accept the money because she felt sorry for Oseola.

8. When she got older, Oseola couldn't afford to stop working.

Step 2:   Work in pairs. Take turns asking tag questions to check the information in Step 1.

Example

STUDENT A: Oseola McCarty didn't clean houses, did she?

STUDENT B: No. She washed clothes for a living.

STUDENT A: That's right.

Step 3:   Now write the correct information above the underlined parts of the statements in Step 1. Check your corrections with another pair of students.

C   STYLE: Prioritizing or Ranking Ideas

When two people are discussing more than one idea, it helps the listener if the speaker prioritizes or ranks the ideas to indicate which are the most important and which are the least important. Here are some expressions that can be used to prioritize or rank ideas.

Highest Priority	Also a Priority	Lowest Priority
Our top priority is …	But it is also important …	Least important is …
First of all, …	In addition, …	Of least concern is …
First and foremost, …	Another consideration is …	
Above all, …	Aside from that, …	

Work in pairs.

Step 1:   Read the ads for volunteer jobs on the next page.

WANTED	**POSITION**	**VOLUNTEER HELP NEEDED**
Part-time worker at neighborhood animal shelter. Help find homes for abandoned animals. Do something useful for your community, and bring the joy of a new pet into someone's life. Responsible for feeding, walking, and taking care of animals. Some contact with the public and experience in office work necessary. Volunteers needed at least 8 hours per week: daily 8 A.M. to 10 P.M.	Volunteer fund-raiser for charitable healthcare organization. Responsibilities include helping to find new donors and helping to raise $1,000,000 for yearly budget. Responsible for formal fund-raising dinner and celebrity baseball night. Handle correspondence and telephone fund-raising drive.	Hospital worker. Volunteer needed to be a companion to ill patients. Read aloud to patients, take them for walks, offer a shoulder to lean on. Our motto: "A friend when you need one." Call 555-5863 or email us at *www.we-care.org*.

Step 2: Read the personal qualities listed below. Discuss which qualities apply to each job. Prioritize the qualities. Add other qualities that may apply. Use expressions from the style box on page 130 and tag questions when possible.

ability to finish tasks	flexibility
ability to work long hours	good communication skills
ability to work with many kinds of people	good listening skills
assertiveness	good office skills
attention to detail	love of animals
cheerfulness	patience
cleanliness	public speaking experience
compassion	sense of humor
emotional strength	stylish appearance

Example

STUDENT A: <u>First and foremost</u>, volunteers at the animal shelter must love animals.

STUDENT B: Of course. <u>But it's also important</u> for them to have good communication skills, isn't it?

STUDENT A: Yes, you're right, because they'll have some contact with the public.

STUDENT B: And <u>aside from that</u>, volunteers need some office skills for the administrative work, don't they?

D SPEAKING TOPIC

Work in a small group. Create a public service announcement (PSA).

Step 1: Select a not-for-profit organization from the following list. Give it a name, and decide on its purpose.

after-school program	nursing home
animal shelter	scholarship fund
art museum	scientific research organization
environmental group	special hospital
homeless shelter	

Step 2: Write your PSA. Your announcement should explain what the organization does and why people should donate time or money to it. Use these guidelines:

1. Make your PSA interesting by using the tag questions from the grammar section on pages 127–130 to get your listeners involved. Make sure your tag questions are grammatically correct and that your intonation conveys the idea of either a question or a comment.
   - "You probably love animals, don't you?"
     (This PSA needs volunteers at an animal shelter).
   - "You've suffered from hay fever, haven't you?"
     (This PSA will ask volunteers to participate in a clinical medical trial for new allergy research).

2. Make your PSA convincing by listing a few reasons why people should help your organization. Use the expressions from the style section on pages 130–131 to prioritize and rank ideas.
   - "First and foremost, you should love working with animals. . . ."
   - "Aside from that, you will feel a great sense of satisfaction. . . ."

Step 3: Prepare a one-minute announcement for a radio station. Write several roles so that everyone in your group can play a part. Record your PSA and play it in class.

Step 4: Listen to all the PSAs. The class will vote on which PSA is the most interesting and which is the most convincing.

E RESEARCH TOPICS

Report on one of these topics related to helping others.

1. Do research on a philanthropic organization or a philanthropist.

Step 1: Choose a not-for-profit organization or a philanthropist you would like to know more about. Select from the groups listed in the boxes below, or think of your own.

Some Not-for-Profit Organizations

UNICEF

Nature Conservancy

Amnesty International

Save the Children

International Committee of the Red Cross

Salvation Army

Oxfam

Sierra Club

Some Philanthropists*

John D. and Catherine T. McArthur

Bill Gates

Brooke Astor

George Soros

John Kluge

Oveta Culp Hoby

Carol F. Sulzberger

Andrew W. Mellon

Charles F. Feeney

Andrew Carnegie

Warren E. Buffet

Robert Wood Johnson

John D. Rockefeller

Ted Turner

---

* You may need to look up the name as a foundation (for example, Robert Wood Johnson Foundation).

Step 2:   Find out about the organization or person by visiting the library, doing research on the Internet, or telephoning (for example, call the office of the organization). Use the following questions as a guide.

Questions to Ask about a Not-for-Profit Organization

1. When was it established?

2. Who established it? Why?

3. What are its goals?

4. How much money does it receive?

5. What are some of its accomplishments?

6. (your own questions)

Questions to Ask about a Philanthropist

1. If the philanthropist is no longer alive, when did he or she live?

2. What is/was the person's life like? What does/did the philanthropist do?

3. Whom does/did the philanthropist help?

4. How were recipients selected?

5. (your own questions)

2. Visit a local organization that is looking for volunteers: a hospital, a church, a mosque, a temple, an arts organization or museum, an AIDS organization, an organization that helps the elderly, a school, or an environmental organization.

Step 1:   Talk to volunteers as well as the staff. Ask questions about:

- number of volunteers

- kind of work the volunteers do

- reason the organization needs volunteers

- requirements for volunteers

- satisfaction of the volunteers

Step 2:   Report to the class about the organization you visited. Listen to each other's reports. Discuss which organization you would be most likely to volunteer for, and give your reasons why.

For Unit 6 Internet activities, visit the NorthStar Companion Website at http://www.longman.com/northstar.

Emotional Intelligence

1 Focus on the Topic

A PREDICTING

Look at the cartoon and the title of the unit. Then discuss these questions with a partner.

1. What kind of job do you think this man has? What does the cartoon show us about intelligence?

2. What do you think "emotional intelligence" means?

B   SHARING INFORMATION

Work in a small group. Discuss your answers to the following questions.

Bill Gates

Serena and Venus Williams

Jennifer López

1. Do you know the people in the photographs? Are they intelligent? Explain.

2. Who are the three most intelligent people you know personally? In what ways are they intelligent? Describe them to your classmates.

C   PREPARING TO LISTEN

BACKGROUND

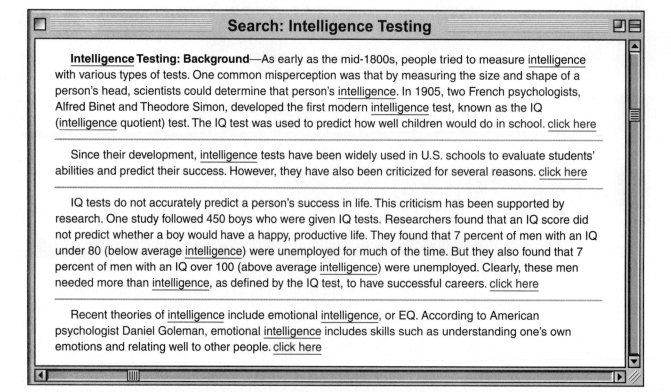

Search: Intelligence Testing

Intelligence Testing: Background—As early as the mid-1800s, people tried to measure intelligence with various types of tests. One common misperception was that by measuring the size and shape of a person's head, scientists could determine that person's intelligence. In 1905, two French psychologists, Alfred Binet and Theodore Simon, developed the first modern intelligence test, known as the IQ (intelligence quotient) test. The IQ test was used to predict how well children would do in school. click here

Since their development, intelligence tests have been widely used in U.S. schools to evaluate students' abilities and predict their success. However, they have also been criticized for several reasons. click here

IQ tests do not accurately predict a person's success in life. This criticism has been supported by research. One study followed 450 boys who were given IQ tests. Researchers found that an IQ score did not predict whether a boy would have a happy, productive life. They found that 7 percent of men with an IQ under 80 (below average intelligence) were unemployed for much of the time. But they also found that 7 percent of men with an IQ over 100 (above average intelligence) were unemployed. Clearly, these men needed more than intelligence, as defined by the IQ test, to have successful careers. click here

Recent theories of intelligence include emotional intelligence, or EQ. According to American psychologist Daniel Goleman, emotional intelligence includes skills such as understanding one's own emotions and relating well to other people. click here

*Complete the following opinion survey about intelligence. Circle how you feel about each statement, from **1** (Strongly Agree) to **4** (Strongly Disagree). Then compare your answers in a small group. Explain your opinions using examples from your experience.*

Intelligence An Opinion Survey	What Do You Believe about Intelligence?			
	Strongly Agree			Strongly Disagree
1. Intelligence can be accurately measured.	1	2	3	4
2. Each person is born with a certain amount of intelligence.	1	2	3	4
3. Scientists and mathematicians are more intelligent than artists and writers.	1	2	3	4
4. Very intelligent people do not have good "people skills" and are not good at relating to others.	1	2	3	4
5. Emotions do not help us think logically.	1	2	3	4
6. People who get good grades in school will also do well in their careers.	1	2	3	4

VOCABULARY FOR COMPREHENSION

Read the following sentences. Circle the letter of the word or expression that is closest in meaning to the underlined word. Compare your answers with those of another student.

1. Some people do not <u>respond</u> in a positive way to criticism. They become either angry or depressed.

   a. agree   **b.** react   **c.** listen

2. How do you <u>handle</u> your anger? One way is to do something physical, like going for a walk. By the time you get back, you won't feel angry anymore.

   a. deal with   **b.** hide   **c.** understand

3. Some people feel that they must <u>make a big fuss</u> in order to get what they want. They become annoyed and aren't satisfied until they get their way.

   a. complain loudly   **b.** become worried   **c.** remain calm

4. We must all learn to accept <u>setbacks</u>. When things go wrong, we should keep going and not let problems stop us.

    a. choices   **b.** surprises   **c.** disappointments

5. Some people always seem to <u>take life in stride</u>. Difficulties don't seem to bother them, and they can look ahead to better times.

    a. balance the positive   **b.** worry about   **c.** exercise regularly
        and the negative   everything

6. Don't <u>give up</u> when you can't solve a problem. Instead, try looking at it in a new way, and eventually you will find a solution.

    a. feel sad   **b.** stop trying   **c.** ask for help

7. I love the class I am taking now. I feel very <u>enthusiastic</u> about it.

    a. intelligent   **b.** thankful   **c.** excited

8. You will get depressed if you always <u>dwell on</u> failures. You should think about the positive things in your life instead.

    a. think about for   **b.** forget about   **c.** look for anxiously
        too long   gladly

9. She's a very <u>sharp</u> manager. She understands problems quickly and always solves them.

    a. smart   **b.** reliable   **c.** easygoing

10. It's common to feel <u>resentful</u> when other people succeed and you don't. But instead of feeling bad, focus on what's possible and best for your own situation.

    a. tired and nervous   **b.** surprised and   **c.** hurt and angry
                                  confused

11. When you make a mistake, it's best to <u>swallow your pride</u>. Then you can try to correct the problem.

    a. tell people about   **b.** express your   **c.** admit you are wrong
        a problem   anger   or need help

12. When friends are upset, it's important to <u>empathize with</u> them. By recognizing their feelings, you will be able to help your friends feel better.

    a. understand   **b.** spend time with   **c.** change

2 Focus on Listening

A   LISTENING ONE: *Can You Learn EQ?*

You will listen to a radio program called *Psychology Talk*. Host Claire Nolan discusses the emotional intelligence quotient (EQ).

 Listen to the introduction, and answer the questions. Compare your answers with those of another student.

1. The main focus of this discussion will be _____.
   a. how to test a person's EQ
   b. whether EQ can be learned
   c. how to use EQ in the workplace

2. Claire Nolan will interview two educators about their ideas on EQ. One educator works with children and the other with adults. Do you think their opinions will be similar or different? Explain.

_____

_____

LISTENING FOR MAIN IDEAS

 Listen to the entire program. Take notes below as you listen to the educators discuss their opinions about EQ. Then compare your answers with those of another student.

	WHAT IS THE PERSON'S JOB?	CAN EQ BE LEARNED OR TAUGHT?	HOW CAN A HIGH EQ HELP A PERSON?
Betty Cortina			
Jim McDonald			

LISTENING FOR DETAILS

 The people in the interview mention qualities that a person with a high EQ might possess. Read the list below. Then listen to the entire interview again, one part at a time. Check the qualities you hear mentioned. Compare your answers with those of another student.

A person with a high EQ can _____.

Part One

_____ 1. respond well to others

_____ 2. talk openly about feelings

_____ 3. be patient and easygoing

_____ 4. make a big fuss

_____ 5. control his or her emotions

_____ 6. apologize easily when wrong

_____ 7. let negative feelings get in the way

Part Two

_____ 8. have a positive, enthusiastic attitude

_____ 9. use time effectively

_____ 10. respond well to change

_____ 11. have creative ideas

_____ 12. accept responsibility for mistakes

_____ 13. see how his or her behavior affects others

_____ 14. work well with other people

REACTING TO THE LISTENING

Emotional intelligence includes qualities or skills such as understanding one's own emotions and relating well to other people. According to Daniel Goleman, there are several main skills of emotional intelligence.

1 *Read the list of skills below. Then listen to the excerpts from the radio interview. They describe situations in which people do not have one (or more) of the skills. Write the skill or skills each person needs to develop and why.*

Skills of Emotional Intelligence

self-awareness: understanding your own emotions
self-control: managing your own emotions
self-motivation: using your emotions to get things done
empathy: understanding other people's emotions
people skills: relating well to other people

Excerpt One

1. Skill(s) needed: _____

_____

2. Reason: _____

_____

Excerpt Two

3. Skill(s) needed: _____

_____

4. Reason: _____

_____

Excerpt Three

5. Skill(s) needed: _____

_____

6. Reason: _____

_____

2 *Discuss these questions.*

1. Do you think it is possible for people to improve their EQ? Explain.

2. In which areas is your own EQ highest? Why do you think this is true? Give examples.

3. The theory of emotional intelligence was developed in the United States. Do you think it would apply across all cultures? Are qualities associated with EQ highly valued in all cultures?

B LISTENING TWO: *Test Your EQ*

You will hear Claire Nolan and Jan Davis discuss the EQ tests.

1 *Before you listen, take this short test to discover your own EQ. Read each situation, and circle the letter of the answer that best describes how you would react. Then write the reason for your choice.*

 2 *Now, listen to Claire Nolan and Jan Davis discuss the answers that show the highest EQ. Go through the test again, and circle the letter of the high EQ answer.*

EQ Test*

1. Your four-year-old son is crying because some other children won't play with him. What do you do?

   a. Don't do anything. Let him solve the problem on his own.
   b. Talk to him and help him figure out ways to get the other kids to play with him.
   c. Tell him in a kind voice not to cry.

   Your answer:　　　　**a**　　**b**　　**c**

   Reason: _____

   High EQ answer:　　**a**　　**b**　　**c**

---

* Adapted from Daniel Goleman, "EQ: What's Your Emotional Intelligence Quotient?" *Utne Reader,* November–December 1995.

2. You're a college student who had hoped to do well in a course, but you just found out you failed the midterm exam. What do you do?

    a. Make a specific plan for ways to improve your grade.
    b. Promise yourself to do better in the future.
    c. Drop the class and study something else.

Your answer: **a**   **b**   **c**

Reason: _____

High EQ answer: **a**   **b**   **c**

3. Your friend is driving. He is angry because a driver in another car almost hit him. You're trying to calm him down. What do you do?

    a. Put in one of his favorite CDs and try to distract him.
    b. Join him in insulting the other driver.
    c. Tell him about a time something like this happened to you and how you felt as angry as he does now.

Your answer: **a**   **b**   **c**

Reason: _____

High EQ answer: **a**   **b**   **c**

4. You are a manager in a company that has employees from different ethnic backgrounds. You hear someone telling a joke about one ethnic group. What do you do?

    a. Ignore it. It's only a joke.
    b. Call the person into your office and tell him or her not to tell ethnic jokes.
    c. Say something to all the employees right away. Tell them that ethnic jokes are not acceptable in your organization.

Your answer: **a**   **b**   **c**

Reason: _____

High EQ answer: **a**   **b**   **c**

5. You've been assigned to lead a team of workers from different departments to solve a problem at work. You're having your first meeting to discuss the problem. What's the first thing you do?

    a. List what the group should do to make the best use of its time.
    b. Have people take the time to get to know each other better.
    c. Begin by asking each person for ideas about how to solve the problem.

Your answer: **a**   **b**   **c**

Reason: _____

High EQ answer: **a**   **b**   **c**

C   LINKING LISTENINGS ONE AND TWO

Work in a small group. Discuss your answers to the following questions.

1. Look at the skills of emotional intelligence listed in the box on page 141. Then look at the EQ Test on pages 142–143. Which skills are being tested in each of the situations described in the EQ test?

2. Look at the survey you completed on page 137.

   a. The chart below includes the same statements that you responded to in the survey on page 137. How would the speakers in the listenings respond to these questions? Would they agree or disagree with them? Write a number from *1* (strongly agree) to *4* (strongly disagree) to show how each speaker would feel about each statement.

   b. Do you still agree with your own original answers?

	BETTY CORTINA	JIM MCDONALD
1. Intelligence can be accurately measured.		
2. Each person is born with a certain amount of intelligence.		
3. Scientists and mathematicians are more intelligent than artists and writers.		
4. Very intelligent people do not have good "people skills" and are not good at relating to others.		
5. Emotions do not help us think logically.		
6. People who get good grades in school will also do well in their careers.		

3 Focus on Vocabulary

1 *Pronounce the adjectives and verb phrases on page 145 with your teacher. Then, working with a partner, read aloud the opinions of people working in various occupations. They are discussing the qualities they need to do their jobs well. Write in the adjective or verb phrase that best completes the statements. Then read aloud the completed statements.*

Adjectives	Verb Phrases	
easygoing	deal with setbacks	put oneself in
enthusiastic	dwell on failure	someone else's shoes
patient	empathize with	act with respect
perceptive	give up	respond well
resentful	make a fuss	swallow one's pride
sharp	make allowances for	take life in stride
high-spirited	put aside negative feelings	

1. "As a software designer in the computer industry, we work long hours, so

   you have to be someone who is _____ the work.

a. (enthusiastic about / resentful of)

   You must _____ to change because in this field we

b. (act with respect / respond well)

   are always facing something new."

2. "A good trial lawyer is a/an _____ person.

a. (high-spirited / easygoing)

   Winning is the most important thing. But you sometimes lose, so you must

   know how to _____."

b. (dwell on failure / deal with setbacks)

3. "A customer service representative talks to people who have problems with

   telephone service. We have to know how to respond when customers

   _____ because their telephones don't work.

a. (are high-spirited / make a fuss)

   Sometimes the customers are very angry at us, but we have to

   _____ and help them anyway.

b. (put aside our negative feelings / give up)

4. "As a psychologist, I try to _____

a. (put myself in my clients' shoes / be easygoing with my clients)

   in order to really understand them. You have to be very

   _____ in order to understand what a person is

b. (enthusiastic / perceptive)

   feeling."

5. "To be a good scientist, you have to be able to admit when you are wrong.

   You must be able to accept criticism, _____,

a. (swallow your pride / make a fuss)

   and continue your work. All in all, you need to be able to

   _____."

b. (take life in stride / be resentful)

2 *Complete the following activities.*

1. Work with a partner. Choose a profession from the previous exercise and write a dialogue using several of the adjectives and expressions you learned in it. Practice the dialogue and perform it for the class.

2. Work in a small group. Take turns discussing a time when you were angry, sad, frustrated, or resentful. Use at least five words and expressions from this unit to illustrate your story. Did you react badly or well? Did you show a high EQ? Would you do anything differently now? Explain. Take notes about each other's stories on a separate piece of paper. Set up a chart like the one below. Share the best stories with the class.

Name	What Happened?	Feelings	Reactions

4 Focus on Speaking

A   PRONUNCIATION: Unstressed Vowels

Words with two or more syllables always have one syllable that is stressed. They usually have one or more syllables that are unstressed.

respond	re-SPOND	syllable	SYL-la-ble

In most words, the vowel sound in the unstressed syllable is reduced. The reduced vowel is pronounced "uh" (like the vowel sound in *but*). This reduced vowel sound is called a *schwa*. The symbol for a schwa is /ə/.

respond	r/ə/-SPOND	syllable	SYL-l/ə/-ble
children	CHIL-dr/ə/n	mistake	m/ə/s-TAKE

Note: Vowels with secondary stress are not reduced. For example, in the compound word *setback,* the vowel in *back* has secondary stress and is not reduced to a schwa.

1 *Listen to words from this unit. Put a line between the syllables. Then listen again, and put a dot over the syllables with the strongest stress. Write /ə/ over the vowel in the unstressed syllables.*

1. con|trol
2. adjust
3. success
4. productively
5. people
6. honest
7. quotient
8. resentful
9. personal
10. ability
11. adult
12. perceptive
13. failure
14. advice
15. emotional

2 *Listen to the words again, and repeat them aloud. Make sure you pronounce the /ə/ sound correctly.*

3 *Listen to the advertisement for a seminar about EQ. Mark the stressed vowels.*

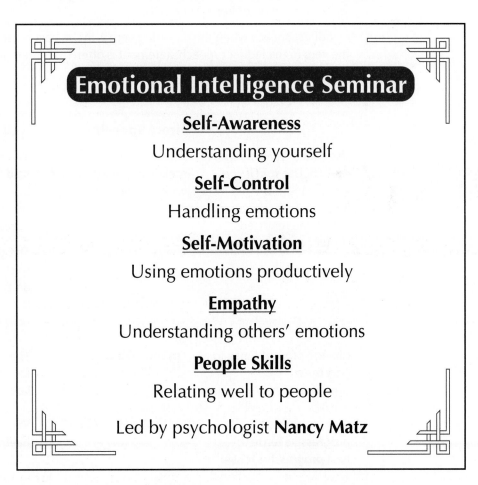

Emotional Intelligence Seminar

Self-Awareness
Understanding yourself

Self-Control
Handling emotions

Self-Motivation
Using emotions productively

Empathy
Understanding others' emotions

People Skills
Relating well to people

Led by psychologist **Nancy Matz**

Work in pairs. Take turns. Read the advertisement aloud to your partner. Your partner will listen for correct pronunciation of the stressed and unstressed syllables.

B GRAMMAR: Direct and Indirect Speech

1 *Work with a partner. Read the sentences below, and answer the questions.*

a. Betty Cortina said that some of her kids were more patient than others.

b. Daniel Goleman said that we could learn to improve our EQ.

1. For both examples, what were the speakers' exact words?

2. In sentence *a*, why is the second verb in the past tense?

3. What tenses are used in sentence *b*? Why?

Direct and Indirect Speech

Direct speech (also called quoted speech) reports the speaker's exact words.
Indirect speech (also called reported speech) reports what the speaker said without using his or her exact words.

In indirect speech when the reporting verb is in the past tense (*said, told, reported*), the verb in the indirect speech statement is often in a different tense from the verb that was used in the direct speech statement.

	Direct Speech	Indirect Speech
Use **said** or **told** to report speech. Use **told** if you want to mention the listener. **That** is optional before the reported sentence.	"An emotionally intelligent person knows when and how to apologize."	The psychology teacher **said** (that) an emotionally intelligent person knows when and how to apologize.
		The psychology teacher **told the students** (that) an emotionally intelligent person knows when and how to apologize.
Change **present tense** to **past tense**.	"I**'m** sorry I**'m** late."	The student said (that) she **was** sorry she **was** late.
Change **present progressive tense** to **past progressive tense**.	"I**'m having** a bad day."	She said (that) she **was having** a bad day.

Change **past tense** and **present perfect tense** to **past perfect tense.**	"The bus **broke** down."	The student said (that) the bus **had broken** down.
	"It **has** never **broken** down before."	She said (that) it **had** never **broken** down before.
The modals **will, can,** and **may** change form in indirect speech.	"I **won't** be late again."	She said (that) she **wouldn't** be late again.
	"I **can** take a taxi next time."	She said (that) she **could** take a taxi next time.
	"I **may** get a new car."	She said (that) she **might** get a new car.
Change **must** to **had to.**	"I **must** find a better way to get to work."	She said (that) she **had to** find a better way to get to work.
Do not change the modals **should, could, might,** or **ought to.**	"I **should** get up earlier."	She said (that) she **should** get up earlier.
Change the pronouns, possessives, and time words to keep the original meaning.	"**I** can't drive **my** car because it broke down **yesterday.**"	The student said (that) **she** couldn't drive **her** car because it had broken down **the day before.**

2 *Work with a partner. Read the statements on page 150 and respond using indirect speech.*

Student A: Read statement 1 aloud. Listen to Student B respond. The correct response is in parentheses. If Student B is correct, say, "That's right." If Student B is incorrect, make the correct statement. Switch roles after statement 4.

Student B: Cover Student A's statements. After Student A reads statement 1, clarify what he or she said by restating, using indirect speech. Student A will tell you if you are correct or not.

Example

STUDENT A: I did poorly on the EQ test!

STUDENT B: I think you said you had done poorly on the EQ test, right?

STUDENT A: That's right.

Student A

1. I don't think the EQ theory will hold up.
   (Student B: You said you didn't think the EQ theory would hold up.)

2. I'm going to work on my EQ.
   (Student B: You said you were going to work on your EQ.)

3. I never learned about EQ in school.
   (Student B: You said you had never learned about EQ in school.)

4. My parents tried their best.
   (Student B: You said your parents had tried their best.)

Now switch roles. Student A, cover Student B's statements.

Student B

5. I am really busy.
   (Student A: You said that you were really busy.)

6. I can't talk to the boss right now.
   (Student A: You said that you couldn't talk to the boss right now.)

7. I haven't finished my work yet.
   (Student A: You said that you hadn't finished your work yet.)

8. I'll call the boss later.
   (Student A: You said that you would call the boss later.)

C STYLE: Restating for Clarification or Emphasis

When we restate for clarification, we say the same thing in different words.
Restating is useful to check how well you have understood what someone said.
To restate, it is important to explain the other person's ideas *in your own words.*
Unlike direct and indirect speech, when you restate, you do not repeat the other
person's exact words. Here are some expressions that can be used to begin a
restatement.

In other words ...	She means/meant that ...
To put it another way ...	He wants/wanted to say that ...
She is/was trying to say that ...	What that means is ...

Work as a class. Read the quotations. Use your own words to restate the ideas. Discuss what the quotations mean.

Example

"The heart has its reasons which reason knows nothing of."

—Blaise Pascal (1623–1662)
French mathematician and philosopher

STUDENT A: What that means is emotions and intellect are not connected.

STUDENT B: Really? I thought it meant that love, which is supposed to be controlled by the heart, is not reasonable.

STUDENT C: In other words, we can't really decide who to love because the heart doesn't listen to reason.

1. "Intelligence is almost useless to someone who has no other quality."

—Alexis Carrel (1873–1944)
French surgeon and biologist

2. "The intellect is always fooled by the heart."

—François La Rochefoucauld (1613–1680)
French writer and moralist

3. "An intellectual is a man who takes more words than necessary to tell more than he knows."

—Dwight D. Eisenhower (1890–1969)
34th president of the United States

4. "The sign of an intelligent people is their ability to control emotions by the application of reason."

—Mary Mannes (1904–1990)
American writer

5. "Genius is 1 percent inspiration and 99 percent perspiration."

—Thomas Alva Edison (1847–1931)
American inventor

6. "When an old man dies, a library burns down."

—Anonymous
African proverb

D   SPEAKING TOPICS

1 *Work with a partner. You will do a role play about EQ.*

1. Choose one of the following four situations. Decide whether you will illustrate high or low EQ for each person in the role play. Review the five skills of emotional intelligence on page 141 to clarify your ideas. Practice the role play with your partner. Then perform your role play for the class. Here is an example of a situation between a worried parent and a teenager who wants to stay out late.

PARENT: I want you to call me up before midnight and tell me what time I should expect you, OK?

TEENAGER: Wait a minute. Are you saying that you expect me to leave my friends and give you a call?

PARENT: That's exactly what I'm saying. Do you understand?

TEENAGER: Yes, I do. And I might be home before midnight anyway. Joe said that the movie ends at 11:00.

Situation One: Two Friends

Student A: You have been waiting for your friend in front of a movie theater for 30 minutes. The movie started 15 minutes ago. Your friend is always late, and you decide it is time to say something about it.

Student B: You are late to meet your friend at the movies. You are running late because your phone kept ringing. You know your friend is going to be mad, but you don't want to be rude to the other people who are calling you.

Situation Two: A Boss and an Employee

Student A: You are very busy and have to give a report at an important meeting tomorrow. One of your employees just gave you information for your report but didn't give you all the details you need. There is very little time, so now you will both have to work late. You are quite annoyed.

Student B: You have just completed a big report for your boss. You worked hard on it and are really satisfied with the results. However, your boss hardly looked at it but told you that it wasn't what he or she was expecting. You are very upset because you did exactly as you were told.

Situation Three: A Married Couple

Student A: You are tired. Your wife or husband begins to criticize you because you left your dirty dishes in the sink. You don't think you've done anything wrong. You think he or she is not being fair. You are annoyed.

Student B: Your husband or wife has left dirty dishes in the sink again. You are tired and don't want to wash them. You think he or she is not being fair. You complain.

Situation Four: Two Friends

Student A: You and your friend were going to go to the beach next weekend. Your friend has decided not to go because he or she has too many things to do. You are disappointed and angry since his or her reasons don't seem very important. You were really looking forward to the weekend.

Student B: You were going to go to the beach with your friend, but you don't want to go now because you have too many things to do: homework, laundry, letters you should have written, and so on. You also have another friend who hasn't been feeling well, and you want to visit that person. A weekend at the beach isn't good right now. You need the time to stay home and do some of these things. You tell your friend.

2. Watch as other pairs perform their role plays. As a class, discuss the role plays. Use indirect speech from the grammar section on pages 148–150 or restating from the style section on pages 150–151 to discuss what people said. Answer these questions:

- Were their responses appropriate?

- Did they show high or low EQ?

- Should they have handled the situation differently? If so, how?

2 *Work in a small group. Create five multiple-choice EQ test questions. Write one question illustrating each of the five skills of emotional intelligence (see page 141). For each question, write one "correct" answer that shows high EQ, and write two "incorrect" answers that show low EQ. Look at the EQ test questions on pages 142–143 for sample questions.*

Share your EQ test questions with another group. Does the other group agree with the "correct" answers? Why or why not?

E ■ RESEARCH TOPIC

Interview a person you admire about emotional intelligence. Report your findings to the class.

Step 1: You will need to explain the theory of emotional intelligence to the person you interview. Work in a small group. Write an example for each skill of emotional intelligence. Use these examples when you explain the theory.

Self-Awareness: understanding your own emotions

Example: _____

Self-Control: managing your own emotions

Example: _____

Self-Motivation: using your emotions to get things done

Example: _____

Empathy: understanding other people's emotions

Example: _____

People Skills: relating well to people

Example: _____

Step 2: Interview the person you chose. First, briefly explain EQ, and then ask the questions that follow. Take notes so you can report your findings to the class.

Name of person interviewed: _____

Occupation: _____

Employer: _____

1. Is high emotional intelligence important for your job (or intended job)? If so, which skills are the most important? _____

_____

2. Can you think of situations in which you've had to demonstrate high EQ? _____

_____

3. How can an employer evaluate the emotional intelligence of someone applying for a job? _____

_____

4. How can a person improve his or her emotional intelligence? _____

_____

5. Should schools teach students the skills of emotional intelligence? Why or why not? If so, what can schools do to help students improve their EQ? _____

_____

6. Should employers teach their employees the skills of emotional intelligence? Why or why not? If so, what can employers do to help their employees improve their EQ? _____

_____

Step 3: Report your findings to the class. Use indirect speech and restating in your report.

For Unit 7 Internet activities, visit the NorthStar Companion Website at http://www.longman.com/northstar.

Goodbye to the Sit-Down Meal

"I just dialed 1-800-BAGUETTE."

1 Focus on the Topic

A PREDICTING

Work with a partner. Look at the cartoon and the title of the unit. Discuss the following questions.

1. How have cooking and eating changed over the past decades where you live?

2. The numbers "1-800" are part of some telephone numbers in the United States. These numbers mean that the call is free for the caller. What does the cartoon say about the changes that have occurred in the way food is prepared and eaten?

B   SHARING INFORMATION

Work in a small group. Look at the six factors that influence food trends. Then read the questions, and discuss the answers with your group.

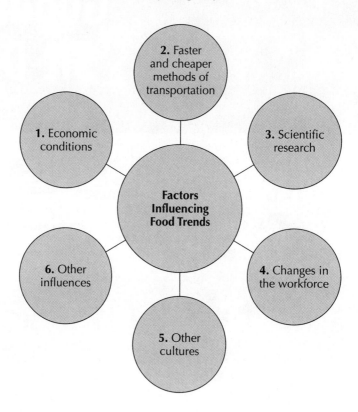

1. *Economic conditions:* How does the amount of money you have affect what you eat?

2. *Faster and cheaper methods of transportation:* Do changes in the way food is shipped affect the way people eat? How? Is international food easy to find in stores where you live?

3. *Scientific research:* Have advances in science affected the way you eat? What research findings have made a difference to you?

4. *Changes in the workforce:* Do your work habits affect your family's or your eating habits? How?

5. *Other cultures:* Have your eating habits or preferences been influenced by other cultures? Do you enjoy international food? Are international restaurants available near you?

6. *Other influences:* What are some of the other factors that affect people's eating habits?

C   PREPARING TO LISTEN

BACKGROUND

If somebody asked you to think about lunch in France, and you let your imagination run wild, what would come to mind? Would lunch take place under a canopy on a pleasant summer afternoon, and would the meal include a fresh baguette and some cheese? Would there be music, candles, celebratory toasts, and fresh, tasty delicacies? If your answer is yes, you're not in the minority. Most people associate France with good food. It's no secret that French culture includes a long tradition of slow, careful preparation of meals that use fresh, local ingredients. Meals are meant to be lingered over and enjoyed with good company and intimate conversation. Even the midday meal has been one to enjoy at leisure, usually at home with family.

It's also no secret that food trends in the United States have been moving toward the complete opposite—ever faster food preparation and consumption. Lunch for many people is eaten in less than an hour, if it is eaten at all. Sitting down to a lengthy lunch or returning home to family to do so is next to impossible unless it is a special occasion. Many people think nothing of eating quickly at their desks as they answer email, and some even eat in their cars.

Is France trying to adapt to the pressures of our overwhelmingly fast-paced society? Is France, like other countries with fine culinary traditions, beginning to abandon some of its precious culinary culture and follow more modern trends?

Work in a small group. Compare a traditional meal in your culture to a modern version of a meal today. What do they have in common? What is different? Which do you prefer? Explain.

VOCABULARY FOR COMPREHENSION

1 *Read the following sentences. Try to determine the meaning of each underlined word from the context of its sentence. Write a definition or similar expression on the line.*

1. One recent <u>phenomenon</u> is bubble gum ice cream. Its popularity is a bit of a surprise to many people.

   something that happens that is strange or hard to understand

2. In the early twentieth century, it was common to spend several hours every day cooking and eating. In recent years, we have <u>witnessed</u> a change in people's eating habits.

   _____

3. There has been a <u>boom</u> in take-out food in the last decade or two. People like to eat at home, but they can't or don't want to prepare meals.

_____

4. Supermarkets in the United States now carry foods that used to be expensive and difficult to find. These <u>delicacies</u> include snails from France, lychee nuts from China, noodles from Japan, and other unusual fruits and vegetables.

_____

5. There is no doubt that a change in eating habits has occurred. This <u>shift</u> is of great interest to sociologists, who see it as being part of larger changes in our lives.

_____

6. Many people think of eating as a special activity to be shared with family and close friends. Preparing and eating food are seen by many as <u>intimate</u> activities.

_____

7. The way people view food is basic and important to each family or culture and is considered a <u>core</u> cultural value.

_____

8. Simply heating up frozen meals has become a popular method of preparing a meal. In the frozen food sections of supermarkets, the shelves are <u>stacked</u> with meals that can be prepared quickly.

_____

9. Other recently popular items include panini, sushi, and Thai noodles. Each of these has become a <u>hit</u> in most cities in the United States today.

_____

10. Some people feel that their neighborhoods are being <u>overrun</u> by fast-food restaurants.

_____

11. Combining foods that don't usually go together can result in some interesting new tastes. This has prompted some cooks and chefs to <u>let their imaginations run wild</u> as they create new products for the public to try.

_____

2 *Match each word on the left with a definition or expression on the right. Write the correct letter in the blank.*

_____ **1.** phenomenon	**a.** be extremely creative
_____ **2.** witnessed	**b.** basic, essential
_____ **3.** boom	**c.** something rare, something very unusual
_____ **4.** delicacies	**d.** change, modification
_____ **5.** shift	**e.** private or personal
_____ **6.** intimate	**f.** something extremely popular
_____ **7.** core	**g.** full of
_____ **8.** stacked	**h.** spread over a place quickly and in great numbers
_____ **9.** hit	**i.** rapid increase, surge
_____ **10.** overrun	**j.** observed
_____ **11.** let one's imagination run wild	**k.** food that is expensive and rare

2 Focus on Listening

A LISTENING ONE: *French Sandwiches*

You will hear the first part of a National Public Radio report by Sarah Chayes on a recent phenomenon in eating habits in France.

 Listen to the first part of the report, and answer the questions.

1. What is changing in France? Why might this be surprising?

_____

_____

2. Why do you believe these changes are taking place?

_____

LISTENING FOR MAIN IDEAS

You will now hear the entire report. Write short answers to the questions below. Compare your answers with those of a partner.

1. What is becoming very popular among French people?

   _____

2. According to the speaker, what are some reasons for the change in French eating habits?

   _____

3. Why has the bakery become so popular recently?

   _____

LISTENING FOR DETAILS

Listen to the report again. As you listen, circle the letter of the answer to each question.

1. How long did people traditionally sit down to eat in France?
   a. one hour
   b. two hours
   c. three hours

2. What does the report say about the reasons for the change in eating habits?
   a. They are contradictory.
   b. They are conservative.
   c. They are complicated.

3. In the past, what products did French bakeries offer?
   a. a wide variety of baked goods and dairy products
   b. a limited number of breads and pastries
   c. a variety of baked goods and general grocery items

4. How does Nicole, a worker in the bakery, feel about making all the different products she now prepares?
   a. She dislikes it.
   b. She likes it.
   c. She's confused by it.

5. How has the owner of the bakery reacted to the demand?
   a. She is being more creative.
   b. She is busier than she wants to be.
   c. She is responding unhappily.

6. In general, what do French working people now do?
   a. pay more for better food
   b. leave early at the end of the day
   c. eat lunch later than usual

7. How have women contributed to the changes?
   a. Fewer women want to cook.
   b. Women are having fewer children.
   c. More women are working.

8. Why have the changes in men's professions been so important?
   a. They have less time.
   b. They are not as hungry.
   c. They prefer to eat out.

9. What is the key to the success of the bakery?
   a. The prices are low.
   b. The bakery uses only French products.
   c. The bakery serves customers quickly.

10. What just closed around the corner from Au Pain Gourmet?
    a. a French salad bar
    b. a hamburger franchise
    c. a foreign bakery

REACTING TO THE LISTENING

 1 *Listen to the excerpts. The reporter uses several words that have more than one meaning. This deliberate use of words with double meanings adds humor and interest to the report. Answer the questions that follow with a partner.*

Excerpt One

You will hear reporter Sarah Chayes explain what happens in Au Pain Gourmet, a bakery in Paris.

1. What does *tough* mean here?
   a. The bread is difficult to chew, like tough meat.
   b. The situation is difficult to accept, but you must.

2. What does the reporter mean?
   a. Nicole earns money doing this.
   b. The bread on the table is not soft.

Excerpt Two

Now you will hear how the bakery owner has adapted to the new demand.

3. What does *swallow* mean here?
   a. to eat
   b. to accept

4. What does the reporter mean?
   a. The size of the sandwich was too large for most people's mouths.
   b. There were too many very different ingredients in the sandwich.

Excerpt Three

You will now hear about the customers' reactions to the new products.

5. What does *hit* mean here?
   a. to strike or crash into
   b. a success, something popular

6. What does the reporter mean?
   a. The lines are long and frustrating, so customers in a hurry occasionally fight.
   b. The sandwiches are enormously popular with the people who go there.

Excerpt Four

You will now hear about a reaction to the change in eating habits.

7. What does *exploding* mean here?
   a. increasing rapidly
   b. blowing up and making a loud noise

8. What does the woman mean?
   a. High oven temperatures have caused accidents in some bakeries.
   b. The trend has suddenly become extremely popular.

2 *Work in a small group. Discuss the following questions.*

1. Why is the bakery doing better than the hamburger place?

2. What do you predict for the future of the bakery?

3. Is there an increase in fast-food products and restaurants in your area? Explain. If there is, how do you feel about it?

B   LISTENING TWO: *Food in a Bowl*

You will hear some comments from *Satellite Sisters*, a radio show featuring five sisters who live in different parts of the world and share their thoughts— via satellite—on everyday life. In this segment, Lian, in California, talks about a food trend.

 Listen to the report and answer the questions. Then discuss your answers in a small group.

1. Why was Lian surprised in the supermarket?
   a. She found unusual food items in bowls.
   b. She thought the food-in-bowls section was too large.

2. Why does Lian think this food-in-bowls trend is happening?
   a. People are too hurried to be careful about eating.
   b. Bowls keep food warmer than plates.

3. Lian jokes that maybe the next new eating style will be _____.
   a. eating while keeping one hand on the phone
   b. eating without using our hands

4. Lian exaggerates by using humor when she says, "just get yourself a nice *trough*, and put the lasagna in there." (A trough is a container that holds food for animals.) Why does she mention an animal food container?
   a. Many people are vegetarians and don't eat animal products.
   b. Lian thinks that people look like animals when they eat the wrong food in bowls.

5. Lian thinks that teaching her children to eat with a knife and fork is _____.
   a. her responsibility
   b. extremely difficult

6. Lian's sister, Julie, in Bangkok, also makes a comment. What is her attitude toward the subject?
   a. She shares Lian's feelings about food in bowls.
   b. She seems to have no problem accepting food in bowls.

7. What does Liz struggle with?
   a. eating food on skewers
   b. finding new ways to cook lamb

C   LINKING LISTENINGS ONE AND TWO

The Satellite Sisters speak to each other in a style that is very different from that of Claude Fishlere and Sarah Chayes. In the conversations on pages 164–165, identify the speakers from the style they use. Then choose words that describe each speaker's style.

When you've finished, read the conversations aloud, playing the role and using the style you have identified. These are the people who may be speaking:

- a bakery owner

- a Satellite Sister

- Claude Fishlere

You can use the words in the box below to describe the speaker's style:

intimate	light	analytical
informal	humorous	informative

Conversation One

A: Would you please describe how you see the changes in eating habits in your culture?

B: Oh, people are just getting really sloppy about their eating habits. They seem to have gotten rid of the concept of a sit-down meal with a knife and fork!

A: Well, that's quite typical behavior for the twenty-first century. Actually, I'm afraid it's a fact of life these days. It shows a complex set of sociological changes in action.

	WHO IS SPEAKING?	WHAT IS THE SPEAKER'S STYLE?
Speaker A		
Speaker B		

Conversation Two

A: Wow! Those sandwiches look *so* good. I'm dying to try one! What's in them?

B: There's shrimp salad with dill, or marinated mushrooms with fresh basil leaves.

A: I think I'll go for the second one. I've never tried anything like that before!

	WHO IS SPEAKING?	WHAT IS THE SPEAKER'S STYLE?
Speaker A		
Speaker B		

Conversation Three

A: I can't stand it! My kids will only eat fast food! I'm worried about their getting fat. That stuff is full of preservatives, too!

B: Oh, I know. Most children are the same! You might offer them something healthful that looks like a snack or a treat—for example, a car-shaped vegetable sandwich.

A: That's a good idea. Maybe I can trick them into eating better food.

	WHO IS SPEAKING?	WHAT IS THE SPEAKER'S STYLE?
Speaker A		
Speaker B		

Conversation Four

A: I'm curious to know which products have been selling well recently. You said you've tried salad sandwiches on whole wheat bread. Did that appeal to the women?

B: Yes. The women seem to go for the healthier products. I think they are really concerned about keeping an eye on their diets.

A: I'd like to see how that trend develops. You see, my sense of it is that this shift toward fast yet healthy food will take some very interesting turns in the future.

	WHO IS SPEAKING?	WHAT IS THE SPEAKER'S STYLE?
Speaker A		
Speaker B		

3 Focus on Vocabulary

1 *Read the following list of words and phrases from Listenings One and Two. Each word or phrase is related to a general social trend, a particular food trend, or both. Complete the chart by putting the words in the correct column. Then compare your answers with those of a partner.*

~~boom~~	franchise	shift
bowl	hands-free	sit-down
delicacies	phenomenon	take-out
demand	products	utensils
exploding	revolution	white-collarization
feminization		

SOCIAL TRENDS	FOOD/FOOD TRENDS
boom	

2 *In English, there are many idiomatic expressions related to food. Here are some examples from Listening One.*

- It puts bread on her table. (meaning: It helps her make a living.)

- It was a bit much for people to swallow. (meaning: People couldn't accept it.)

In the sentences that follow, match each underlined food expression with its definition from the list on page 167. Write the correct number in the blank.

1. Men used to be the main <u>breadwinners</u>, while women raised the children.

2. In the past, only men were responsible for the family income. Now women have to <u>bring home the bacon</u>, too.

3. Hey, there's a new DVD player out that's really great, but it's $300. That's a lot of <u>dough</u>.

4. We've got a lot of work to do outside today. Let's <u>get cooking</u> before it gets dark.

5. <u>There's trouble brewing</u> in my office. I've heard some people might get fired soon.

6. Thanks for your offer, but I'll finish this report on my own. <u>Too many cooks spoil the broth</u>.

7. He's really hard to get along with. He always <u>stirs up</u> trouble.

8. There was an interesting show on TV last night about problems in our city. It really gave me <u>some food for thought</u>.

9. She writes books for fun, but teaching is really her <u>bread and butter</u>.

10. Don't just wait by the window for your letter to arrive. Keep yourself busy. You know <u>a watched pot never boils</u>.

   _____ **a.** creates

   _____ **b.** it's better to do some things alone

   _____ **c.** make money

   _____ **d.** things seem to take longer if you focus on what you want to happen

   _____ **e.** money

   _____ **f.** something to think about

   _____ **g.** problems are developing

   _____ **h.** main source of income

   _____ **i.** start working

   _____ **j.** salary earners

3 *Work with a partner. Take turns asking and answering the following questions. Use the underlined words in your answers. Use detailed examples. Switch roles after question 5.*

Example

STUDENT A: In the last two weeks, how many <u>take-out</u> meals have you had?

STUDENT B: I must admit, we often get <u>take-out</u> meals because we are so busy.

1. What do you think of when you imagine <u>hands-free</u> meals?

2. Which eating <u>utensils</u> are most important to you?

3. What are your favorite <u>delicacies</u>?

4. Have you been affected by the <u>feminization</u> of the workforce?

5. Is there an <u>exploding</u> awareness of health issues in your community?

Now switch roles.

   6. Is eating less a recent phenomenon among only <u>white-collar</u> men?

   7. Do you prefer a crowded, noisy restaurant or a quiet, <u>intimate</u> one?

   8. Has there been a recent <u>demand for</u> international foods in your area?

   9. Do you find the <u>shift</u> toward fast food hard to swallow?

   10. Have you ever tried to prepare a meal that would be <u>a big hit</u>?

   4 *Tell the class any interesting information that your partner told you. Use the vocabulary items that you have learned in this unit.*

4 Focus on Speaking

A PRONUNCIATION: Spelling and Sounds—*oo* and *o*

English uses six letters (*a, e, i, o, u,* and *y*) to spell 14 vowel sounds. Some spellings are confusing, because the same spelling can be pronounced in different ways. The spellings **oo** and **o** are examples of confusing spellings. When you learn words with these spellings, pay attention to the sound of the vowel.

• **oo** spellings are usually pronounced /ʊ/ as in **good** or /uw/ as in **school**.

• **o** spellings can have several pronunciations:

   1. /ɑ/ not, stop, hot

   2. /ow/ no, ago, rose

   3. /ə/ some, done, Monday

   1 *Listen and repeat the following words. The bold, underlined letters show the vowel sounds. One of the words in each set has a different vowel sound from the other two. Circle the word with the different vowel sound.*

   1. <u>o</u>ne, s<u>o</u>me, l<u>o</u>ck

   2. f<u>oo</u>l, w<u>oo</u>l, sh<u>oo</u>t

   3. b<u>o</u>dy, r<u>o</u>de, b<u>o</u>th

   4. d<u>oo</u>r, b<u>oo</u>t, fl<u>oo</u>r

   5. sh<u>oo</u>k, l<u>oo</u>k, b<u>oo</u>st

   6. n<u>oo</u>n, c<u>oo</u>k, b<u>oo</u>m

2 *The following words are all spelled with **oo**. Listen, and repeat the words.*

~~food~~	book	flood	cool
too	cook	look	blood
boom	noodles	noon	tool

*Now work with a partner. How is **oo** pronounced? Write the words from the box in one of the columns below. Then read the words in each column. Your partner will check your pronunciation.*

/uw/ too	/ʊ/ good	other (not /uw/ or /ʊ/)
food		

 3 *The following words are all spelled with **o**. Listen, and repeat the words.*

~~popular~~	shock	money	frozen	explode
oven	possible	whole	women	job
done	home	come	go	do

*Now work with a partner. How is **o** pronounced? Write the words from the box in one of the columns below. Then read the words in each column. Your partner will check your pronunciation.*

/ɑ/ not	/ow/ no	/ə/ Monday	other (not /ɑ/, /ow/, or /ə/)
popular			

4 *Work with a partner. Mark the correct sounds for all **o** and **oo** words in the box below. Use the symbols /ʊ/, /uw/, /ɑ/, /ow/, and /ə/.*

food	go	flood	cool	too
cook	look	blood	boom	noodles
noon	tool	popular	shock	money
frozen	explode	oven	possible	whole
women	job	done	do	come

*Practice asking each other the questions below. Try to use the words from the box in your answers. Correct each others' pronunciation of **o** and **oo** sounds.*

1. When it's too hot to cook, what do some people do?

2. Can you think of any popular books about technology or science fiction?

3. What are some tools used around the home, and what are some of their uses?

4. When was the last time you emailed or phoned home?

B   GRAMMAR: Phrasal Verbs

1 *Work with a partner. Read the sentences below, and answer the questions.*

a. In France, more and more people are buying their lunch at the local bakery and <u>taking it out</u>.

b. Demand for fast lunches is growing, and Au Pain Gourmet has to <u>keep up</u> with the trend.

c. Women now <u>make up</u> almost half of the labor force.

d. Children usually leave daycare in the late afternoon, and parents like to <u>pick them up</u> as early as they can.

1. What are some synonyms for the underlined verbs?

2. In sentence *a*, what does the pronoun *it* refer to? In sentence *d*, what does the pronoun *them* refer to?

Phrasal Verbs

A **phrasal verb** is two or three words put together to make one verb. Two-word phrasal verbs consist of a verb and a particle (an adverb or preposition). This combination of words often has a meaning that is very different from the meanings of its separate parts.

VERB	+	PARTICLE	MEANING
keep		up with	Stay at the same level
take		out	Bring food from a restaurant to another place
make		up	Compose
pick		up	Collect

Phrasal Verbs

Some phrasal verbs contain three words.

Some phrasal verbs are **transitive**. They take a direct object.

Many transitive phrasal verbs are **separable**. The direct object can come between the verb and particle, or after the particle.

However, when the direct object is a pronoun, it must go between the verb and particle.

If the direct object is a long phrase, it always comes after the particle.

Examples

Au Pain Gourmet is having difficulty **keeping up with** the demand.

Parents **pick** their children **up** as early as possible.

Workers often **take** their lunch **out** to the park.

They **take** it **out** to the park.

NOT

They ~~**take out** it~~ to the park.

Are you going to the deli? Can you please **pick up** a sandwich with Swiss cheese, mustard, and lettuce and tomato?

NOT

Can you please ~~pick a sandwich with Swiss cheese, mustard, and lettuce and tomato up~~?

(continued)

Phrasal Verbs	Examples
Other transitive verbs are **inseparable**. The direct object always comes after the particle.	Au Pain Gourmet is having difficulty **keeping up with** the demand. NOT Au Pain Gourmet is having difficulty ~~keeping~~ the demand ~~up with~~.
Some phrasal verbs are **intransitive**. They do not take a direct object.	Outside the store, customers were **lining up**.

2 *Work with a partner. Complete the following telephone conversations using the phrasal verbs in parentheses. Use the correct pronoun, and place the pronoun between the verb and the particle when necessary. Then read the conversations aloud.*

STEPHEN: Hi, Julie? It's Stephen. I'm sorry to _____ just before
          1. (call up / *pronoun*)

          the math test, but you said you wanted to try that new sandwich

          place you read about—Au Pain Gourmet.

JULIE: Oh, I read about it in the paper. Apparently people are lining up

          around the block to give it a try. It has really _____.
                                                            2. (catch on)

STEPHEN: Yeah, I would like to _____, too. I'd like to
                                3. (check out / *pronoun*)

          _____ tomorrow morning, but we have to finish our
          4. (ask over / *pronoun*)

          homework. Then we can go out for a walk and get one of those

          baguette sandwiches.

JULIE: Stephen, I don't know . . . see . . . Bill was talking about getting

          together . . .

STEPHEN: What was that? Oh, your friend Bill? Well, can't you

          _____? Just _____ until another time.
          5. (turn down / *pronoun*)   6. (put off / *pronoun*)

JULIE: Well, I . . .

(An hour or two later . . .)

JULIE: Hi, Bill? This is Julie. How are you?

BILL: Hey, Julie! How are you? I'm looking forward to . . .

JULIE: Bill, hold on a minute . . . Listen, I know you offered to cook lunch for me tomorrow, but I'm afraid I have to cancel.

BILL: You mean _____?
      7. (call off/*pronoun*)

JULIE: Yes, I know I'm _____, but I was _____ and
      8. (letting down/*pronoun*)   **9.** (think over/*pronoun*)
      I don't know if I can spare the time. I'm working on a big math project
      for school, and we have to _____ on Monday. Maybe
      10. (hand in/*pronoun*)
      some other time?

BILL: But Julie! Well, OK. I'll just wait until you're available since you're the only girl I want to date.

JULIE: Bill, I'm sorry. I was hoping I could _____, but I . . .
      11. (work out/*pronoun*)
      What's that noise?

BILL: Oops, hang on a minute. I have another call. Could you hold for a minute?

JULIE: Well, actually, can you _____ later?
      12. (call back/*pronoun*)

BILL: I can't, but we'll see each other around. I'll talk to you soon, OK?

JULIE: OK, 'bye.

(Bill switches to the other line.)

BILL: Hello?

SALLY: Hi, Bill. It's Sally.

BILL: Hey, Sally.

SALLY: Oh, I hear the radio in the background there. Are you listening to

WYYN, too?

BILL: Yeah, I just _____ a few minutes ago.
13. (turn on/*pronoun*)

SALLY: Did you hear about that new sandwich shop? Listen, why don't we

_____ tomorrow? We could go for lunch.
14. (try out/*pronoun*)

BILL: Sounds great. But everyone is going there. It'll be really crowded. I'm

not sure if I want to hang out with everyone in the class.

SALLY: This is a really new concept in food. As for the people from our class . . .

there's no way we will _____ .
15. (run into/*pronoun*)

BILL: Cool! See you tomorrow, then!

3 *Match the phrasal verbs from the conversations above with the definitions. Write the correct letter in the blank.*

Phrasal Verbs	**Definitions**
_c_ 1. ask over	a. cancel
____ 2. call back	b. investigate
____ 3. call off	c. invite to one's home
____ 4. call up	d. phone
____ 5. catch on	e. become popular
____ 6. check out	f. return a phone call
____ 7. hand in	g. submit work (to a teacher)
____ 8. let down	h. understand (after thinking about)
____ 9. put off	i. start (a machine)
____ 10. run into	j. experiment to see if you like it
____ 11. think over	k. reject
____ 12. try out	l. disappoint
____ 13. turn down	m. postpone
____ 14. turn on	n. meet by accident
____ 15. work out	o. consider

4 *Work in a group of four. Imagine that Bill, Sally, Julie, and Stephen all meet each other at the sandwich shop. Write down the conversation they have, and then act it out for the class. Use the phrasal verbs you have learned in this unit.*

C STYLE: Calling Attention to a Particular Item

When you are speaking to a group of people and need to demonstrate a process or show visual material, you often need to focus your audience's attention on what you are doing. Here is an example from a food demonstration.

"Do you see what I'm holding? It's just a potato peeler. But I'm going to use this peeler to cut thin strips of carrot for a salad. <u>Watch me carefully</u> . . ."

Here are some expressions you can use to focus your audience's attention on a particular process or item.

Watch me carefully . . .	Have you ever seen anybody do this before?
Look at what I'm doing . . .	This ingredient is very special. Look at it.
Do you see this utensil?	Look at what I'm holding.
Have you ever seen this before?	Are you catching on?
Can you try it out?	

Work in a small group. Take turns explaining how to use one of the utensils or gadgets listed below. As you explain, use the expressions you learned for calling attention on a particular item.

Example

"Now, do you see these? These are called *chopsticks*. Watch me carefully and I'll show you how to use them. First you hold one like this . . . Have you ever seen this before? Now look at my fingers. Look at what I'm doing with these two fingers . . .

chopsticks
vegetable steamer
pressure cooker
bamboo mat for making sushi
electric whisk
cookie cutter
coffee grinder
spice grater
(your choice) _____

D   SPEAKING TOPIC

In recent years, TV shows that demonstrate how to cook a meal have become popular in many parts of the world. Imagine that you are going to create an episode of your own TV food show. Work in a small group. Plan an unusual dish, such as the four-course sandwich you heard about in Listening One.

Step 1:   Decide what you are going to cook. Make sure you agree on something nutritious, interesting, possibly unfamiliar, and relatively easy to cook.

Step 2:   Write the script. Make your show as interesting and entertaining as possible by using humor, facts about the food, and visuals. As you demonstrate how to cook the dish, make sure you use the expressions from the style section on page 175 to focus your audience's attention on what you are doing. Use some of the phrasal verbs you learned in the grammar section on pages 170–174. Here is an example.

> STUDENT A: <u>Look at what I'm doing</u>. I have to beat the egg whites until they look solid. Oops . . . I've dropped the whisk. Can you <u>pick it up</u> for me?

> STUDENT B: Er . . . I have flour all over my hands. Can't you <u>pick it up</u> yourself?

Step 3:   Perform your food show for the class or videotape it and show it to the class.

Step 4:   Watch the other class members' food shows. Place checks in the chart below to rate each show. Then, with the class, discuss what makes a good food show.

	EXCELLENT	GOOD	OK	NOT VERY GOOD
Instructions				
Level of interest				
Acting				
Humor				

E RESEARCH TOPICS

Report on one of these topics related to food.

1. Choose a supermarket and analyze the food trends in your area.

   Step 1: Do the research. Like Lian, the Satellite Sister, wander through the frozen food aisles in the supermarket. Answer the following questions.

   - What types of foods are most plentiful? For instance, are there several brands of one particular product?

   - Which types are at the best eye level for sales? Check whether the "specials" are clearly visible.

   - What trends can you identify? For example, look at the diet foods or foods from certain areas of the world. See if you can tell what is becoming more popular and what is losing popularity.

   Step 2: Prepare a short presentation to give to the class. You can choose to be academic and analytical, like Claude Fishlere, or funny, like the Satellite Sisters.

   Step 3: Present your report to the class. Tell your classmates what you saw and what trends you spotted. Listen to the reports of other groups. Ask questions if you do not understand.

2. Watch a food show on TV and answer the questions below. Report back to the class with your findings.

   - Who presented the show?

   - What did he or she prepare?

   - Were the presenter's instructions easy to follow?

   - Was the show entertaining?

   - Will you try the recipe you saw on the show?

For Unit 8 Internet activities, visit the NorthStar Companion Website at
http://www.longman.com/northstar.

Finding a Niche: The Lives of Young Immigrants

1 Focus on the Topic

A PREDICTING

Look at the photograph and the title of the unit. Then discuss these questions with a partner.

1. How are the experiences of visiting another country and immigrating to another country similar? How are they different?

2. A *niche* is a small, special place that can be physical or psychological. What do you think "finding a niche" means? In particular, what do you think it means to immigrants?

B   SHARING INFORMATION

Work in a small group. Discuss the following questions.

1. Have you ever moved to a different country? Describe the experience. How long did you live there? What was the purpose of your stay? What difficulties did you have? What did you learn? If you have never moved to a different country, do you know people who have? Describe their experience.

2. If you had to immigrate at the age you are now, what would concern you most? Language? Work? Explain. How would your concerns be different from those of a ten-year-old child?

3. Do you agree or disagree with the following statements? Write **A** (agree) or **D** (disagree).

_____ **a.** Teenage immigrants should learn math and science in their first language, rather than in the language of their new country.

_____ **b.** As immigrant teens learn their new language, they become less proficient in their first language.

_____ **c.** One of the main responsibilities of teachers is to make sure that students maintain their own language and culture, even if it means that those students learn English more slowly.

_____ **d.** It is important that teenage immigrants study the same curriculum as students who speak English so that those immigrants will completely adapt to their new home.

C   PREPARING TO LISTEN

BACKGROUND

The United States has always attracted immigrants from around the world; consequently some cities are made up of people from every nation imaginable. Queens, one of the five boroughs of New York City, is one of the most ethnically diverse areas of the country. Many of the newcomers are teenagers who have not yet completed their schooling. Unfamiliar with the language and the culture, they face the enormous task of learning to adapt to their new realities.

Due to the diverse backgrounds and needs of these immigrants, teachers and school administrators face the complex task of helping these students find their niche in the United States. The New York City public school system has an innovative program: the International High School in Long Island City, Queens. Its mission is to help new immigrant students develop not only academic but also cultural skills that are necessary for success in high school, college, and beyond. Only students who have been in the United States for less than four years are eligible for admission. Since it was established in 1985, the school has received a great deal of recognition for its success in teaching young people.

Work with a partner. On the first day of class, teachers at the International High School are often faced with students from around the world. Look at the map, and answer the questions. Share your answers with the class.

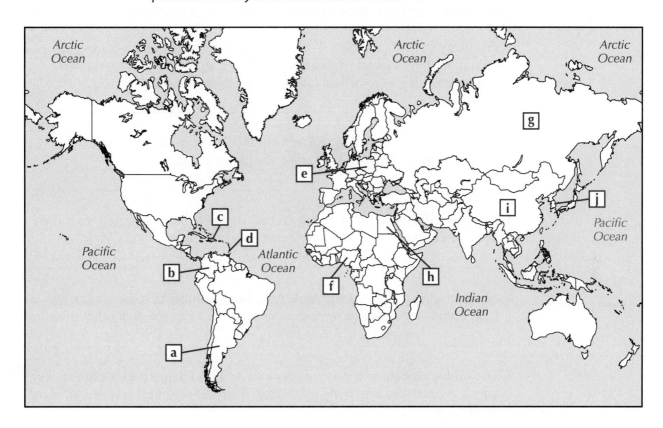

1. What do you know about the countries listed below? Match the countries on the map with their names below.

a Argentina   _____ Korea

_____ China   _____ Nigeria

_____ Colombia   _____ Poland

_____ the Dominican Republic   _____ Russia

_____ Egypt   _____ West Indies

2. What languages do students from these countries probably speak?

3. What special challenges might these students face? Why?

VOCABULARY FOR COMPREHENSION

1 *Read the following sentences. Determine the meaning of each underlined word from the context of its sentence. Write a definition or similar expression on each line.*

1. For many immigrants, New York is home. It is a place where many immigrant businesses have started and where immigrant neighborhoods have grown. It's a city where immigrant communities <u>flourish</u>.

   _____

2. Some young immigrants experience conflict between the need to learn English and the desire to maintain their <u>native tongue</u>.

   _____

3. It can be difficult for young immigrants who have been <u>uprooted</u> from their home environments to adjust to their new environment.

   _____

4. Many of these young people come from large families that are very <u>tight-knit</u>. Family members know each other very well and see each other often.

   _____

5. For adults, moving to a new country can be a bit strange and confusing. For young people who are trying to develop their self-confidence, however, it can be very <u>intimidating</u>.

   _____

6. Priscilla was nervous because she thought she would not be allowed to speak her native tongue in class. She was <u>relieved</u> when she learned that this was not true.

   _____

7. At home, immigrant teens can speak their own language or dialect freely, but at school this practice is sometimes <u>suppressed</u>.

   _____

8. My mother is going to visit France. She wants to <u>bone up on</u> her French because she hasn't practiced it since high school.

   _____

9. Hiroko is <u>unique</u> because she is the only student in her class who was born in the United States.

_____

10. American television reflects mostly <u>mainstream</u> American culture. It doesn't necessarily show the rich ethnic variety of the American population.

_____

11. Excellent study habits help <u>set</u> great students <u>apart</u> from average ones.

_____

12. In the United States, strong differences among ethnic groups become less obvious as those groups are <u>assimilated</u> into mainstream culture.

_____

2 *Match each word on the left with a definition or expression on the right. Write the correct letter in the blank.*

_____ **1.** flourish

_____ **2.** native tongue

_____ **3.** uprooted

_____ **4.** tight-knit

_____ **5.** intimidating

_____ **6.** relieved

_____ **7.** suppress

_____ **8.** bone up on

_____ **9.** unique

_____ **10.** mainstream

_____ **11.** set apart

_____ **12.** assimilated

a. special; individual

b. removed from; torn from

c. the common way of thinking or acting

d. not allow to be expressed

e. frightening

f. make someone or something different

g. grow and develop well

h. review; study again

i. adapted and adjusted

j. happy that you don't have to worry about something

k. first language

l. close; connected

2 Focus on Listening

A   LISTENING ONE: *A World within a School*

You will hear a report by Richard Schiffman, with host Mary Ambrose, from the Public Radio International program *The World*. Schiffman interviews teachers and students at the International High School in Queens, New York. Ambrose says that the International High School "seems to work."

Students helping each other as students do at The International High School.

 Listen to the introduction, and answer the questions.

1. Why do you think that the program at the International High School is successful? _____

   _____

2. How do you think the program differs from other high school programs that involve immigrant students? _____

   _____

LISTENING FOR MAIN IDEAS

 You will hear the entire report. Check (✓) the statements that are true.

At the International High School, _____.

_____ 1. students speak their native languages

_____ 2. students work in groups

_____ 3. students are not all immigrants to the United States

_____ 4. students help each other in their native language

_____ 5. teachers want students to feel comfortable

_____ 6. students improve their English and their native language

_____ 7. teachers think that speaking two languages causes problems

_____ 8. students try to be assimilated quickly into American culture

LISTENING FOR DETAILS

 Listen to the report again. In the chart, check (✓) whether each person is a student or teacher. List what they like about the school, and summarize their comments. Check your answers with a partner.

PERSON BEING INTERVIEWED	Student	Teacher	WHAT THIS PERSON LIKES ABOUT THE SCHOOL
Jennifer Shenke	❏	❏	
Priscilla Billarrel	❏	❏	
Aaron Listhaus	❏	❏	
Evelyna Namovich	❏	❏	
Kathy Rucker	❏	❏	

REACTING TO THE LISTENING

 1 *The reporter selects quotations from three teachers to support his ideas about the International High School. Listen to each excerpt. Decide which aspect of the school this teacher emphasizes. Then decide how length and pitch are used for emphasis.*

Excerpt One

1. This teacher emphasizes _____.
    a. future career possibilities
    b. academic success
    c. psychological comfort

2. To emphasize this idea, what transition word is higher in pitch and longer? Which sound effect is used?

_____

Excerpt Two

3. This teacher emphasizes _____.
   a. future career possibilities
   b. academic success
   c. psychological comfort

4. To emphasize this idea, what two sets of key words are longer in length and higher in pitch?

   school and _____; special and _____

Excerpt Three

5. This teacher emphasizes _____.
   a. future career possibilities
   b. academic success
   c. psychological comfort

6. To emphasize this idea, what two key words are higher in pitch and longer?

   _____

2 *Work in a small group. Discuss the following questions, and compare your answers with those of your classmates.*

1. Would you like to go to school at the International High School? Explain.

2. How do you think some parents might feel about sending their children to this school? Do you think they would worry that their children are not speaking the new language all the time they are at school? Explain.

3. Do you think this teaching method would work at a college or university? Explain.

B   LISTENING TWO: *The Words Escape Me*

You will now hear a song by a New York–area band called Gabriel's Hold. The lyrics express some feelings from the perspective of a young person coming to live in a new country. (You can visit http://www.gabrielshold.com for more information about the band.)

1 *Listen to the song, and circle the answer to each question.*

1. What is the young man concerned about?
   a. learning a language
   b. getting a job
   c. missing a train

2. What does the singer compare his experience to when he says, "Frozen in a fast frame, action is blurred"?
   a. being in a cold place
   b. being in a fast car
   c. being in a movie

3. The singer questions a decision he made when he says, "What was I thinking?" What is he referring to?
   a. deciding to take the train in a foreign country
   b. deciding to come to the new country to live
   c. deciding to speak in a loud voice

4. What does the singer mean when he says, "I can also use your words to order only fish"?
   a. He knows how to say *fish,* so that's why he orders it.
   b. He likes to eat only fish.
   c. He goes to restaurants that serve only fish.

5. What does the expression "get the jokes" mean?
   a. like the jokes
   b. hear the jokes
   c. understand the jokes

6. Why does he feel that people think he's not smart?
   a. He can't communicate his knowledge in his new language.
   b. He does badly on examinations in his new language.
   c. He's not good at reading in his new language.

7. Why does the singer imagine people saying "Get out, get out"?
   a. He is late and he has to leave his house now.
   b. He is not confident around people, and he imagines they don't like him.
   c. He had a fight with someone he lives with.

8. How would you describe the singer's general tone in the song?
   a. frustrated
   b. enthusiastic
   c. sad

2 *Complete the song lyrics below by filling in the missing words. Then listen and check your work. Compare your answers with those of a classmate.*

The Words Escape Me

WORDS AND MUSIC BY STEVE COLEMAN

1 I was standing on a train platform in a

(1) _____ land.

2 I was 21 years old,

3 Excited to be involved, and to do my part, to understand everything I was told.

4 But they moved too quickly, talked too fast, moved too quickly.

5 I couldn't even catch my (2) _____.

6 Frozen in a fast frame, action is blurred.

7 Loud, too loud, I can't understand your

(3) _____.

8 What was I thinking? I can't do this, learn this.

9 Think I'll just go home.

10 But I can't go home.

11 I worked out some bugs,[1] and know where I live.

12 I can also use your words to (4) _____ only fish.

13 I try to eat their food; I (5) _____ the meals from home.

---

[1] *worked out some bugs:* solved some small problems.

14 I eat too little; I eat too much.

15 I'm studying hard, but I don't get the (**6**) _____.

16 They think I'm stupid; I can't tell them I'm not.

17 Writing in this book makes me feel at home.

18 The words I can't (**7**) _____, they're hiding my best, you know.

19 What was I thinking? I can't do this, learn this.

20 Think I'll just go home.

21 But I can't go home.

22 Hey, yeah, words escape me, [repeat]

23 And I can't use my (**8**) _____. [repeat] I can't use it like you. [repeat]

24 *Learn the language, talk the language, learn the language, boy.* [repeat]

25 *Get out, get out, get out, get out, boy.* [repeat]

26 Oh, I'm too tired, I'm too old, it's too simple, it's too cold. I can't even . . .

27 *Get out, get out, get out, get out, boy.*

28 Writing in this (**9**) _____ makes me feel at home.

29 The words I can't escape, they're hiding my best, you know.

30 What was I (**10**) _____? I can't do this, learn this.

31 Think I'll just go home.

32 But I can't go home.

33 Hey, yeah, words escape me, [repeat]

34 And I can't use my tongue. [repeat]

C LINKING LISTENINGS ONE AND TWO

Work in a small group. Imagine that a new student at the International High School and the singer of "Words Escape Me" meet in New York. What might they say to each other? Complete the chart with your ideas about how these people would answer the questions. Then role play their meeting for the class.

TOPICS	NEW STUDENT AT THE INTERNATIONAL HIGH SCHOOL	SINGER OF "WORDS ESCAPE ME"
1. What difficulties have you faced since you first arrived here?		
2. How are you feeling about your new life in the United States?		
3. What might help you to adapt better and find a niche in this country?		

3 Focus on Vocabulary

1 *Read this story about culture shock. Fill in the blanks with words from the box before each paragraph. Compare your answers with those of a classmate.*

Culture Shock: The Problems of Young Immigrants

support	uprooted	encourage
set him apart	value	blend in
intimidated	interpret	

   In his home country of Mexico, Esteban was an active, outgoing young man. He was optimistic, full of life, and had many friends. Esteban was also an excellent student. When he was 16, his father was transferred to the United States, and the family moved with him. This was a very difficult adjustment for Esteban, who felt (**1**) _____ from his home. At school, the American

kids were friendly to him, but he couldn't seem to (2) _____.
Instead of feeling excited by his new classes, he felt (3) _____.
His teachers tried to (4) _____ him. They suggested that
he join clubs in order to meet other students. Esteban appreciated their
(5) _____, but his feeling of being a foreigner
(6) _____ from the others. Sometimes he had difficulty
communicating with his classmates, and there was no one who spoke his language
and could (7) _____ for him. He felt that no one would ever
listen to him or (8) _____ his opinion.

challenged	tight-knit	extended
niche	relieved	deal with
suppressed	adaptation	

His unhappiness (9) _____ to his family life, too. Although
Esteban's family was very (10) _____, he did not want to talk
to them about his problems. Instead, he (11) _____ his sad
feelings so his parents wouldn't worry about him. He thought that if only he
knew more English, he would be able to make friends more easily and feel
more comfortable. Esteban's frustration grew. Eventually, he felt unable to
(12) _____ even the smallest day-to-day tasks. Sometimes
he disliked the United States and English and felt that he would never adjust.

Although Esteban thought most of his problems were a result of his poor
English, social scientists and psychologists know better. Esteban was
experiencing culture shock without knowing it. His insecurities and confusion
were a temporary but normal stage in the (13) _____
process. His beliefs were suddenly being (14) _____ by a new
set of values in his new country. All this was happening without his awareness.
Esteban's reaction was natural. Gradually, Esteban began to feel more
comfortable in the United States, and he started to enjoy his school life and his
new friends. He was (15) _____ after a few months when he
realized that he was no longer unhappy. Though he would always love his native
country first, he had found his (16) _____ in his new home
and was able to enjoy his life once again.

2 *Work with a partner. Read the statements in the chart below, and decide how strongly you agree or disagree with each one. Circle a number from 1 to 5 to describe the strength of your opinion. (1 means "strongly agree," 3 means "not sure," and 5 means "strongly disagree.") Then explain your choices to your partner using words from the box below.*

uproot	tight-knit families	encourage
foreign	mainstream culture	challenge
set apart	deal with	intimidating
unique	flourish	relieved
support	value	blend in

1. Adolescents have a much harder time adapting to life in a new country than adults or young children.   1   2   3   4   5

2. Sports, food, and music are among the most important areas where immigrants make an impact on their new country.   1   2   3   4   5

3. The most powerful emotion that an immigrant experiences in a new culture is fear.   1   2   3   4   5

4. After a person lives in a different country for some time, that person is never completely the same.   1   2   3   4   5

5. The experiences that immigrants first have when they get to a new country can have a crucial impact on their adjustment to their new lives.   1   2   3   4   5

4 Focus on Speaking

A   **PRONUNCIATION: Discriminating between *sh, z, ch,* and *j***

The sounds *sh* /ʃ/, *z* /ʒ/, *ch* /tʃ/, and *j* /dʒ/ are difficult to pronounce correctly, especially when they are close together:

It's hard to mea**s**ure how immigra**t**ion affects a cul**t**ure, but it's an interesting sub**j**ect.
       /ʒ/   **/ʃ/**   **/tʃ/**   **/dʒ/**

These four sounds are similar in some ways but different in others. The outside of the mouth looks the same for all four sounds. The lips are a little rounded and protrude (stick out) a little. Inside the mouth, the tongue pulls back from the top teeth with all four sounds.

The first sound in **ch***ild* /tʃ/ starts with /t/. The first sound in *just* /dʒ/ starts with /d/. You cannot hear the /t/ or /d/ as separate sounds, but you must say them to pronounce these words correctly.

The first sounds in **sh***ip* /ʃ/ and **ch***ild* /tʃ/ are voiceless. The vocal chords do not vibrate. The bold sounds in *plea**s**ure* /ʒ/ and *just* /dʒ/ are voiced. The vocal chords vibrate. When these sounds end words, do not release them strongly. Keep the sound short and say the next word.

Voiceless /ʃ/	Voiced /ʒ/	Voiceless /tʃ/	Voiced /dʒ/
she	plea**s**ure	**ch**ild	**j**ust
wa**sh**	bei**ge**	wa**tch**	a**ge**

1 *Listen to the list of words. Put a check (✓) in the column that describes the sound of the boldfaced letters.*

	/ʃ/ SHE	/ʒ/ PLEASURE	/tʃ/ CHILD	/dʒ/ JUST
1. interna**ti**onal	✓			
2. langua**ge**				✓
3. en**j**oy				
4. ad**j**ust				
5. mea**s**ure				
6. lec**tu**re				
7. tradi**ti**onal				
8. cul**tu**re				
9. u**s**ual				
10. puni**sh**ment				
11. spe**ci**al				
12. sub**j**ect				
13. **Ch**ile				
14. televi**si**on				
15. edu**c**ators				
16. occa**si**on				
17. commu**ni**cation				
18. encoura**ge**				
19. trea**s**ure				
20a. ni**ch**e				
20b. ni**ch**e				
21. flouri**sh**				

2 *Work with a partner, and practice pronouncing* **sh, z, ch,** *and* **j.**

Student A: Read the comments or questions.

Student B: Use the words in parentheses to help you with your answers. Pay attention to your pronunciation of these sounds. Switch roles after item 6.

Example

Student A: The United States attracts people from all over the world.

Student B: (That's right . . . salad bowl) "That's right, it's a real salad bowl."

Student A

1. Do the students seem to like the International High School?

2. Is it typical for immigrants to feel uncomfortable at first?

3. Immigrants have to learn to adjust in many ways.

4. The high school we heard about seems unique.

5. Do the teachers at that school often lecture?

6. Ms. Shenke uses an unusual approach.

Student B

1. (Yes . . . enjoy it)

2. (Yes . . . usually the case)

3. (Yes . . . find their niche)

4. (Yes . . . special)

5. (No . . . only occasionally)

6. (Right . . . doesn't lecture)

Now switch roles.

Student B

7. The report said that the school was multilingual.

8. Did the report mention a country in South America?

9. The teachers at this school don't seem to believe in discipline through fear, do they?

10. Is it hard to tell how successful a new approach is at first?

11. Can you think of another word for *instructor*?

12. It's important to talk to others when you have a problem, don't you think?

Student A

7. (That's right . . . different languages)

8. (Yes . . . Chile)

9. (No, they don't. Instead . . . encouragement)

10. (Yes . . . takes time to measure results)

11. (Yes . . . *educator*)

12. (Yes . . . communication)

B   GRAMMAR: Present and Past—Contrasting Verb Tenses

1 *Work with a partner. Read the sentences below, and answer the questions.*

    a. When <u>we're working</u> in class, we <u>help</u> each other. We'<u>re</u> all immigrants here, we all <u>know</u> what it feels like to be different, so we <u>support</u> one another.

    b. Sometimes it <u>was</u> so difficult because I <u>didn't know</u> what the subject <u>was</u> all about, what the teacher <u>was speaking</u> about.

    c. This project <u>has been</u> really successful. The students <u>have learned</u> a lot of math. They'<u>ve been working</u> together really well.

    1. Which sentences are about actions in the present?

    2. Which are about actions in the past?

    3. Which sentences focus on activities that are continuing in the present?

Present and Past—Contrasting Verb Tenses

Present Progressive and Simple Present	Examples
The **present progressive** is used to describe what is happening right now, an action that is in progress.	The students in one group **are speaking** Polish.
The **simple present** is used to describe a general fact or habit.	The students at the International High School **speak** many different languages.
The **present progressive** can be used with the **simple present** to describe a present action that is continuing while another present action takes place.	While we**'re working** in class, we **help** each other.
The **simple present** is also used with non-action verbs to refer to actions taking place at the moment of speaking.	The students **seem** to be enjoying the project they **are working** on right now.

Past Progressive and Simple Past

	Examples
The **past progressive** is used to describe an action that was in progress at a specific time in the past.	The students **were designing** a temple during math class.
The **simple past** is used to describe an action that was completed in the past.	The students **finished** building their temples by the end of class.
The **past progressive** can be used to describe two actions in progress at the same time.	While the students **were working**, they **were speaking** their native languages.
The **past progressive** is used with the **simple past** to describe one action that was interrupted by another action.	The teacher **was walking** around the room when a student **asked** a question.
The **simple past** is used to describe two actions that happened in a sequence, one after the other.	Another student **stopped** working and **helped** her classmate with the answer.

Present Perfect and Present Perfect Progressive

	Examples
The **present perfect** and **present perfect progressive** are used to talk about things that started in the past, continue to the present, and may continue in the future.	She **has lived** in the United States since her twenty-first birthday. She **has been living** in the United States since her twenty-first birthday.
The **present perfect** is used to talk about things that happened at an unspecified time in the past or a time period that is not finished.	She **has taken** several tests. She **has taken** several tests this year.

2 *Read the following interview with Lisa Chin, a Chinese American physician. Then complete the sentences using the correct forms of the verbs.*

INTERVIEWER: Dr. Chin, your mother was an immigrant. Her family was uprooted because of war. You were saying that she came to this country under very different conditions than we have now. What was it like for her as a young girl?

DR. CHIN: Well, her experience wasn't unique in those days. When

my mother _____ to this country from
                          1. (come)

China, she _____ , let's see, I guess
                    2. (be)

about eight years old. She _____ any
                                3. (not/speak)

English. When she _____ to school, there
                          4. (go)

_____ any special classes for immigrants.
        5. (not/be)

Immigrant students _____ to join the regular
                            6. (have)

classes, even if they couldn't speak English. My mother said this

_____ very difficult for her at first.
        7. (be)

INTERVIEWER: Did she tell you what those school days were like for her?

DR. CHIN: Oh, yes. She talks about it a lot now. On the first day of

school, she _____ anything the teacher
                    8. (not/understand)

_____ about. But when my mother
        9. (talk)

_____ a friend to explain in Chinese,
        10. (ask)

the teacher _____ angry and
                    11. (become)

_____ her to speak only English.
        12. (tell)

INTERVIEWER: That sounds like a lot of pressure for such a young girl.

DR. CHIN: I'm sure it was. My grandparents also _____
                                              13. (want)

her to learn English quickly. They _____
                                        14. (feel)

that it was important for her to blend in. They

_____ that learning English would help my
        15. (think)

mother succeed. Soon, my mother _____ the
                                        16. (feel)
same way. In fact, today she _____ Chinese
                                  17. (not/speak)
very well at all, and she can't read or write it.

INTERVIEWER: Since then, the world _____ quite a bit. With
                                      18. (change)
all the new technology, it _____ difficult to
                                19. (not/be)
travel and communicate with people all over the globe. How do
you think all this has affected your family?

DR. CHIN: That's a good question. Well, I guess we _____
                                                        20. (be)
truly part of a global economy now. People's attitudes are
different in many ways. For example, attitudes about language

_____ a lot since I was young. Many people
        21. (change)
feel that it _____ an advantage to speak
                    22. (be)
two or more languages. I can see that change when I

_____ at my children.
        23. (look)

INTERVIEWER: When you look at your children?

DR. CHIN: My kids _____ English at home all their lives,
                        24. (speak)
but today they both _____ a "two-way"
                          25. (attend)
bilingual Chinese school. That's where English-speaking children
study Chinese, and Chinese-speaking children study English.
So my children are Chinese-American, but they

_____ to speak Chinese for the first time
        26. (learn)
now. They _____ the school because all the
                27. (love)
students _____ very good friends. They
                28. (become)
_____ each other the new language. My
        29. (teach)
children _____ their friends learn English,
                30. (help)
and their friends _____ them Chinese at the
                        31. (teach)
same time.

INTERVIEWER: How do you think it helps the kids?

DR. CHIN: Well, I really believe that in the future, knowing a second language will help my children get better jobs and, well, find their niche with so many different people . . .

INTERVIEWER: You mean sort of a multicultural society?

DR. CHIN: Yes, exactly.

INTERVIEWER: So, how is your mother doing now?

DR. CHIN: Well, she's doing really well, actually. You know, she

_____ Chinese since she was a girl, so
               32. (not/speak)

she _____ how to speak it any more.
        33. (not/remember)

Now she _____ that she hadn't forgotten it.
                 34. (wish)

In fact, she _____ language lessons recently,
                  35. (take)

trying to bone up on her Chinese!

3 *Work with a partner.*

Student A: Ask Student B the questions about the reading. Use the correct verb tense. Listen to Student B's responses, and ask follow-up questions to find out more information. Switch roles after question 6.

Student B: Respond to Student A's questions. Use an appropriate verb tense. Some questions are not answered directly in the reading, so you must express your own opinion based on what you have read.

Example

Student A: Where/be/Dr. Chin's mother born?

Where was Dr. Chin's mother born?

Student B: She was born in China.

Student A

1. How long/she/be/in the United States?

2. How/she/feel/about speaking Chinese when she was a girl in school in the United States?

3. How/she/feel/about it now?

4. Why/her feelings/change?

5. What new technology/change/the way people learn other languages?

6. How/you/feel/when people speak a language you don't understand?

Now switch roles.

Student B

7. What/be/Dr. Chin's native language?

8. What/be/the benefits of a bilingual school?

9. How/the bilingual school/help/Dr. Chin's children?

10. What types of jobs/require/a bilingual person?

11. How/Dr. Chin's views about language/differ/from her grandparents' views?

12. In your opinion, what kind of school/be/best for immigrant children?

C | STYLE: Hesitating in Response to a Question

When you respond to a question, or when someone asks for your opinion, you sometimes need extra time to think about your answer and to decide what to say. Here are some expressions to use when you hesitate in response to a question.

I need a moment to think about that …	Umm, that's a good question …
I'm not sure …	Well, er …
Let me think a minute …	Well, let's see …

1 *Study this short conversation. Circle the expressions that are used to show hesitation.*

A: I just read a report about where most immigrants to the United States came from in the early twentieth century. You'll never guess where most of them came from!

B: Let me think a minute. Was it Latin America?

A: Umm, it wasn't. In fact, it was Europe.

B: Really! I'm very surprised.

2 *Work with a partner. You will exchange information about the country of origin of those who immigrated to the United States from 1820–1975.*

Student A: Ask Student B the questions at the top of the next page.

Student B: Cover the questions. Listen to Student A ask the questions. Look at the first chart, on the next page, and find the answer. Use an expression to hesitate as you respond with the answer.

Student A

1. Where did most of the immigrants come from during this period?

2. Did many immigrants come from Latin America during this time?

3. What time period does the chart cover?

4. Does the chart show how old the immigrants were?

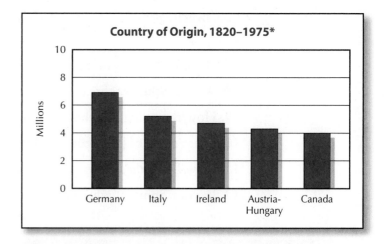

Now switch roles. You will exchange information about the country of origin of those who immigrated to the United States from 1976–1986.

Student B: Ask Student A the questions below.

Student A: Cover the questions. Listen to Student B ask the questions. Look at the chart below, and find the answer. Use an expression to hesitate as you respond with the answer.

Student B

5. Did any of the countries in the first chart continue sending immigrants to the United States during this period?

6. What country sent the most immigrants during this time?

7. Was Europe still the continent that most immigrants came from?

8. How many immigrants came from Korea?

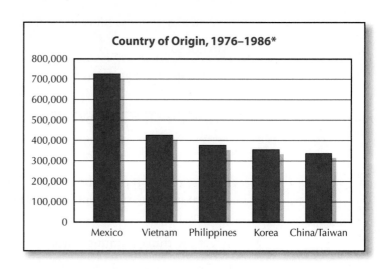

---

* Source: Eric Foner and John A. Garraty, eds., *Reader's Companion to American History* (Boston: Houghton Mifflin, 1991), p. 534.

D SPEAKING TOPIC

Imagine that the school board in your town is considering starting a school to educate immigrant students. Divide the class into four groups: teachers, students, parents, and school board members.

Step 1: Define the problem. Each group should select a city, town, or neighborhood in the country where the members live now. Identify the largest groups of immigrants. Then discuss what kind of problems they might have and what their children might need in order to adjust to their new lives.

Step 2: Establish the school's objectives. Discuss the objectives below. If your group decides on more objectives, add them to the list. Then decide how important each objective is. Write *1* (very important), *2* (somewhat important), or *3* (not important) in the space after each objective. As you discuss the objectives, use the correct verb tenses from the grammar section on pages 196–200.

Objective	Importance
• to keep their native language and culture alive	_____
• to be assimilated into the new culture	_____
• to learn the new language as quickly as possible	_____
• to learn general subjects (math, history, and so on)	_____
• (other objectives) _____	_____

_____

_____

Example

STUDENT A: I think our school should help students to keep their native language alive. After all, it's the language that they *have heard since they were born.*

STUDENT B: Yes, that's really important. I was talking to some parents, and they want their children to know both languages.

Step 3: Develop a plan. Keeping your objectives in mind, plan the daily schedule of your new school together. Write down the name of the classes, and then describe both the teaching style (lecture, group work, hands-on activities) and the language(s) that will be used. Make sure your choices support the objectives of the school that you agreed upon in Step 2. As you plan the schedule, talk with other group members and ask questions. If you need a moment to think, use expressions to hesitate from the style section on pages 201–202.

Example

STUDENT A: The students should do a lot of group work.

STUDENT B: Group work? *Umm* . . . I don't know if that's such a good idea. Won't the students just work with other people who speak the same language as themselves?

STUDENT A: Good point. *Well, let me think a minute.* Maybe the teachers should put the students into groups. That way, they can control which group different students are in.

Step 4: Present your plan to the rest of the class. Be sure to explain the following:

- the objectives of your school

- why you chose those objectives

- the daily schedule, including teaching methods and language(s)

- how the daily schedule will help to achieve the goals or objectives

After all the groups have presented their plans, discuss the similarities and differences among the plans.

E   RESEARCH TOPIC

Interview someone who has lived or is now living in a country where he or she had to learn a new language.

Step 1: Work in a small group. Before you conduct your interview, write questions that address each of the topics below. Make sure everyone in your group asks the same questions of the people they interview.

- reasons for living in the other country

- reaction to the new language

- reaction to some traditions in the new culture

- reaction to working or going to school in the new culture

- other aspects of the experience

- what is missed from the home culture

Step 2: After completing your interview, compare what you learned with the other members of your group. Discuss the similarities and differences among the experiences of all the people you interviewed.

For Unit 9 Internet activities, visit the NorthStar Companion Website at http://www.longman.com/northstar.

Technology: A Blessing or a Curse?

1 Focus on the Topic

A PREDICTING

Look at the cartoon and the title of this unit. Then discuss these questions with a partner.

1. Why do you think the man is hiding from his laptop computer and his cell phone?

2. What do you think "technology: a blessing or a curse?" means?

B   SHARING INFORMATION

Work with a partner. Complete the chart with your opinion on how the technology items listed have either improved or diminished the quality of our lives. When you are finished, share your views with the class.

ITEM	WAYS IT HAS IMPROVED OUR QUALITY OF LIFE	WAYS IT HAS DIMINISHED OUR QUALITY OF LIFE
Personal computer		
Cell phone		
ATM (automated teller machine)		
Personal stereo equipment		
The Internet		
E-mail		
Satellite TV		
Others (your ideas)		

C   PREPARING TO LISTEN

BACKGROUND

Technology might be a big part of modern life, but it is clear that its impact is still controversial. Work in a small group. Take turns reading aloud the lines from this excerpt of the poem "The Paradox of Our Times." Then answer the questions that follow.

The Paradox of Our Times

BY JEFF DICKSON

The paradox of our time in history is that
we have taller buildings, but shorter tempers;
wider freeways, but narrower viewpoints.

We spend more, but have less;
we buy more, but enjoy it less.

We have bigger houses and smaller families;
more conveniences, but less time.

We have more degrees,[1] but less sense;
more knowledge, but less judgment;
more experts, but more problems;
more medicine, but less wellness.

We drink too much, smoke too much, spend too recklessly,
laugh too little, drive too fast, get too angry too quickly,
stay up too late, get up too tired,
read too seldom, watch TV too much,
and pray too seldom.

We have multiplied our possessions, but reduced our values.

We talk too much, love too seldom, and hate too often.

We've learned how to make a living, but not a life;
we've added years to life, not life to years.

We've been all the way to the moon and back,
but have trouble crossing the street to meet a new neighbor.

---

[1] **degrees:** credentials given to those who complete courses of study at a university

1. This poem includes many words that contrast with each other. Underline the contrasting words in each line. What is a paradox? How do the contrasts show a paradox? What is "the paradox of our times"?

2. Does the poem express the way you feel sometimes? Explain your answer.

3. Select one or two lines that seem most interesting to you. Read them aloud. Discuss with the group what they mean and whether you agree with them.

4. The poet effectively uses comparisons of unlike things for emphasis. What else makes the poem effective?

VOCABULARY FOR COMPREHENSION

Circle the letter of the word or phrase that is closest in meaning to the underlined words.

1. To sleep well, you need to get some peace and quiet. However, in the city, noise can <u>shatter</u> the peace.

    a. increase   **b.** annoy   **c.** destroy

2. Sometimes the dog in the next apartment barks all day. It makes me cranky after a few hours. A whole day of it <u>sends me over the edge</u>, and I call the police.

    a. hurts me   **b.** makes me tired   **c.** makes me angry

3. People who live near airports often complain about <u>sonic</u> pollution. They say that the air traffic disturbs their sleep and prevents them from living a normal life.

    a. noise   **b.** air   **c.** solar

4. Some areas have <u>banned</u> talking on cellular phones while driving because it is so dangerous.

    a. prohibited   **b.** permitted   **c.** requested

5. The use of the Internet at work has <u>prompted</u> companies to make new rules. For example, in some companies, employees can't use the Internet for personal business during work hours.

    a. reminded   **b.** caused   **c.** allowed

6. Many city noises are loud and sudden. They <u>jolt</u> people out of their sleep.

    a. ease   **b.** help   **c.** startle

7. I haven't been sleeping well at night lately. I have a <u>nagging</u> headache, and taking aspirin doesn't help.

    a. constant   **b.** slight   **c.** feverish

8. At the end of the cowboy movie, the sheriff gathered <u>a posse</u> of men. He needed help to catch the gang of bad guys.

    a. a group   **b.** a couple   **c.** hundreds

9. When people feel that they have been hurt needlessly, they often get angry and sometimes take <u>retaliatory</u> steps. They do something to hurt the person who has hurt them.

    a. punishing   **b.** immediate   **c.** official

10. Neighborhood <u>vigilantes</u> take the law into their own hands. Instead of calling the police, they find a way to punish an offender by themselves.

    a. guards who catch criminals   **b.** part-time officers who catch criminals   **c.** unofficial group of people who catch criminals

11. When my alarm clock <u>goes off</u> in the morning, I never feel like getting out of bed. I'm always too tired.

   a. starts making   **b.** stops making   **c.** fails
   noise   noise

12. Last night, I heard a loud noise outside of my kitchen. I was so scared that I called <u>911</u> for the police to come. They discovered that a cat had knocked down the recycling container.

   a. emergency services   **b.** the operator   **c.** directory assistance

13. Some neighborhood kids found an old car and destroyed it. The front was completely <u>mutilated</u>.

   a. damaged   **b.** constructed   **c.** criticized

14. If you park in a no-parking zone, the traffic police can <u>tow away</u> your car. You can't pick it up until you pay a fine.

   a. remove   **b.** destroy   **c.** park

15. I think a very heavy truck just went by. I felt the <u>vibrations</u> shaking the whole house.

   a. sounds   **b.** movements   **c.** echoes

2 Focus on Listening

A   LISTENING ONE: *Noise in the City*

You will hear a segment of a report from *Living on Earth* by Neal Rauch of National Public Radio. Rauch interviews several residents of a large city. Steve Curwood is the host of this news program, which often reports on environmental issues.

Listen, and answer the questions. Compare your answers with those of another student.

1. What could be causing the noise you heard? _____

2. How do you think people feel when they hear this noise? _____

3. What might they do after hearing the noise? _____

4. Where do you think this report takes place? _____

LISTENING FOR MAIN IDEAS

*You will now hear the entire report. Read each statement, and write **T** (true) or **F** (false).*

_____ 1. All New Yorkers agree about banning this form of sonic pollution.

_____ 2. When a car alarm goes off too often, vigilante groups sometimes do something to damage the car.

_____ 3. Car alarms are very effective at preventing theft.

_____ 4. Car alarms can seriously affect people's health and quality of life.

_____ 5. There are no laws or penalties to punish drivers whose car alarms go off for too long a time.

_____ 6. Police can break into a car if the alarm goes off for too long.

LISTENING FOR DETAILS

Read the following questions. Then listen to the report again. As you listen, take notes on the opinions of the people below. Then compare your answers with those of a classmate.

1. Judy Evans, scenic designer and artist

   a. Why are car alarms such a problem at night?

   _____

   b. What usually happens when a person makes a lot of noise in public?

   _____

2. The "egg man," a music producer and composer

   a. What do he and his neighbors do when they hear a car alarm go off?

   _____

   b. What do other vigilante groups sometimes do?

   _____

3. Lucille DiMaggio, a target of vigilante retribution

   a. What happened to her car?

   _____

   b. What happened when she set off her car alarm in the restaurant parking lot?

   _____

4. Judy Evans, scenic designer and artist

   a. What happened on a different night when she heard a car alarm going off?

   _____

b. What should happen to car alarms in densely populated neighborhoods?

_____

5. Catherine Abate, New York state senator

a. How does the noise from alarms affect people?

_____

b. How can loud noise be particularly harmful to young people?

_____

6. Neil Rauch, radio reporter

a. How have existing laws helped cut down on car alarm noise?

_____

b. How would it be helpful if car alarm owners were to adjust their alarms to be less sensitive to vibrations?

_____

REACTING TO THE LISTENING

 1 _Listen to the excerpts from the radio report. Pay attention to each speaker's tone of voice and choice of words. Evaluate how serious or humorous the speaker sounds as he or she makes a complaint or gives an opinion, and check (✓) the appropriate column._

	MOSTLY SERIOUS	SOMEWHAT SERIOUS	SOMEWHAT HUMOROUS	MOSTLY HUMOROUS
Excerpt One: Judy Evans				
Tone of voice	❏	❏	❏	❏
Choice of words	❏	❏	❏	❏
Excerpt Two: Lucille DiMaggio				
Tone of voice	❏	❏	❏	❏
Choice of words	❏	❏	❏	❏
Excerpt Three: Senator Abate				
Tone of voice	❏	❏	❏	❏
Choice of words	❏	❏	❏	❏
Excerpt Four: "Egg man"				
Tone of voice	❏	❏	❏	❏
Choice of words	❏	❏	❏	❏

2 *Work in a small group. Discuss the following questions.*

1. What do you think of vigilante groups that take action against something that bothers them in their neighborhood? Are these groups a good idea? Have you heard about retaliatory steps being taken by other groups? What alternatives could people choose instead of those mentioned in Listening One?

2. Some Broadway theater actors have been known to stop their performances if they hear cell phones ringing in the audience. How do you feel about that?

3. Modern life is full of noises, as the radio report said, and many of them are annoying. Close your eyes for one minute and sit quietly. Concentrate on the sounds around you. Then write down all the sounds you have heard. Are they pleasant or irritating? Did you notice anything new? Then do the same thing in another place—at home, at work, on a bus or train, in a park.

B LISTENING TWO: *Technology Talk*

You will hear a radio report about other types of technology that drive people crazy. Four people phoned in to the radio show *Technology Talk* to complain.

 1 *Listen to the report, and write down the type of technology each caller is talking about. Write the reasons for each caller's annoyance or frustration. Compare your answers with those of a classmate.*

Caller 1

Technology: _____

Reason it drives the caller crazy: _____

Caller 2

Technology: _____

Reason the caller finds it frustrating: _____

Caller 3

Technology: _____

Reason the caller is frustrated: _____

Caller 4

Technology: _____

Reason it drives the caller crazy: _____

2 *Read the cartoon title and captions. What is a "midlife crisis"? Who or what does it usually refer to? What is the humor or message of the cartoon?*

C   LINKING LISTENINGS ONE AND TWO

Work in a small group. Look at the first row of the chart, and review the responses to the car alarm problems that were presented in Listening One. Then fill in the rest of the chart with possible responses to the problems in Listening Two. Compare and discuss your ideas.

TECHNOLOGY	PROBLEM	MILDLY AGGRESSIVE RESPONSE	MORE AGGRESSIVE RESPONSE	VERY AGGRESSIVE RESPONSE	EXTREMELY AGGRESSIVE RESPONSE
Listening One: Car alarms	Faulty car alarms sound and are not turned off quickly	Leave note on car saying, "Fix your car alarm. It disturbed hundreds of people last night."	Break egg on windshield	Put grease on windshield	Break windshield
Listening Two: Automated phone systems					
Listening Two: Cell phones					
Listening Two: Remote controls					
Listening Two: E-mail and junk e-mail					

3 Focus on Vocabulary

1 *Listen to some common noises. What do you think makes each noise? Write your response in the left column of the chart.*

NOISE	WHAT PROBABLY MAKES THIS NOISE	ADJECTIVES TO DESCRIBE THE NOISE
1. Bang		
2. Shatter		
3. Ring		
4. Rattle		
5. Beep		
6. Creak		
7. Whistle		
8. Tick		
9. Screech		
10. Honk		

2 *Listen to the noises again. Choose one or two adjectives that describe each noise from the box below (or from other adjectives that you know). Write them in the right column of the chart. Then compare your answers with those of another student.*

aggravating	faint	low	shrill
annoying	frightening	nagging	soft
awful	irritating	nasty	startling
comforting	jolting	piercing	sudden
constant	loud	rhythmic	surprising

3 *Work with a partner to complete Dialogues One and Two.*

Student A: Look at Dialogue One. Complete each statement by choosing the correct word or phrase from the box. Read the statement to Student B. Then listen to Student B's response, and check that Student B has used the word or phrase in parentheses. Continue with items 2 and 3. Do the same with Dialogue Two.

Student B: Follow the directions on page 228.

banned	frazzled	I've had it
defective	frustrated	jolts
disturbing the peace	getting under my skin	offense
drive you crazy	go off	retaliatory steps
pay a fine	irritated	

Dialogue One

1. My new clock radio is really _____. I wish I'd never bought it. (go off)

2. Oh, sure it does. It goes off too often! And it makes a really loud noise. It _____ me out of my sleep. (defective)

3. I can't. It's not broken. I just can't figure out how to set it. And the instructions are too complicated. I just get _____ and give up whenever I try to read them. (frazzled)

Dialogue Two

4. Hi. What's up? You look really _____. (I've had it.)

5. Yeah. They really play their music too loud. I guess it can _____ if you hear it all day. (retaliatory steps)

6. You're kidding! You called the police? Are those kids breaking the law? I mean, is it really a(n) _____ to play loud music? (disturbing the peace)

7. I guess those kids should _____ for breaking the law. Maybe then they would think twice about making so much noise next time. (banned)

4 Focus on Speaking

A   PRONUNCIATION: Stressed Adverbial Particles

Native English speakers often stress adverbial particles like *up, down, off, on, back,* and *out.*

I'm fed UP!

- These particles are stressed when they are used as adverbs after verbs.

Come BACK!

- They are also stressed when they are part of separable two word verbs.

Turn it DOWN.

- These particles are *not* stressed when they are used as prepositions or as part of an infinitive.

Listen <u>to</u> the noise!
I want <u>to</u> move!

- Join the vowel sounds in the words *up, on, in, out,* and *off* closely to the preceding word.

Come ON!

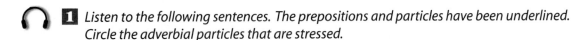 **1** *Listen to the following sentences. The prepositions and particles have been underlined. Circle the adverbial particles that are stressed.*

1. I tried <u>to</u> read the instructions, but then I gave <u>up</u>.

2. I asked him <u>to</u> turn it <u>down</u>, but he said he didn't want <u>to</u>.

3. Come <u>in</u> and sit <u>down</u>. You look really worn <u>out</u>.

4. I want <u>to</u> buy a new car. This one keeps breaking <u>down</u>.

5. I'm taking this new gadget <u>back</u>. I can't get it to work, and I'm really fed <u>up</u>.

2 *Listen to the following complaint about technology. Circle the particles that are stressed. Join the vowel sounds in **up, on, in,** and **off** closely to the preceding word.*

> I give up! I've had it with these modern appliances! I bought a new alarm clock, but it goes off whenever it feels like it. Last night it went off at midnight. I got up before I realized what time it was. First I got angry and threw it out. Then I took it out of the garbage and decided to take it back. I want to get my money back!

3 *Work with a partner. Match the comments by putting the appropriate letters in the blanks. Then practice the dialogues. Make sure you stress the particles when necessary.*

_____ 1. When did the police show up?

_____ 2. Do you want to go out tonight?

_____ 3. My new alarm clock goes off all the time.

_____ 4. I'm fed up with those new token machines.

_____ 5. Ugh! I have six new voice messages and no time to make calls.

a. I can't. I have to get up early.

b. I know. They are always breaking down.

c. Why don't you take it back to the store?

d. But they're probably new customers. You have to call them back.

e. Forty minutes after I called them up.

B   GRAMMAR: Future Perfect and Future Progressive

1 *Work with a partner. Read the sentences below, and answer the questions.*

a. By the time I figure out how to work the remote, the news will already have started.

b. We will be hearing from more listeners right after this break.

1. Are these sentences about activities in the past, present, or future?

2. How are the two verb tenses different from each other?

Future Perfect and Future Progressive

Both the **future perfect** and the **future progressive** are commonly used to speak about events in the future.

Future Perfect

The **future perfect** is used to talk about a future action that will *already have been completed* by a certain time in the future. The future perfect is often used with the simple present tense to show the relationship between two future events. The event that will take place first uses the future perfect. The event that will take place second uses the simple present tense.

To form the future perfect, active voice: Use *will* + *have* + **past participle**

To form the future perfect, passive voice: Use *will* + *have been* + **past participle**

Examples

By the time I **figure out** how to use the remote, the news **will** already **have started.** (*or* the news **will have** already **started**)

By tomorrow evening, **I will have (will've) sent** about 20 email messages.

By the end of the week, about 50 email messages **will have (will've) been sent.**

Future Progressive

The **future progressive** is used to describe actions that will be in progress at a specific time in the future.

To form the future progressive: Use *will* + *be* + **present participle**

Examples

If the trend **continues,** and cell phones **become** more and more popular, people **will be spending** most of their waking hours on the phone.

In the future, we**'ll be using** a lot of new technology.

2 *Work with a partner. Play the "Mystery Item" game using the future perfect. Student A, look at the directions on this page. Student B, look at page 229.*

Student A: Read the clues about technological items that are common today. Fill in the blanks with future perfect forms of the verbs in parentheses. Be sure to use the correct structure, active or passive. Then read the first two clues about the mystery item to Student B. If Student B cannot guess what the item is, read the third and fourth clues.

Mystery Item 1: Clues

1. By this time next year, you _____ the battery in (replace)
   your mystery item.

2. About 80 million of them _____ by the end of this (make)
   year, and almost everybody has at least one of these items.

3. This mystery item was invented in Germany around 1500.

4. Today it is the number one jewelry item in the world.

Mystery Item 2: Clues

1. You definitely use this item; in fact, you probably _____ (use)
   it once or twice by the end of the day.

2. By the end of the day, these items _____ millions of (use)
   gallons of water around the world.

3. The modern version of this item saves a lot more water than previous versions did.

4. It has greatly improved since it was first invented, and now you would probably find it very hard to live without this item.

Mystery Item 3: Clues

1. There is a good chance that someone in your family

   _____ your mystery item before nine o'clock tonight. (turn on)

2. This mystery item will not go out of style. In fact, by the end of this century,

   this item _____ any less important than it is today. (not/become)

3. Millions of people use the item every second.

4. This item was first available only in black and white.

Answers: (1) watch, (2) toilet, (3) TV

3 *Work with a partner. Discuss what type of technology people will be using in the next 10 to 20 years and beyond. Look at the items below, and make predictions about what people will and won't be doing. Use the future progressive when you make your predictions.*

Example: By the end of this decade, people will probably be vacationing in outer space.

- vacation in outer space
- use video telephones
- live past the age of 100
- select their children's genetic characteristics
- drive electric or solar-powered cars

- use robots to do housework
- use computers to learn English
- do all shopping online
- use only cell phones
- get a complete education online

C   STYLE: Expressing Frustration

There are many ways of expressing frustration. For example, in this unit, you have heard many people complain about their problems with different types of technology. The box below presents some phrases (preceded or followed by a noun or noun phrase) that can be used to express frustration. Words such as *really, very, so,* or *extremely* are often added to intensify the meaning. Here are some examples:

- What's one thing about modern technology that <u>really drives you crazy</u>?

- I know that a lot of people like the convenience of cellular phones, but <u>I find them truly irritating</u>.

- I'm so <u>frustrated</u> with my new Internet provider. There are too many advertisements. They're <u>driving me crazy</u>!

I'm annoyed with/by …	…bothers me.
I'm irritated with/by …	…gets under my skin.
I'm frustrated with …	…drives me crazy. [very informal]
I'm fed up with …	…drives me nuts. [extremely informal]
I'm sick and tired of …	…sends me over the edge.
I've had it with …	

Work with a partner. Role-play one of the following situations between neighbors, or create your own situation in which one of you complains. Use expressions of frustration from the style section on page 221 in your dialogues. Then perform your role play for the class.

Situation 1

Neighbor One: Your next-door neighbor plays loud music during the evening. He doesn't turn it off until midnight. You don't like his taste in music, so it bothers you even more. You have told him politely several times that you have to get up early in the morning. Each time, he gets the message and turns it down, only to do the same thing the following night.

Neighbor Two: When you get home from a long, tiring day at the office, you like to play a little soft music. Your neighbor is supersensitive and sometimes asks you to turn it down. You always do. Tonight he was banging on the wall to get you to turn it down. You think that's really rude.

Situation 2

Neighbor One: Your neighbor has an air conditioner that hums and clanks loudly all night. You can't sleep with the constant noise. You've mentioned it casually to your neighbor before, but your hint hasn't done any good. Your neighbor hasn't gotten the message. You've decided to be more direct to solve the problem.

Neighbor Two: Your neighbor mentioned your noisy air conditioner once before, but you can't do anything about it right now. You've explained that a new one is very expensive, and you can't buy one now. It's been hot lately, and you can't sleep without air-conditioning. You thought that your neighbor understood your situation after you explained it. Everything seemed OK until today.

Situation 3

Neighbor One: Your neighbor has a loud car alarm that plays several musical tunes. It goes off all the time, even if no one is near the car. You can't stand it anymore. You are going to your neighbor's apartment to say something.

Neighbor Two: Your car alarm seems to be a little defective. Sometimes it goes off when it's not supposed to. You've taken it to be repaired, but it still seems to be a little too sensitive.

D SPEAKING TOPIC

Work with a partner. Think of a frustrating problem in modern life that could be solved by a new gadget. (A gadget is a small tool or machine that makes a job easier.) Then invent a gadget to solve the problem. Don't worry about practicality; just let your imagination run wild. Create a commercial for your product.

Step 1: Draw a sketch of your invention. Design an advertisement for it. Use the vocabulary you have learned in this unit to describe the gadget. Be sure to:

- describe the problem, using expressions of frustration from the style section on page 221.

- explain what your product is and how it will work.

- predict how your product will improve life in the future, using the future progressive and future perfect, from the grammar section on pages 218–221.

Step 2: Present your commercial to the class.

Step 3: Evaluate the products other students have invented. Comment on what you like about them and suggest ways their products could be improved.

E RESEARCH TOPIC

Work with a partner to investigate recent developments in technology.

Step 1: Visit the library or do some research online. Investigate recent developments in one of the following areas:

nano technology   electronics
cloning   artificial intelligence
robotics   (your idea) _____
genetic engineering

Be sure to include the following in your report:
- history of the development
- people responsible for the development
- ways the development has affected and will affect your culture

Step 2: Present a summary of your findings to the class. Be prepared to answer questions about your project.

For Unit 10 Internet activities, visit the NorthStar Companion Website at
http://www.longman.com/northstar.

Student Activities

3. Focus on Vocubulary, pages 80–81

Student B, complete the following sentences with the correct words from the box below. Then listen to Student A read each statement. Read your sentences in response. As you listen to Student A, listen for the words in parentheses. Ask Student A to repeat if you do not hear the correct word. Tell Student A the word you are listening for if you still don't hear the word.

evacuate	panic	route	warning	power outage

1. (vulnerable) So would I. It would be hard not to _____ if you saw yourself heading straight for the center of a dangerous storm—in an airplane!

2. (sophisticated) I know what you mean. What if lightning caused a _____ on the plane and the pilot couldn't work the controls?

3. (vital) I know the local authorities need that information to decide whether to _____ the area, but I couldn't do that job!

Work with the same partner. Imagine you are friends on vacation together. You have learned that a severe storm is approaching, and you are preparing to wait out the storm in a small beach house.

Student B, complete the sentences on page 226 with the correct words from the box. Then listen to Student A read each statement. Read your sentences in response. As you listen to Student A, listen for the words in parentheses. Ask Student A to repeat if you do not hear the correct word. Tell Student A the word you are listening for if you still don't hear the word.

| second-guess | manual | stock up on | evacuate | contaminate |

1. (provisions) It's OK. There's a _____ one in the drawer. Look! It's really raining hard!

2. (flooded) You know, we're going to need clean water if that happens. We'd better _____ drinking water.

3. (forecast) Of course you're right. We acted as if nothing could stop our vacation. I'll never _____ the weather forecast again!

4B. Grammar, pages 87–88

Guessing Game

Group B, complete the sentences below with the correct adjective clause. Then listen to Group A's sentences, and identify the item or person they describe. If your Group answers correctly, you receive one point. If you answer incorrectly, Group A receives one point.

Example

Group A: They're the people who fly into the eye of a hurricane.

Group B: Hurricane Hunters.

Group B is correct and gets one point.

Then play again. Take turns reading your sentences to Group A. Group A must identify the item or person you've described. (The words in parentheses are suggested answers.)

The team with the most points wins.

1. It's a kind of equipment _____ is used to track hurricanes. (answer: satellite, radar)

2. It's a country _____ is affected by hurricanes. (answer: the United States, etc.)

3. They're the people _____ are most affected by hurricanes. (answer: residents)

4. What's the name of a scientist _____ studies weather conditions? (answer: meteorologist)

5. It's a word _____ means to predict the weather. (answer: forecast)

6. They're the people _____ fly into the eye of the storm. (answer: Hurricane Hunters)

7. It's a year _____ there was a big hurricane. (answer: 1938, etc.)

UNIT 5: You Will Be This Land

4A. Pronunciation, page 105

Student B: Listen to and answer Student A's questions. Then ask Student A the questions below. Listen to Student A's response, and check for both the answer in parentheses and the pronunciation.

1. What tool do you use to clean your teeth? (toothbrush)

2. What's the opposite of catch? (throw)

3. What's another way to say "inside"? (within)

4. Whose is it if it's not ours, yours, his, or hers? (theirs)

5. What's two plus one? (three)

6. What's the opposite of "these"? (those)

7. What do you put through a needle for sewing? (thread)

8. What's the opposite of "this"? (that)

UNIT 10: Technology: A Blessing or a Curse?

3. Focus on Vocabulary, page 216

Student B: Look at Dialogue One below. Complete each statement by choosing the correct word or phrase from the box. Listen to Student A, who will begin a dialogue. Check that Student A has used the correct word or phrase in parentheses. Then read item 1 to Student A, who will check your answer. Continue with items 2 and 3. Do the same with Dialogue Two.

banned	frazzled	I've had it
defective	frustrated	jolts
disturbing the peace	getting under my skin	offense
drive you crazy	go off	retaliatory steps
pay a fine	irritated	

Dialogue One

1. (getting under my skin) Why? Doesn't the alarm

_____ when it should?

2. (jolts) Maybe it's broken. Why don't you take it back? Most stores will give

you your money back if a product is _____.

3. (frustrated) Well, you sound really worn out. If you get too

_____, you might get sick. You need to get some sleep.

Dialogue Two

4. (irritated) I am. In fact, _____ with the

neighborhood kids and their boom boxes.

5. (drive you crazy) And all night. I've already called the police. They tried to

calm me down and told me not to take _____.

6. (offense) Actually, it is. Playing loud music is _____,

and that's against the law.

7. (pay a fine) You're right. I think boom boxes should be

_____ in public places.

4B. Grammar, page 220

Student B: Read the clues about technological items that are common today. Fill in the blanks with future perfect forms of the verbs in parentheses. Be sure to use the correct structure, active or passive. Then read the first two clues about Mystery Item 4 to Student A. If Student A cannot guess what the item is, read the third and fourth clues.

Mystery Item 4: Clues

1. Most kids love these. It is likely that your children _____ you to buy
   (ask)
   them one of these items by the time they are five or six years old.

2. Now these items are made with 18 or 21 gears. Maybe by the mid-twenty-
   first century, a new version with 100 gears _____.
   (invent)

3. A Scottish blacksmith first came up with the idea for this item. That is
   surprising, because there are so many hills in Scotland that these items are
   difficult to use there.

4. This mystery item usually has two wheels, and you ride it.

Mystery Item 5: Clues

1. Most likely, by the time you retire, you _____ to buy a pair.
   (have)

2. At present, they are made mainly of glass, metal, and plastic, but it's likely
   that by the mid-21st century, manufacturers _____ other materials.
   (introduce)
   Despite the design changes, they will still probably look the same.

3. In the late Middle Ages, they were worn as ornaments for the face.

4. They first appeared in Italy, in the late 13th century, and were used in China
   around the same time.

Mystery Item 6: Clues

1. By 8:00 A.M. tomorrow, your mystery item _____.
   (turn on)

2. By 8:00 A.M. tomorrow, millions of Americans _____ one on for the
   (switch)
   news and weather.

3. You listen to this mystery item.

4. It usually gets both FM and AM frequencies.

Answers: (4) bicycle, (5) glasses, (6) radio

Grammar Book References

NorthStar: Listening and Speaking, High Intermediate, Second Edition	*Focus on Grammar 4,* Third Edition	Azar's *Understanding and Using English Grammar,* Third Edition
Unit 1 Passive Voice	**Unit 18** The Passive: Overview	**Chapter 11** The Passive: 11-1, 11-2
Unit 2 Gerunds and Infinitives	**Unit 9** Gerunds and Infinitives: Review and Expansion	**Chapter 14** Gerunds and Infinitives (1) **Chapter 15** Gerunds and Infinitives (2)
Unit 3 Present Unreal Conditionals	**Unit 23** Present and Future Unreal Conditionals	**Chapter 20** Conditional Sentences and Wishes: 20-1, 20-3
Unit 4 Adjective Clauses	**Unit 13** Adjective Clauses with Subject Relative Pronouns **Unit 14** Adjective Clauses with Object Relative Pronouns or *When* and *Where*	**Chapter 13** Adjective Clauses
Unit 5 Advisability in the Past—Past Modals	**Unit 16** Advisability in the Past	**Chapter 9** Modals (1): 9-7, 9-8, 9-11 **Chapter 10** Modals (2): 10-3
Unit 6 Tag Questions	**Unit 7** Negative *Yes/No* Questions and Tag Questions	**Appendix** Unit B: Questions: B-5
Unit 7 Direct and Indirect Speech	**Unit 25** Direct and Indirect Speech	**Chapter 12** Noun Clauses: 12-6, 12-7

NorthStar: Listening and Speaking, High Intermediate, Second Edition	Focus on Grammar, High Intermediate, Second Edition	Azar's Understanding and Using English Grammar, Third Edition
Unit 8 Phrasal Verbs	**Unit 11** Phrasal Verbs: Review **Unit 12** Phrasal Verbs: Separable and Inseparable	**Appendix** Unit E: Preposition Combinations See also Appendix 1: Phrasal Verbs, in *Fundamentals of English Grammar,* Third Edition
Unit 9 Present and Past— Contrasting Verb Tenses	**Unit 1** Simple Present and Present Progressive **Unit 2** Simple Past and Past Progressive **Unit 3** Simple Past, Present Perfect, and Present Perfect Progressive	**Chapter 2** Present and Past, Simple and Progressive: 2-1, 2-2, 2-5, 2-9, 2-10 **Chapter 3** Perfect and Perfect Progressive Tenses: 3-1, 3-2
Unit 10 Future Perfect and Future Progressive	**Unit 5** Future and Future Progressive **Unit 6** Future Perfect and Future Perfect Progressive	**Chapter 4** Future Time: 4-5, 4-6

Audioscript

UNIT 1 For News Resisters, No News Is Good News

2A. LISTENING ONE: *News Resisters*

Bob Edwards: Since you're listening to this program, odds are you're not taking the advice of Dr. Andrew Weil. He's written a book titled *8 Weeks to Optimum Health* and he recommends reducing your daily intake of news.

Andrew Weil: And then I asked people over the course of eight weeks to extend this to two days a week, three days a week and so forth until the last week you get up to a whole week of no news.

BE: Weil is not the only one trying to get people to take a break from coverage of daily events. NPR's Margot Adler reports on a growing number of people who bring new meaning to the phrase "no news is good news."

LISTENING FOR MAIN IDEAS

BE: Since you're listening to this program, odds are you're not taking the advice of Dr. Andrew Weil. He's written a book titled *8 Weeks to Optimum Health* and he recommends reducing your daily intake of news.

AW: And then I asked people over the course of eight weeks to extend this to two days a week, three days a week and so forth until the last week you get up to a whole week of no news.

BE: Weil is not the only one trying to get people to take a break from coverage of daily events. NPR's Margot Adler reports on a growing number of people who bring new meaning to the phrase "no news is good news."

Margot Adler: When I was a kid, I loved a baseball novel called *The Southpaw*. It was the first volume of a baseball quartet written by Mark Harris. One of the books, *Bang the Drum Slowly,* became a famous movie. What I only learned recently was that Harris wrote a long essay in the *New York Times* back in the early '70s in which he said reading a daily newspaper was a useless addiction. Thirty years later, Harris still believes that.

Mark Harris: Somebody gets up in the morning and the first thing he or she has to do is get that newspaper, and then they have to have it with the coffee and it's kind of two addictions go together.

MA: Harris left his job with the newspaper and turned to writing novels because, he said, you could focus on much more interesting things that are never considered newsworthy. For example, you could focus on the person who loses in sports or comes in second. He also turned to teaching. Academia turns out to be a place filled with news resisters. Take Gabrielle Spiegel, the chair of the history department at Johns Hopkins University. Perhaps it's understandable that a medievalist who says her period of study ends around 1328 would find daily news, in her words, "ephemeral, repetitive and inconsequential."

Gabrielle Spiegel: But I think my underlying reason is that, you know, life is short. There's only a certain amount of time that you have to spend on things, and I have always believed that

there are two things you really need to get through life, and I say this to my children in a sort of nauseatingly repetitive way. The first is a really rich fantasy life so you can imagine what the possibilities are, and the other is a sense of humor so you can deal with what is. And actually I'd rather spend my time on my fantasy life and reading novels than reading newspapers. And I really do think that's why I don't read newspapers.

MA: John Sommerville is a professor of history at the University of Florida and the author of works on the history of religion in England. He has written a book called *How the News Makes Us Dumb: The Death of Wisdom in an Information Society,* and he argues that bias is fixable, but the real problem isn't. His main argument against daily news is the daily part. He argues that dailiness, as he puts it, chops everything down to a standard size, making it harder to get perspective, to know the appropriate size and scale of any problem.

John Sommerville: That one feature by itself, regardless of the competence and the professionalism of the journalist, it's lethal. If dumbness is the inability to make connections, logical connections and historical connections, then you can see how taking in everything on a daily basis is going to hurt our ability to make the connections.

MA: Sommerville prefers quarterlies and says somewhere between weekliness and monthliness you move from entertainment to reflection. And while he does occasionally read newsmagazines, he prefers to read them a month after they come out to maintain perspective. As a historian of religion, Sommerville believes there is a natural antagonism between the news's emphasis on the immediate, and religion, which points toward the more eternal. And it does seem that those involved in spiritual practices are often the most resistant to the daily news barrage.

Tupton Shudrun is a Buddhist nun, a teacher and a student of the Dalai Lama. She says that when you study meditation, you become aware of how your mind is influenced by outside events. She says the media presents problems well, but doesn't give time or space to those helping to remedy the situation.

Tupton Shudrun: And it creates a sense of despair that I think is unrealistic, and that sense of despair immobilizes us from actually contributing to the benefit of society and doing something to help others.

MA: The venerable Tupton Shudrun says she reads a newsmagazine occasionally because as a teacher she needs to get the general feeling of the country, but she chooses what she reads. She, like Weil, advises students to decide consciously how much news to take in and not to assume that the media has a lock on what's important and how to measure success. She also says many people keep themselves plugged in because they don't know how to be alone with themselves. Historian Gabrielle Spiegel agrees.

GS: I think we live in a society that offers us very, very little time alone. And the way children are raised, you know, set in front of televisions, they don't have a lot of time to be by themselves. When my children were little, we used to have a thing called Mommy's hour in which, you know, they had to go in their rooms and just think for an hour or two a day so I could think for an hour or two a day.

MA: While studies show that the majority of Americans don't want to disengage from daily news, when we e-mailed the news staff at NPR for suggestions of people to interview for this story, we got an enormous response, and a surprising number wrote things like, "I would if I could," or "Psst, don't tell anyone." Margot Adler, NPR News, New York.

LISTENING FOR DETAILS

(*Repeat Listening for Main Ideas*)

REACTING TO THE LISTENING

Exercise 1

Excerpt One

Academia turns out to be a place filled with news resisters. Take Gabrielle Spiegel, the chair of the history department at Johns Hopkins University. Perhaps it's understandable that a medievalist who says her period of study ends around 1328 would find daily news, in her words, "ephemeral, repetitive and inconsequential."

Excerpt Two

As a historian of religion, Sommerville believes there is a natural antagonism between the news's emphasis on the immediate, and religion, which points toward the more eternal. And it does seem that those involved in spiritual practices are often the most resistant to the daily news barrage.

Tupton Shudrun is a Buddhist nun, a teacher and a student of the Dalai Lama. She says that when you study meditation, you become aware of how your mind is influenced by outside events.

Excerpt Three

While studies show that the majority of Americans don't want to disengage from daily news, when we emailed the news staff at NPR for suggestions of people to interview for this story, we got an enormous response, and a surprising number wrote things like, "I would if I could," or "Psst, don't tell anyone."

2B. LISTENING TWO: *CornCam*

Exercise 1

Cheryl Corley: In the Midwest, people say during the summer you can drive past a cornfield in the morning, and by the time you drive home in the evening, the corn will seem taller. Watching the corn grow is a beloved and necessary pastime in the Midwest, but its appeal is spreading, thanks to CornCam. In May of last year, editors for *Iowa Farmer Today* mounted a camera behind one of their toolsheds. They pointed it at the adjacent field and fed the images to the publication's website. Since then, CornCam has gained a loyal audience, with more than 600,000 visitors to the site last year. Dan Zinkat is crops editor at *Iowa Farmer Today,* and one of CornCam's creators. So what exactly is CornCam?

Dan Zinkat: Uh, CornCam is a uh, digital camera that takes an image of a cornfield every fifteen minutes and updates it, in, in its simplest form.

CC: Well, well, who tunes in to watch this?

DZ: Mmmm, people from around the world, literally. We've had, uh, hits from Beijing, Russia, England, South Africa. . . . I think most of them are people who live in the cities. We do get

a fair number of commercial farmers who are pretty proud to see someone focusing on corn.

CC: Can it be that riveting, really? What's the appeal?

DZ: I, I think it's riveting in kind of a quiet sense. I think many people tell us that watching the, the cornfield reminds them of growing up on a farm or a small town. Or others tell us they live in big cities on the East Coast or the West Coast, and they think the uh, cornfield is somewhat relaxing and soothing.

CC: Mmm hmm. Well, just how fast does corn grow?

DZ: Well, given the right uh, temperatures, enough moisture in the ground, timely rainfall, you could conceivably have corn grow up to six inches a day, but that's in, in a short-lived period—usually in July.

CC: Mmm hmm. . . . All right, well thanks so much, Dan.

DZ: You're quite welcome, Cheryl. Thank you.

CC: Dan Zinkat is crops editor for *Iowa Farmer Today.*

4A. PRONUNCIATION: *Reducing and Contracting Auxiliary Verbs*

Exercise 1

1. The United <u>States has</u> become a nation of people addicted to the news.

2. <u>Americans are</u> offered news in many forms.

3. <u>Critics have</u> been concerned about the amount of news we watch.

4. Many <u>viewers have</u> tuned into the CornCam website.

5. <u>Academics are</u> worried about the amount of news we consume.

Exercise 2

Americans <u>are</u> offered many sources of news, some of which <u>are</u> available 24/7. The country <u>has</u> become a nation of "news junkies," or people who <u>are</u> addicted to the news. Some academics <u>have</u> started to ask serious questions about the role of the news media in society. Some people believe that the media <u>is</u> focusing on negative stories. Therefore, it focuses less on the important issues that we face. We'<u>re</u> being entertained by gossip about celebrities and politicians, but we'<u>ve</u> stopped worrying about serious problems that affect our society.

UNIT 2 The Achilles Heel

2A. LISTENING ONE: *Dreams of Flying and Overcoming Obstacles*

Bob Edwards: This is the time of year when high school seniors rush to the mailbox to find out which colleges have accepted them. One thing they'll be judged on is their application essay, so *Morning Edition* asked students to share those essays. More than 150 students, parents and teachers from around the country responded. Five were chosen for broadcast. There'll be one each day this week. Richard Van Ornum of Cincinnati is first.

LISTENING FOR MAIN IDEAS

Bob Edwards: This is the time of year when high school seniors rush to the mailbox to find out which colleges have accepted them. One thing they'll be judged on is their application essay, so "Morning Edition" asked students to share those essays. More than 150 students, parents and teachers from around the country responded. Five were chosen for broadcast. There'll be one each day this week. Richard Van Ornum of Cincinnati is first.

Richard Van Ornum: When I was little, I dreamed I was flying. Each night, I was up in the air, though never over the same landscape. Sometimes in the confusion of early morning, I would wake up thinking it was true and I'd leap off my bed, expecting to soar out of the window. Of course, I always hit the ground, but not before remembering that I'd been dreaming. I would realize that no real person could fly and I'd collapse on the floor, crushed by the weight of my own limitations. Eventually, my dreams of flying stopped. I think I stopped dreaming completely.

After that, my earliest memory is of learning to count to 100. After baths, my mother would perch me on the sink and dry me, as I tried to make it to 100 without a mistake. I had to be lifted onto the sink. An accident with a runaway truck when I was four had mangled my left leg, leaving scars that stood out, puckered white against my skin. Looking at the largest of my scars in the mirror, I imagined that it was an eagle. It wasn't fair, I thought, I had an eagle on my leg, but I couldn't fly. I could hardly walk, and the crutches hurt my arms.

Years later, in Venice, I had the closest thing to a revelation I can imagine. Sitting on the rooftop of the Cathedral of San Marco, I wasn't sure what life had in store for me. I was up on a ledge in between the winged horses that overlook San Marco square. To the left, the Grand Canal snaked off into the sea, where the sun cast long crimson afternoon shadows across the city. Below me, in the square, pigeons swirled away from the children chasing them and swooped down onto a tourist who was scattering dried corn.

Somewhere in the square, a band was playing Frank Sinatra. It was "Fly Me to the Moon," I think. Up on the roof of the cathedral, it seemed to me the pieces of my life suddenly fell together. I realized that everyone is born with gifts, but we all run into obstacles. If we recognize our talents and make the best of them, we've got a fighting chance to overcome our obstacles and succeed in life. I knew what my gifts were: imagination and perseverance. And I also knew what my first obstacle had been: a runaway truck on a May morning with no compassion for preschoolers on a field trip. But I knew that the obstacles weren't impossible. They could be overcome. I was proof of that, walking.

That night, for the first time in years, I dreamed I was flying. I soared through the fields of Italy, through the narrow winding streets of Venice and on beyond the Grand Canal, chasing the reddening sun across the sea.

BE: The college essay of Richard Van Ornum, who attends the Seven Hills School in Cincinnati.

LISTENING FOR DETAILS

(*Repeat Listening for Main Ideas*)

REACTING TO THE LISTENING

Exercise 1

Excerpt One

When I was little, I dreamed I was flying. Each night, I was up in the air, though never over the same landscape. Sometimes in the confusion of early morning, I would wake up thinking it was true and I'd leap off my bed, expecting to soar out of the window. Of course, I always hit the ground, but not before remembering that I'd been dreaming. I would realize that no

real person could fly and I'd collapse on the floor, crushed by the weight of my own limitations.

Excerpt Two

Looking at the largest of my scars in the mirror, I imagined that it was an eagle. It wasn't fair, I thought. I had an eagle on my leg, but I couldn't fly. I could hardly walk, and the crutches hurt my arms.

Excerpt Three

I knew what my gifts were: imagination and perseverance. And I also knew what my first obstacle had been: a runaway truck on a May morning with no compassion for preschoolers on a field trip. But I knew that the obstacles weren't impossible. They could be overcome.

Excerpt Four

Years later, in Venice, I had the closest thing to a revelation I can imagine. Sitting on the rooftop of the Cathedral of San Marco, I wasn't sure what life had in store for me. I was up on a ledge in between the winged horses that overlook San Marco square. To the left, the Grand Canal snaked off into the sea, where the sun cast long crimson afternoon shadows across the city. Below me, in the square, pigeons swirled away from the children chasing them and swooped down onto a tourist who was scattering dried corn.

2B. LISTENING TWO: *The Achilles Track Club Climbs Mount Kilimanjaro*

Narrator: They climbed one of the world's tallest mountains— a group of disabled climbers from the New York area. It's a story of reaching new heights, and overcoming great odds. Monica Pellegrini introduces us to those inspirational athletes.

Climber 1: I thought a few times going up that I wouldn't make it. . . . um . . . I almost turned back around twice.

Monica Pellegrini: Mount Kilimanjaro, in the northern part of the African nation of Tanzania. Scaling it is no small task for your average climber, but for a group of seven from New York's Achilles Track Club, it was a much greater challenge. They are all disabled in some way. Five are blind. One is deaf and asthmatic. The other, a cancer survivor and amputee.

Climber 2: It was a lot more difficult than I had expected. Er . . . a difficult climb, and the altitude really did affect a lot of us. But we persevered, and the majority of the athletes were able to make it.

MP: The accomplishment makes the group the largest of disabled athletes to ever climb Mount Kilimanjaro—an expedition they call a testament to the human spirit, and a chance to empower themselves and others.

Climber 3: I just wanted to reach deep down, and grab all the energy I had, and keep on going. Because behind accomplishing this physical challenge for myself, I knew there was a greater message we were all carrying.

MP: The group kept a diary of their travels online, and even when the going got tough, they buckled down, turning to each other for inspiration as they continued on the trail to the peak.

Climber 4: I heard it was going to be hard. I just didn't imagine it was going to be so tough.

MP: Tough, yes, but an experience that will not be forgotten any time soon.

C1: When you're experiencing this wide open space, wind, the sunshine, the strength of the sun like you've never felt before . . .

MP: The adventure began on August 28th and ended this past Sunday, when the group, along with their 18 volunteer guides from the Achilles Track Club, reached the summit.

C1: Getting to the top was definitely the high point.

MP: Monica Pellegrini, UPN 9 news.

4A. PRONUNCIATION: *Thought Groups*

Exercise 1

1. When Richard was little, he dreamed he was flying.

2. He looked at his scar and imagined it was an eagle.

3. When he visited Venice, he realized that he had great gifts.

4. He suddenly realized that he could overcome his obstacles.

5. The essay he wrote about his experience

   was chosen for broadcast.

UNIT 3 Early to Bed, Early to Rise . . .

2A. LISTENING ONE: *Teen Sleep Needs*

Michelle Trudeau: Teenagers, when allowed to, sleep nearly nine and a half hours every night—as much as young children. But unlike young children, even when teens do get their full sleep, they're still out of sync with everybody else. They have waves of sleepiness in the daytime, and then surges of energy in the evening, making them wide awake late at night. But not, Carskadon has discovered, for the reasons most of us assume.

LISTENING FOR MAIN IDEAS

MT: Teenagers, when allowed to, sleep nearly nine and a half hours every night—as much as young children. But unlike young children, even when teens do get their full sleep, they're still out of sync with everybody else. They have waves of sleepiness in the daytime, and then surges of energy in the evening, making them wide awake late at night. But not, Carskadon has discovered, for the reasons most of us assume.

Mary Carskadon: We kind of always thought that adolescents stayed up late because they liked to—which they do—and because there's plenty of things to do—which there are. . . .

MT: But there's also a big push from biology that makes teenagers such night owls. It comes from that mighty sleep hormone, melatonin.

MC: Melatonin is a wonderfully simple signal that turns on in the evening,

MT: You're getting sleepy. . . .

MC: And it turns off in the morning.

MT: And you awaken. During adolescence, melatonin isn't secreted until around 11:00 P.M., several hours later than it is in childhood. So the typical teenager doesn't even get sleepy until that melatonin surge signals the brain that it's night, no matter how early the teen goes to bed. And the melatonin doesn't shut off until nine hours later, around 8:00 A.M. But of course most high schools start around 7:30. The result is all too evident. A teenager's body may be in the classroom, but his brain is still asleep on the pillow.

Student: I'll wake up and I'll just feel miserable, just kind of like ugh, what's wrong with me, you know?

William Dement: An adolescent, and particularly the adolescent in high school, is almost bound to get severely sleep deprived.

MT: That's William Dement of Stanford University. Bill Dement *is* Dr. Sleep, captivated by the mysteries of sleep for decades, creating the specialty of sleep medicine. As a scientist, Dement has contributed more to our understanding of what happens to each of us at night during those hours of unconsciousness than perhaps any other researcher. These days, Dement makes frequent forays out of his lab—an ambassador at large from the field of sleep research. Teenagers, parents, and school authorities need to know more about the science of sleep, he says, and how important it is to young people's health.

WD: I've been accepting every invitation that I get to speak to high school students. So I go to a high school and it'll be 10:30 in the morning, or 2:00 in the afternoon, whenever it is, several hundred students in an auditorium, and I'll just watch them, as I'm talking.

MT: Doing a little spontaneous field research.

WD: And after ten minutes of sitting, particularly if the lights are dim, I would say, almost without exception, they are all struggling to stay awake. Ten minutes!!

MT: This shows up in lab studies too. The typical teenager when monitored in a quiet environment during morning hours will fall asleep in less than three and a half minutes.

WD: It's just like magic. It's like somebody turned on some kind of gas . . . in the auditorium. And they all look gassed.

MT: Not gassed, just severely sleep deprived. Short about two hours of sleep every school night, accumulating into what Dement calls "sleep debt." And most teenagers are up to their drooping eyelids in sleep debt: An estimated 85 percent of high school students are chronically sleep deprived, unable to stay fully awake throughout the school day. And it's not just falling asleep in class; it's also riding a bike, playing sports, using tools, driving. . . .

Calene: Uum, he hit a tree one night when he was driving.

MT: Calene, a South High student, talking about his friend.

C: And he told me he fell asleep for couple of seconds, and next thing he knew, he hit a tree.

Ronald Dahl: You can have a second where your eyelid blinks and you are not taking information or making judgment.

MT: Researcher Ronald Dahl from the University of Pittsburg.

RD: But that occurs when you're at the wheel, you travel 60 feet in that second.

C: The report was that if he would have hit, like, three inches to the left, he would have probably been dead. You know, three inches could have changed everything.

MT: Reaction time, alertness, concentration, all slowed down by insufficient sleep. The Federal Department of Transportation estimates teenage drivers cause more than half of all fall-asleep crashes.

RD: But in addition to those straightforward effects on attention and the ability to stay awake and alert, there are more subtle effects on emotion.

MT: Dahl is studying how adolescents balance their cognitive thoughts and their emotions. When tired, he says, teens are more easily frustrated, more irritable, more prone to sadness. And their performance on intellectual tasks drops.

LISTENING FOR DETAILS

(*Repeat Listening for Main Ideas*)

REACTING TO THE LISTENING

Exercise 1

Excerpt One

MC: Melatonin is a wonderfully simple signal that turns on in the evening,

MT: You're getting sleepy . . .

MC: And it turns off in the morning.

MT: And you awaken.

Excerpt Two

WD: An adolescent, and particularly the adolescent in high school, is almost bound to get severely sleep deprived.

MT: That's William Dement of Stanford University. Bill Dement *is* Dr. Sleep.

Excerpt Three

Student: I'll wake up and I'll just feel miserable, just kind of like ugh, what's wrong with me, you know?

Excerpt Four

WD: And after ten minutes of sitting, particularly if the lights are dim, I would say, almost without exception, they are all struggling to stay awake. Ten minutes!!

2B. LISTENING TWO: *Get Back in Bed*

Lian: This is Lian, and, like many of our listeners out there, I'm tired. I'm tired in the morning, I'm tired in the afternoon, and I'm really tired at night. And frankly, I'm tired of being tired. My excuse is that I have two small children who sleep a little, and wake up a lot. Dr. Walsleben, why are we all so tired?

Dr. Joyce Walsleben: We're probably tired because we don't make sleep a priority. And I think as a young mother and a career woman, your days are pretty well filled, and I would suspect that you probably think you can do without sleep or at least cut your sleep short, and one of the things that happens is we forget that sleep loss accumulates, so even one bad night, teamed with another will make an effect on our performance the following day. The other aspect, which you did touch on, is that even though we may sleep long periods of time, the sleep may not be really of good quality.

L: How serious a problem is sleep deprivation?

JW: Well, it can be very serious, because lack of sleep can affect our performance. It's not . . . We can get cranky and all of that, but if our performance is poor, and we are in a very critical job, we can have a major incident. And there have been many across society in which sleep and fatigue were issues.

The *Exxon Valdez* was one in which the captain got a lot of attention, but the mate who was driving the ship had been on duty for 36 hours. . . . But you can read your local papers; every weekend, you'll see a car crash with probably a single driver, around 2 or 3 A.M., no reason why they would happen to drive off the road, and we all believe that that's probably a short sleep event that occurred when they weren't looking for it.

L: Dr. Walsleben, I know how this sleep deprivation affects me. By the end of the day, with my children, I'm tired and cranky, I'm not making good parenting decisions, I don't have a lot to give my husband when he comes home, and then I just feel too tired to exercise. So I think, "Oh, I'll eat or I'll have a big cup of coffee, and that will give me the energy that I don't have naturally." Are these pretty common effects of sleep deprivation amongst your patients?

JW: They're very common, and so many people accept them . . .

L: I would even say by Friday afternoon, I'm afraid to get behind the wheel of a car, because I just feel like I am not a safe driver on the road. That's how tired I am by Fridays.

JW: I think it's great of you to have recognized that . . . and that's a real, major concern for most of America's workers. By Friday, everyone seems to be missing, probably, five hours of sleep.

4A. PRONUNCIATION: *Contrastive Stress*

Exercise 1

1. I <u>need</u> to go to <u>bed</u>, but I'm <u>feeling</u> <u>energetic</u>.
2. <u>Adolescents</u> wake up <u>late</u>, but <u>children</u> wake up <u>early</u>.
3. <u>Lian</u> is fast <u>asleep</u>, but her <u>children</u> are <u>awake</u>.
4. My <u>husband</u> has <u>insomnia</u>, but <u>I</u> need to <u>sleep</u>.
5. I'm <u>sleepy</u> in the <u>morning</u>, but wide <u>awake</u> at <u>night</u>.

UNIT 4 The Eye of the Storm

2A. LISTENING ONE: *Preparing for a Hurricane*

1. The sky is clear blue, and the ocean is deceptively calm here in Southern Florida. It's the kind of day when you would expect . . .
2. But the beaches are . . .
3. Traveling inland, though, you'll find a totally different mood. Parking spaces are . . .
4. . . . and there are long lines at . . .
5. You see, despite the calm weather now, people here are . . .

LISTENING FOR MAIN IDEAS

Allison Sasso: This is Allison Sasso reporting for station KTFH in Florida. The sky is clear blue, and the ocean is deceptively calm here in southern Florida. It's the kind of day when you would expect the beaches to be packed with tourists, enjoying the surf and sun. But the beaches are eerily silent, except for a few seagulls circling the waves.

Traveling inland, though, you'll find a totally different mood. Parking spaces are hard to find, and there are long lines at every checkout counter as people stock up on batteries, water bottles, and flashlights. You see, despite the calm weather now, people here are getting ready for a hurricane, the first of this hurricane season.

Meteorologist Kyle Zachster works for the weather service. Kyle, what can we expect in Homestead?

Kyle Zachster: Well, Allison. Hurricane Haley is about 70 miles off the coast, with winds reported to be up to 100 miles per hour. It has already damaged islands in the Caribbean.

AS: Local residents at this shopping center are busy. Adam Rashap, what are your plans? Are you going to leave?

Adam Rashap: Huh? No, I'm staying here to protect my house. We'll be all right. Hurricanes are not usually as bad as they predict. Everyone panics and gets ready, but it's never really a big deal.

AS: But authorities say people should stay informed and *not* second-guess the authorities. Despite reconnaissance aircraft, a sophisticated satellite, and radar used by the National Weather Service, forecasting the path of a hurricane is not an easy task. Kyle?

KZ: We input a lot of data into the computer to get a forecast, but there's still an element of interpretation. Often the storm will change route or intensity unexpectedly . . . ummm . . . Folks have to realize that they can be very, very vulnerable. The worst thing is to be caught off guard.

AS: What can people do to prepare?

KZ: Well, Allison, they can stock up on supplies. People should have plenty of water on hand, at least a couple of gallons per person, and more if possible. Sewers can back up, and water gets contaminated. You need food for at least three days, more if possible. For your canned goods, make sure there's a can opener—manual, not electric. You'll need a flashlight and a battery-powered radio.

AS: Kyle, you also said people need a sturdy pair of work boots. Why?

KZ: Yes. If your place has been damaged, you don't want to be walking into anything dangerous when you come back. Snakes, for instance, get dislocated by the hurricane, just like people, and end up in unexpected places.

AS: A nasty surprise! Let's find out what someone else is going to do. Dale Henly, what are your plans?

Dale Henly: Well, uh, we don't live here. We're down for a vacation with the kids—from Minnesota—no hurricanes there! My husband and the kids are pretty excited, um, but honestly, I'm scared stiff! If we have to evacuate, I'll be relieved.

AS: Most tourists aren't prepared to face a hurricane. But if you plan to visit a coastal spot in the late summer, then you *could* hit some very foul weather.

KZ: That's right. The main thing for tourists is to know what plans or provisions the hotel has and what they can do if there's a power outage or if the water's bad. You need to know where you're going if you have to leave, because roads get flooded, and highways get backed up.

AS: What about money?

KZ: Sure. You might need additional cash. People forget that ATMs won't work without power.

AS: Here is a woman who has lived here for more than 50 years, Barbara Swanson. Mrs. Swanson, are you going to stay or leave?

Barbara Swanson: Eh, we're not sure, yet. I've been glued to the news all day. I always get a little jittery when I hear talk of hurricanes. We lost our house to a hurricane back when I was first married.

AS: So you might tough it out this time. I see your son is loading wood on top of the car. Is that to protect the windows?

BS: Yes, just in case. Seems he got the last six pieces in the store. Um, everybody's doing the same thing, I guess.

AS: In Homestead, all residents can do is watch, wait, and try not to panic. This is Allison Sasso reporting.

LISTENING FOR DETAILS

(Repeat Listening for Main Ideas)

REACTING TO THE LISTENING

Excerpt One

Adam Rashap: Huh? No, I'm staying here to protect my house. We'll be all right. Hurricanes are not usually as bad as they predict. Everyone panics and gets ready, but it's never really a big deal.

Excerpt Two

KZ: We input a lot of data into the computer to get a forecast, but there's still an element of interpretation. Often the storm will change route or intensity unexpectedly . . . ummm . . . Folks have to realize that they can be very, very vulnerable. The worst thing is to be caught off guard.

Excerpt Three

Dale Henly: Well, we don't live here. We're down for a vacation with the kids—from Minnesota—no hurricanes there! My husband and the kids are pretty excited, but honestly, I'm scared stiff! If we have to evacuate, I'll be relieved.

Excerpt Four

AS: So you might tough it out this time. I see your son is loading wood on top of the car. Is that to protect the windows?

Barbara Swanson: Yes, just in case. Seems he got the last six pieces in the store. Everybody's doing the same thing, I guess.

2B. LISTENING TWO: *Hurricane Hunters*

Alex Zhao: This is Alex Zhao reporting live from aboard a reconnaissance squadron known as the Hurricane Hunters. The sun is shining in South Florida as the aircraft gets ready. It's carrying six officers from the postcard-like weather here directly into the eye of Hurricane Haley, as the big storm turns northward. They'll fly through the hurricane and relay vital information back to the mainland—information on wind speed, pressure, and organization of the storm.

Today I get to go with them . . . into the eye of the storm. Two of the crew members, Andrea Davis and Miguel Ríos are with me now. Andrea, look how dark it is over there. Where are we headed?

Andrea Davis: We're heading right into the storm's eye, Alex. It's about 12 miles wide.

AZ: Now the plane is becoming dark as we enter the eye wall, which is what we call the thick clouds around the center of the storm. The ends of the wings seem to have disappeared in the clouds and the rain. Inside the eye wall, you can't see anything at all. But wait . . . it's suddenly so bright! In fact, the sun is shining so intensely it's almost blinding.

AD: Yes, we've broken into the eye. Now we're going to drop equipment from the plane to record data.

AZ: Miguel, can I ask you something? Isn't this job dangerous?

Miguel Ríos: Well yes, but it's necessary. Machines can't do what we do. Technology tells you where the storm is located, but it's not as accurate as having people on board. For instance, we can tell certain things about the speed and direction of the storm by looking down onto the ocean surface. It's pretty exciting.

AZ: Really? I'm amazed you don't panic. I think you are all very brave. I wouldn't want to do this every day!

AD: Well, it *can* get intense, but when we get this information back to the mainland, who knows? We could end up saving some lives.

AZ: It's heartening to know you're risking your lives to keep the rest of us safe. Thank you so much for taking me on your trip—into the eye of the storm! I'm Alex Zhao, reporting.

4A. PRONUNCIATION: *Listing Intonation*

Exercise 1

1. People are buying batteries, water bottles, and flashlights.

2. The sky is blue, the ocean is calm, and the beaches are empty.

3. My house was flooded, my furniture was ruined, and my car is gone.

4. The hurricane has passed by Cuba, Puerto Rico, and Southern Florida.

5. There were big hurricanes in 1938, 1965, and 1997.

UNIT 5 You Will Be This Land

2A. LISTENING ONE: *Interview with a Medicine Priest*

Barbara Cassin: Hi. I'm here with David Winston, a Cherokee medicine priest. David, thank you for coming to talk to us today.

David Winston: Oh, you're very welcome.

BC: Would you tell us a little bit about the Cherokee beliefs regarding the environment and conservation?

DW: Yes, I'd be happy to. Uh, basically, Cherokee tradition tells us that we are part of nature and we depend on nature for our life, so we don't, uh, compete with it and we're not trying to tame it, we're trying to live with it.

BC: It's different from our contemporary view, I guess, that nature exists for the benefit of people.

DW: Well, yeah. We believe that we're, as I said, we're a part of what we call the Great Life, and as part of the Great Life we are as important as everything else, but certainly no more important than anything else. And we feel that within the Great Life, there are what we call the Laws of Nature.

BC: . . . The laws of nature . . . could you tell us more about that?

DW: Yeah, we believe that there are many laws of nature, but there are three great Laws of Nature, and those are the laws that tell us how we have to live in relationship to everything else.

LISTENING FOR MAIN IDEAS

BC: Hi. I'm here with David Winston, a Cherokee medicine priest. David, thank you for coming to talk to us today.

DW: Oh, you're very welcome.

BC: Would you tell us a little bit about the Cherokee beliefs regarding the environment and conservation?

DW: Yes, I'd be happy to. Uh, basically, Cherokee tradition tells us that we are part of nature and we depend on nature for

our life, so we don't, uh, compete with it and we're not trying to tame it, we're trying to live with it.

BC: It's different from our contemporary view, I guess, that nature exists for the benefit of people.

DW: Well, yeah. We believe that we're, as I said, we're a part of what we call the Great Life, and as part of the Great Life we are as important as everything else, but certainly no more important than anything else. And we feel that within the Great Life, there are what we call the Laws of Nature.

BC: . . . The laws of nature . . . could you tell us more about that?

DW: Yeah, we believe that there are many laws of nature, but there are three great Laws of Nature, and those are the laws that tell us how we have to live in relationship to everything else. The First Law of Nature is that you don't take any life without real reason. And a real reason would be for food, for medicine, for protection . . . uh, those would be the reasons for taking life. But basically, life is sacred.

BC: Uh-huh. So you shouldn't kill needlessly. Would that include plants?

DW: Absolutely. We believe everything is alive. In fact, we believe stones are alive, trees are alive, plants are alive, animals are obviously alive. And so to us, taking the life of a plant is just as grave a responsibility as taking the life of an animal. And all of those things should be done in a sacred way and in a good way. So for instance, when you go to gather a plant, you don't want to go and say, "Wow, here's a whole patch of plants," and go and gather them all. You gather a few, and then you gather a few from another spot, leaving the majority of the plants so that they can grow and continue to provide not only for themselves, but for us, and for our children, and for their children.

BC: Interesting. And what about the Second Law?

DW: The Second Law is that everything we do should serve the Great Life.

BC: Hmmm. The Great Life. What exactly do you mean by that?

DW: Well, what we mean is . . . is that we believe that there's one spirit that fills all things, humans, plants, rocks, whatever. And the sum of all of that and more is what we call the Great Life. And so we all are part of this same Great Life. And everything we do affects the Great Life, and everything that happens within the Great Life affects us. So it's very, very important that within the Second Law of Nature, that what we do will not harm other parts of the Great Life.

BC: I . . . I wonder if you could give an example.

DW: Well, I could give a lot of examples. And on a very personal, simple level, an example could be for instance . . . uh, lots of people might go out and get an electric toothbrush. Uh, maybe it works a little bit better, it's certainly easier. The toothbrush does all the work for you. But I have a manual toothbrush and I've used one for my whole life, and it works just fine. To use the electricity necessary to power that electric toothbrush requires coal or nuclear power that harms the air, it harms the water, it harms the Great Life.

BC: I see, so we don't really need it . . . OK, so that's two. And what about the Third Law?

DW: The Third Law basically is . . . is that we don't pollute where we live. And where we live is not just our home, it's not just our intimate, small community, it's not just our country. It's this planet, this sacred altar we call the Earth. We don't pour chemical wastes down the drain because they all wind up in the water. So basically we don't pollute the Earth.

BC: I see. Well, they make sense, but it seems it's a little difficult to live by those three laws today. I mean, in this industrialized society, how could you apply the rules?

DW: Well, it's more challenging, certainly. The Cherokees didn't have a problem with . . . uh . . . plastic. We didn't have plastic. We didn't have a lot of the things that exist today. We still have a lot of options. There's small things that each one of us can do . . . things like recycling, things like choosing what we buy and buying things carefully. There are other things we can do—instead of using the car for every short trip to the store, save them up so we use the car as little as possible. We can do things like organic gardening. We can do things to create greater community within our communities. There are a lot of things that we can do to bring these laws into our lives. And ultimately, our lives really depend on these. The Great Life can live without us, but we can't live without the Great Life.

BC: Well, you've certainly given us a lot to think about today. Thanks, David Winston, for talking to us.

DW: You're welcome. Un dun Koh ha hee.

LISTENING FOR DETAILS

(*Repeat Listening for Main Ideas*)

REACTING TO THE LISTENING

Exercise 1

Excerpt One

BC: . . . The laws of nature . . . could you tell us a little more about that?

DW: Yeah, we believe that there are many laws of nature, but there are three great Laws of Nature, and those are the laws that tell us how we have to live in relationship to everything else. The First Law of Nature is that you don't take any life without real reason. And a real reason would be for food, for medicine, for protection . . . uh, those would be the reasons for taking life. But basically, life is sacred.

Excerpt Two

DW: The Second Law is that everything we do should serve the Great Life.

BC: Hmmm. The Great Life. What exactly do you mean by that?

DW: Well, what we mean is . . . is that we believe that there's one spirit that fills all things, humans, plants, rocks, whatever. And the sum of all of that and more is what we call the Great Life. And so we all are part of this same Great Life. And everything we do affects the Great Life, and everything that happens within the Great Life affects us. So it's very, very important that within the Second Law of Nature, that what we do will not harm other parts of the Great Life.

Excerpt Three

BC: I see, so we don't really need it . . . OK, so that's two. And what about the Third Law?

DW: The Third Law basically is . . . is that we don't pollute where we live. And where we live is not just our home, it's not just our intimate, small community, it's not just our country. It's this planet, this sacred altar we call the Earth. We don't pour chemical wastes down the drain because they all wind up in the water. So basically we don't pollute the Earth.

2B. LISTENING TWO: *Ndakinna—A Poem*

Exercise 1

Ndakinna by Joseph Bruchac

Ndakinna means "our land" in Abnaki. Ndakinna, that's what we call, "America."

You cannot understand
this land with maps,
lines drawn as if earth
were an animal's carcass
cut into pieces, skinned,
though always less eaten
than thrown away.

See this land instead
with a wind-eagle's eyes,
linked with rivers and streams
like sinews through leather,
sewed strong to hold the people
to the earth.

Do not try to know the land by roads.

Let your feet instead
caress the soil
in the way of deer,
whose trails follow
the ways of least resistance.

When you feel this land
when you taste this land
when you hold this land as lungs hold breath
when your songs see this land,
when your ears sing this land,

You will be this land.

You will be this land.

Exercise 2

(*Repeat Exercise 1*)

Exercise 3

(*Repeat Exercise 1*)

4A. PRONUNCIATION: th *Sounds*

Exercise 1

1. three
2. they
3. there
4. think
5. so
6. ladder
7. worthy
8. dough
9. sued
10. day
11. bathe
12. other
13. breeze
14. Zen

Exercise 5

(*Repeat 2B Exercise 1*)

UNIT 6 It's Better to Give Than to Receive

2A. LISTENING ONE: *Oseola McCarty—An Unusual Philanthropist*

Barbara Walters: Deep in the heart of Mississippi, hidden behind wind-whipped sheets and sun-drenched linens, lives this year's most talked-about philanthropist. No one noticed the frail woman who spent most of her 86 years doing other people's laundry. Quietly, in between bundles of wash and ironing, Ms. Oseola McCarty tucked away $250,000.

LISTENING FOR MAIN IDEAS

Barbara Walters: But why would a poor washing woman give away her life's savings? This story touched us the moment we first heard it, and the more we thought about it, the more we believed that Ms. Oseola McCarty had to be on our list.

Deep in the heart of Mississippi, hidden behind wind-whipped sheets and sun-drenched linens, lives this year's most talked-about philanthropist. No one noticed the frail woman who spent most of her 86 years doing other people's laundry. Quietly, in between bundles of wash and ironing, Ms. Oseola McCarty tucked away $250,000.

Oseola McCarty: I was surprised myself. I didn't know I had that much money.

BW: The woman who never went to high school, never went to college, stunned the academic world by pledging most of her life's savings to fund scholarships for promising black students at the university down the road.

OM: I didn't have no children. I didn't have nobody else to give it to.

BW: Ms. McCarty's own education was cut short. She left after sixth grade to care for her ailing grandmother. And she worked, taking in bundles of laundry from doctors, lawyers, and policemen, slowly building a nest egg of dollars and change at the bank downtown.

Announcer: The president of the United States.

BW: News of the gift has traveled far.

President Clinton: If this country had more people like you, we'd have very few problems, and we'd be even greater than we are.

OM: I didn't know I was so powerful until people began to tell me.

BW: The trip to the White House this September was her first time out of the South in 50 years. These days, times are not so lonely at the frame house on Miller Street. There's a new visitor: She's Stephanie Bullock, the first recipient of the Oseola McCarty scholarship, and thanks to her benefactor, a college freshman.

Stephanie Bullock: I always knew that I was going to go to college. Didn't know how—but I was going to go. Ms. McCarty will be at my graduation, sitting right over there with my family.

OM: There's more in giving than it is to receive. And I tried it out.

BW: Her washing tools are retired now. Her hands are knarled by arthritis. But the years of crisp collars and pressed pleats now leave a legacy all their own.

OM: I don't regret it one minute. I just wished I had more to give.

BW: Ms. McCarty has started something big. Local business people around her town are now contributing to the Oseola McCarty scholarship fund. She finds it all quite amusing, and told us that the locals weren't about to let some wash-and-iron woman show them all up. Good for you, Oseola.

LISTENING FOR DETAILS

(Repeat Listening for Main Ideas)

REACTING TO THE LISTENING

Exercise 1

Excerpt One

Barbara Walters: No one noticed the frail woman who spent most of her 86 years doing other people's laundry. Quietly, in between bundles of wash and ironing, Ms. Oseola McCarty tucked away $250,000.

Oseola McCarty: I was surprised myself. I didn't know I had that much money.

BW: The woman who never went to high school, never went to college, stunned the academic world by pledging most of her life's savings to fund scholarships for promising black students at the university down the road.

Excerpt Two

OM: I didn't have no children. I didn't have nobody else to give it to.

BW: Ms. McCarty's own education was cut short. She left after sixth grade to care for her ailing grandmother. And she worked, taking in bundles of laundry from doctors, lawyers, and policemen, slowly building a nest egg of dollars and change at the bank downtown.

Excerpt Three

OM: There's more in giving than it is to receive. And I tried it out.

BW: Her washing tools are retired now. Her hands are knarled by arthritis. But the years of crisp collars and pressed pleats now leave a legacy all their own.

OM: I don't regret it one minute. I just wished I had more to give.

2B. LISTENING TWO: *Please Donate or Volunteer—Public Service Announcements*

Exercise 1

Public Service Announcement 1: Volunteering

In America, the Constitution doesn't require you to offer food to the hungry or shelter to the homeless. There is no ordinance forcing you to visit the lonely. Nothing says you have to provide clothing to the poor. In fact, one of the nicest things about living in America is that you really don't have to do anything for anybody. Yet, 80 million Americans volunteer their time and money anyway. Thank you for all you've given. Imagine what more could do. Call 1-800-55-GIVE-5. A public service message from Independent Sector and the Ad Council.

Public Service Announcement 2: Traffic

If you can drive a car, you can drive one for someone who can't. If you can pick up a few groceries, you can pick them up for someone who can't. To find out how easy it is to help, call the Points of Light Foundation, at 1-800-59-LIGHT. Do something good. Feel something real. A public service message from the Points of Light Foundation and the Ad Council.

4A. PRONUNCIATION: *Intonation of Tag Questions*
Exercise 1

1. Oseola McCarty saved her money for about 50 years, didn't she?

2. Wealthy philanthropists save a lot of money on taxes, don't they?

3. A lot of Americans donate to charity, don't they?

4. People give more today than they used to, don't they?

5. Children in your country are encouraged to volunteer, aren't they?

4B. GRAMMAR: *Tag Questions*
Exercise 2
Step 2

A: You've heard about Oseola McCarty's gift to the university, haven't you?

B: Yes, I have. It's an amazing story, isn't it?

A: Uh, huh. Some people are more generous than others, aren't they?

B: That's the truth. Most people wouldn't give away all their money, would they?

A: Of course not. Even very wealthy people don't give a very high percentage of their money away, do they?

B: Right. I remember reading that low-income people give an average of 3.6 percent of their income and wealthy people only 1.6 percent. That's surprising, isn't it?

A: But it's not true for everyone. Look at media tycoon Ted Turner. He gave one billion dollars to the United Nations, didn't he?

B: That's right. It's hard to imagine having that much money to give, isn't it?

A: It sure is. But more wealthy people should give away more of their money, shouldn't they?

B: I agree, but I wonder how I'd feel if I were rich!

UNIT 7 Emotional Intelligence

2A. LISTENING ONE: *Can You Learn EQ?*

Claire Nolan: Hi. This is Claire Nolan, and this is *Psychology Talk*. Today we are going to be discussing EQ—Emotional Intelligence. We've been hearing a lot about EQ lately, and in fact, you've probably seen Daniel Goleman's best-selling books about EQ in the bookstore. Your Emotional Intelligence quotient seems to include both how well you handle your own emotions, and how well you respond to others. And Goleman had some really interesting advice. He said that even if you don't respond well to pressure, you don't handle stress very easily, or you have problems when you interact with other people, you can learn to change. Today I'm going to be talking to two educators to get their perspective on learning to improve your EQ. Listeners, don't go away!!

LISTENING FOR MAIN IDEAS

Part One

Claire Nolan: Hi. This is Claire Nolan, and this is *Psychology Talk*. Today we are going to be discussing EQ—Emotional Intelligence. We've been hearing a lot about EQ lately, and in fact, you've probably seen Daniel Goleman's best-selling books about EQ in the bookstore. Your Emotional Intelligence quotient seems to include both how well you handle your own emotions, and how well you respond to others. And Goleman had some really interesting advice. He said that even if you don't respond well to pressure, you don't handle stress very easily, or you have problems when you interact with other people, you can learn to change. Today I'm going to be talking to two educators to get their perspective on learning to improve your EQ. Listeners, don't go away!!

CN: Welcome back to *Psychology Talk*! Now, our first guest is Betty Cortina. Betty, you're an elementary school teacher. Now, you told me before that you think some kids have higher EQs than others, is that right?

Betty Cortina: Oh, sure! Even at five or six years old, some kids tend to be much more patient and easygoing than others. And then others are prone to shout and make a big fuss. I mean, it's not bad to be high spirited, but if you can't control your emotions, even at that age, you can have a lot of problems.

CN: Like what?

BC: Well, if you can't deal with setbacks, you don't make progress, and if you're always impatient, your peers don't like you.

CN: Can you give us an example?

BC: Sure. One example is how kids deal with frustration. Imagine a child who's having trouble with a math problem. She gets frustrated with the problem, throws down her pencil, and yells, "This is a stupid problem!" Another child, with a higher EQ, might be able to handle the situation better.

CN: So how can you teach the angry child to approach the situation differently?

BC: The child could learn to take a break, or she could ask for help. And she will be more successful because she won't let her negative feelings get in the way of her task.

CN: I guess I can understand that—I suppose kids have to learn to take life in stride, and not to give up when they reach an obstacle.

Part Two

CN: But what about adults? Can you improve your EQ when you grow up, or have we all missed our chance? Jim McDonald, you're our next guest. Do you want to respond to that question?

Jim McDonald: No, you haven't missed your chance, Claire! Of course children can learn to control their emotions, but adults can learn EQ too! Now, as you know, I run management training programs for a bank here in the city, and I agree, this EQ idea is definitely important. Let's face it, when the going gets tough, it's much better for an employee to have a positive, enthusiastic attitude. Business is like life—everyone makes mistakes, but you have to make allowances for that. You can't always dwell on failures, and you have to realize that everyone, including you, makes mistakes sometimes.

CN: Can you give us an example?

JM: Well, I work with a lot of managers, and the good ones are sharp, perceptive people who respond well to whatever's going on around them. They're the ones who probably learned EQ when they were children. But then other people tend to get angry and resentful right away if there's a problem. They say things like "It wasn't my fault," or "I didn't know about that."

CN: What about those people? Can they change?

JM: Yes they can. What we try to show people is that you have to swallow your pride, and admit it if you made a mistake. And then you also need to learn to empathize with others. You have to put yourself in others' shoes. Then you can understand the reasons they behave the way they do.

CN: Well, thank you both. And I'll remember to keep EQ in mind! Maybe I can improve my own Emotional Intelligence!

LISTENING FOR DETAILS

(Repeat Listening for Main Ideas)

REACTING TO THE LISTENING

Exercise 1

Excerpt One

CN: We've been hearing a lot about EQ lately, and in fact, you've probably seen Daniel Goleman's best-selling books about EQ in the bookstore. Your Emotional Intelligence quotient seems to include both how well you handle your own emotions, and how well you respond to others. And Goleman had some really interesting advice. He said that even if you don't respond well to pressure, you don't handle stress very easily, or you have problems when you interact with other people, you can learn to change.

Excerpt Two

BC: Sure. One example is how kids deal with frustration. Imagine a child who's having trouble with a math problem. She gets frustrated with the problem, throws down her pencil, and yells, "This is a stupid problem!" Another child, with a higher EQ, might be able to handle the situation better.

Excerpt Three

JM: Well, I work with a lot of managers, and the good ones are sharp, perceptive people who respond well to whatever's going on around them They're the ones who probably learned EQ when they were children. But then other people tend to get angry and resentful right away if there's a problem. They say things like "It wasn't my fault," or "I didn't know about that."

2B. LISTENING TWO: *Test Your EQ*

Exercise 2

Claire Nolan: This is the second portion of *Psychology Talk.* Jan Davis will tell me how I scored on the EQ test I've just taken.

Jan Davis: OK, number 1, the situation with the crying child. The best answer is B: "Talk to him and help him figure out ways to get the other kids to play with him."

CN: Why is that?

JD: Emotionally intelligent parents use situations like this to teach their children about emotions. They help their children understand what made them upset, what they are feeling, and what they can do to feel better. Now, moving on to number 2, the college student who fails the exam. The answer is A: "Make a specific plan for ways to improve your grade." People with a high EQ are self-motivated and know how to overcome problems.

CN: Instead of dwelling on failure, the student thinks of specific ways to solve the problem.

JD: Right. Number 3, about dealing with the angry driver. The answer is C: "Tell him about a time something like this happened to you and how you felt as angry as he does now." Studies of anger have shown that the best way to calm an angry person is not only to empathize with him, but also to suggest a different way of looking at the problem.

CN: So here, you have to be skillful at managing another person's emotions.

JD: Number 4, the ethnic joke. The answer is C: "Say something to all the employees right away. Tell them that ethnic jokes are not acceptable in your organization."

CN: Hmmm. I put B.

JD: The reason C is right is that the best way to create a feeling of openness and acceptance of different ethnic groups is to make rules about how people should behave. You can't always change how people feel about each other, but you can control how they act toward each other. And by acting with respect, people can often learn to put aside their negative feelings.

CN: Interesting!

JD: Finally, number 5, solving the problem at work.

CN: Let me guess. The answer is B: "Have people take the time to get to know each other better."

JD: Yes, B is correct. Studies show that people are more creative and work better together if they feel comfortable and connected to each other, so you should spend time on that first.

CN: So now that we have the answers, what does this test mean? What does it show us about ourselves?

JD: Well, these questions can give you an idea of your strengths and weaknesses. It's a tool we can use to become more perceptive about our emotional skills, and hopefully improve our EQ.

4A. PRONUNCIATION: *Unstressed Vowels*

Exercise 1

1. con<u>t</u>rol
2. ad<u>ju</u>st
3. suc<u>ce</u>ss
4. pro<u>du</u>ctively

5. <u>p</u>eople

6. <u>h</u>onest

7. <u>q</u>uotient

8. re<u>s</u>entful

9. <u>p</u>ersonal

10. a<u>bi</u>lity

11. a<u>d</u>ult

12. per<u>cep</u>tive

13. <u>f</u>ailure

14. adv<u>ic</u>e

15. <u>e</u>motional

Exercise 2

(*Repeat Exercise 1*)

Exercise 3

Emotional Intelligence Seminar

Self-Awareness: Understanding yourself

Self-Control: Handling emotions

Self-Motivation: Using emotions productively

Empathy: Understanding others' emotions

People Skills: Relating well to people

Led by psychologist Nancy Matz

UNIT 8 Goodbye to the Sit-Down Meal

2A. LISTENING ONE: *French Sandwiches*

Bob Edwards, Host: France, home of the two-hour, sit-down mid-day meal, is witnessing a boom in take-out sandwiches. At noon, customers line up outside Paris bakeries, waiting to buy long, thin versions of a shrimp salad and avocado sandwich, or other iconoclastic delicacies.

The variation in eating habits is reflecting a deeper change in French society. NPR's Sarah Chayes reports.

LISTENING FOR MAIN IDEAS

Bob Edwards, Host: France, home of the two-hour, sit-down mid-day meal, is witnessing a boom in take-out sandwiches. At noon, customers line up outside Paris bakeries, waiting to buy long, thin versions of a shrimp salad and avocado sandwich, or other iconoclastic delicacies.

The variation in eating habits is reflecting a deeper change in French society. NPR's Sarah Chayes reports.

Sarah Chayes: As with any major shift in something as intimate as eating, the story is complicated. Sociologist Claude Fishlere makes a living studying food habits here.

Claude Fishlere: It starts with a change in the workforce. So it's a feminization, white-collarization, if I can say so . . . services rather than industry. . . .

SC: The result has been a revolution in one of France's core industries—the bakery. Formerly, bakeries here offered a limited range of albeit excellent products—about four kinds of bread, breakfast and dessert pastries. Now, that's just the start.

SC: Au Pain Gourmet, a bakery on the corner of a market street, in the ordinary working-class tenth arrondissement of Paris. It's eight in the morning, and Nicole already has the slicer going, cutting bread for lunch sandwiches. She's making tuna vegetables on whole wheat bread.

Nicole: (speaks French)

SC: "I hate making sandwiches," she says. Tough. It puts bread on her table, too. Au Pain Gourmet, with its glass cases stacked full, does so much sandwich business, it had to hire Nicole especially to make them. Owner Audile Gazier says she's just responding to the demand . . . and letting her imagination run wild. She even tried making a four-course sandwich meal— with the appetizer, then the main dish, then cheese, and chocolate spread alternating down one baguette. It was a bit much for people to swallow.

Audile Gazier: (speaks French)

SC: She says, nowadays people want to eat faster at noon, and leave early at the end of the day. Life is changing, she says; we have to keep up. The changes include women making up almost half the labor force now, and making their tastes known, and men, more likely to be working behind a computer than behind a jackhammer, not needing to eat so much. Sociologist Fishlere:

CF: They also have to pick up the children as early as possible, from the *crèche*.

SC: . . . daycare center.

CF: Daycare center. So basically, they look for something that's very close to what is called fast food. And, eh, the interesting point is that the um, supply that has developed goes well beyond your, uh, basic McDonald's hamburgers.

Unidentified Woman #1: (speaks French)

SC: For example, Au Pain Gourmet's plethora of multishaped, multicontent sandwiches. They're obviously a hit with the lunchtime customers who line up all the way onto the sidewalk. They agree this recent phenomenon is growing.

Unidentified Woman #2: Yes, more and more. It's exploding, this kind of eating.

Unidentified Man: Every baker offers sandwiches.

Unidentified Woman #3: Because before, it was only with ham and butter and now we have salad and tomatoes and Roquefort. Because we eat sandwich, but it's French products in it.

SC: French products in it. That may be the key. Instead of being overrun by McDonald's, as some feared, the French have adapted the idea of fast food and made it their own. Around the corner from Au Pain Gourmet, a quick burger franchise just closed. Sarah Chayes, NPR News. Paris.

LISTENING FOR DETAILS

(*Repeat Listening for Main Ideas*)

REACTING TO THE LISTENING

Exercise 1

Excerpt One

SC: It's eight in the morning, and Nicole already has the slicer going, cutting bread for lunch sandwiches. . . . "I hate making sandwiches," she says. Tough. It puts bread on her table, too.

Excerpt Two

SC: Owner Audile Gazier says she's just responding to the demand . . . and letting her imagination run wild. She even tried making a four-course sandwich meal—with the appetizer, then the main dish, then cheese, and chocolate spread alternating down one baguette. It was a bit much for people to swallow.

Excerpt Three

SC: They're obviously a hit with the lunchtime customers who line up all the way onto the sidewalk. They agree this recent phenomenon is growing.

Excerpt Four

Unidentified Woman #2: Yes, more and more. It's exploding, this kind of eating.

Unidentified Man: Every baker offers sandwiches.

2B LISTENING TWO: *Food in a Bowl*

Lian Dolan: A couple of years ago, I started noticing a food trend. And it started at Teryaki Hut. And I noticed a big sign in the window that said: Teryaki Bowl. And I thought: Ah, Teryaki Bowl, OK.

And then I saw at El Pollo Loco, which is kind of a fast food Mexican chain—more bowls, more food in bowls—beef bowls, chicken bowls, rice bowls, and I thought: Well rice, that makes sense, that's a cultural thing. You've got to eat rice in a bowl, that makes sense.

But the other day, I was wandering through the frozen food aisle, and I looked up, and now, there's a whole "Food in Bowl" section. And this has nothing to do with cultural food. I just . . . I don't think lasagna needs to be in a bowl. I don't know. Are we just eating too much food, too fast, that we can't eat on a plate anymore . . . that we need a bowl because we can get that closer to our mouth for more shoveling in?

What is the next trend, hands-free eating, like hands-free cell phones? Just forget it. Forget the utensils, just get yourself a nice trough, and put the lasagna in there.

I'm Lian Dolan in Pasadena, and I feel it's my duty as a mother to educate my children to eat on a plate with a knife and a fork.

Julie Dolan: I'm Julie Dolan in Bangkok. And we've got rice bowls, monk bowls. It's pretty much bowl city, here.

Liz: I'm Liz Dolan in New York. And of all the challenging methods of presenting food, I've actually been having the most trouble lately wrestling with things on skewers. Last week I actually beaned someone with a lamb kebab!

4A. PRONUNCIATION: *Spelling and Sounds— "oo" and "o"*

Exercise 1

1. one some lock
2. fool wool shoot
3. body rode both
4. door boot floor
5. shook look boost
6. noon cook boom

Exercise 2

food, too, boom, book, cook, noodles, flood, look, noon, cool, blood, tool

Exercise 3

popular, oven, done, shock, possible, home, money, whole, come, frozen, women, go, explode, job, do

UNIT 9 Finding A Niche: The Lives of Young Immigrants

2A. LISTENING ONE: *A World within a School*

Mary Ambrose: Students in cities like New York are used to hearing wide variations of English. In a town where immigrant communities flourish, many dialects and languages mix with standard English. In fact, there's an international high school that encourages immigrant students to use and develop their native tongues while learning English. It's a new approach, and as Richard Schiffman reports, it seems to work.

LISTENING FOR MAIN IDEAS

Mary Ambrose: Students in cities like New York are used to hearing wide variations of English. In a town where immigrant communities flourish, many dialects and languages mix with standard English. In fact, there's an international high school that encourages immigrant students to use and develop their native tongues while learning English. It's a new approach, and as Richard Schiffman reports, it seems to work.

Richard Schiffman: The philosophy of this school is that you learn by doing, and not by hearing the teacher lecture. In this math class, for example, six teams of young people are gathered around lab tables, building their own miniature temple out of cardboard. But to find out what really sets this school apart, you need to get up close.

The four teenage boys at this table are planning their temple in Polish. At the other tables, they're speaking Spanish, English, and Mandarin Chinese. This is not just a bilingual classroom; it's a multilingual one, and the pupils here are all recent immigrants to the United States. Their teacher, Jennifer Shenke, walks around the room, quietly helping out.

Jennifer Shenke: They love building things. This has been really successful, and they've learned a lot of math that they didn't have before, umm, just doing scale and proportion. And, and I feel pretty good about that because they, they didn't know that they were learning it until they had learned it.

RS: Shenke is happy that her pupils are learning math and enjoying themselves in the process, and she's especially pleased that they're teaching one another. She knows that many in her classroom wouldn't be able to follow her if she lectured. So she depends on the pupils who know more English and more math to help teach those who know less. That's what's happening now at the lab tables. They're helping each other out in their own languages. . . .

Priscilla Billarrel: . . . I think what we share the most is a feeling of not fitting in.

RS: Priscilla Billarrel left Chile when she was 14 years old. She says that although they come from all over the world, the students at the International High School understand each other very well.

PB: Since we all are immigrants in here, we all know what['s] to be different feels like, so we support one another. Whenever we have problems with pronunciation[s], or we're missing words or something, whatever we're saying, we correct one another kindly. We don't make fun of each other. That's what I really like about this school. . . .

RS: . . . New York City can be an intimidating place, even for those who have spent their whole lives here. But for young people who have just been uprooted from tight-knit, extended families and traditional communities abroad, the city can seem positively unfriendly. Teacher Aaron Listhaus says that young immigrants don't just need a place to learn English and other subjects. They need, above all else, a place that feels completely safe and welcoming.

Aaron Listhaus: It's particularly important for these students to have a comfort level in a place called school and for that school to feel like home . . . to feel like their needs are going to get met, um, they're going to be listened to, they're going to be valued for who they are and the diverse backgrounds that they come from, and that those things are viewed as what makes them special rather than what makes them a problem.

RS: The fact that immigrant youngsters speak a language other than English, Listhaus says, is seen by most educators as a problem that needs to be corrected. The usual approach is to teach students exclusively in English, and to suppress the use of their native language. Evelyna Namovich, who came to the U.S. three years ago from Poland, remembers what it was like to find herself in a typical New York City school.

Evelyna Namovich: Sometimes it was so difficult because I didn't know what was the subject all about, what was she speaking about, and I would need somebody to translate, even a little bit for me, you know. And we couldn't, because we would have to write something like . . . an essay, er, like punishment, if we spoke Polish.

RS: Evelyna says she was relieved when she transferred to the International High School, where she not only wasn't punished for speaking Polish, she was encouraged to bone up on her native language at the same time as she was learning English. Instructor Aaron Listhaus says that it's important that young immigrants don't lose their languages, as his own immigrant parents from Eastern Europe did.

AL: My parents have a hard time speaking in their native languages at this point. And to me there's something sad about that. Language is more than just the way that you communicate with the world; it's the way that you interpret the world in your own head. So to me, there's something more than just communication that's lost when you lose your native language.

RS: And teacher Kathy Rucker adds that speaking another language also has a practical economic value.

Kathy Rucker: People in the future are going to have to communicate in more than one language, it seems to me, because there's so much rapid travel, there's so much international business.

RS: . . . Today, as also in the past, immigrants to the U.S. often feel the need to assimilate as quickly as possible into mainstream American culture. But there is one place, at least, where new immigrants are being encouraged to keep what is unique to them.

From the International High School in New York, I'm Richard Schiffman, for *The World*.

LISTENING FOR DETAILS

(*Repeat Listening for Main Ideas*)

REACTING TO THE LISTENING

Exercise 1

Excerpt One

Jennifer Shenke: They love building things. This has been really successful, and they've learned a lot of math that they didn't have before, ummm, just doing scale and proportion.

And, and I feel pretty good about that because they, they didn't know that they were learning it until they had learned it.

Excerpt Two

Aaron Listhaus: It's particularly important for these students to have a comfort level in a place called school and for that school to feel like home . . . to feel like their needs are going to get met, um, they're going to be listened to, they're going to be valued for who they are and the diverse backgrounds that they come from, and that those things are viewed as what makes them special rather than what makes them a problem.

Excerpt Three

Kathy Rucker: People in the future are going to have to communicate in more than one language, it seems to me, because there's so much rapid travel, there's so much international business.

2B. LISTENING TWO: *The Words Escape Me*
Exercise 1

I was standing on a train platform in a foreign land.
I was 21 years old,
Excited to be involved, and to do my part, to understand
    everything I was told.
But they moved too quickly, talked too fast, moved too quickly.
I couldn't even catch my breath.
Frozen in a fast frame, action is blurred.
Loud, too loud, I can't understand your words.
What was I thinking? I can't do this, learn this.
Think I'll just go home,
But I can't go home.
I worked out some bugs, and know where I live.
I can also use your words to order only fish.
I try to eat their food; I miss the meals from home.
I eat too little; I eat too much.
I'm studying hard, but I don't get the jokes.
They think I'm stupid; I can't tell them I'm not.

Writing in this book makes me feel at home.
The words I can't escape they're hiding my best, you know.
What was I thinking? I can't do this, learn this.
Think I'll just go home.
But I can't go home.
Hey, yeah, words escape me, [repeat]
And I can't use my tongue. [repeat] I can't use it like you.
    [repeat]
Learn the language, talk the language, learn the language, boy.
    [repeat]

Writing in this book makes me feel at home.
The words I can't escape are hiding my best, you know.
What was I thinking? I can't do this, learn this.
Think I'll just go home.
But I can't go home.
Hey, yeah, words escape me, [repeat]
And I can't use my tongue. [repeat]
I can't use it like you. [repeat]
Exercise 2 (*Repeat Exercise 1*)

4A PRONUNCIATION: *Discriminating between* sh, z, ch, *and* j

Exercise 1

1. international
2. language

3. enjoy

4. adjust

5. measure

6. lecture

7. traditional

8. culture

9. usual

10. punishment

11. special

12. subject

13. Chile

14. television

15. educators

16. occasion

17. communication

18. encourage

19. treasure

20a. niche

20b. niche

21. flourish

UNIT 10 Technology: A Blessing or a Curse?

2A LISTENING ONE: *Noise in the City*

Neal Rauch: It's late. You're tired. Finally, after an exhausting day, you're ready to surrender to the world of dreams. Your head sinks into your pillow. Then . . .

LISTENING FOR MAIN IDEAS

Steve Curwood: Modern life is full of nasty noises, especially in the cities. Sirens can shatter serenity at any moment and jackhammers, loud music, and useless mufflers can all send us over the edge. For many people in New York City, there's one form of sonic pollution at the top of the list. They're calling for its banning, even though some nervous New Yorkers savor the sound for security reasons. And as Neal Rauch reports, even as the controversy prompts loud debate, some aren't waiting for laws to be passed.

Neal Rauch: It's late. You're tired. Finally, after an exhausting day, you're ready to surrender to the world of dreams. Your head sinks into your pillow. Then . . .

Judy Evans: After being awakened at night many times so that awful feeling, you know, you've just gotten to sleep and then the alarm goes off.

NR: Each night hundreds of people like Judy Evans, a scenic designer and artist who lives in Brooklyn, are jolted out of their sleep by the nagging wail of a car alarm.

JE: You just wait it out but you don't know if that's going to happen again. You don't know when you're going to be reawakened for a second or a third time even.

NR: Often she is, and sometimes a defective alarm will go on for hours.

JE: If one person were standing on the corner with a horn making that kind of noise, they would be arrested. They would be disturbing the peace.

Man: It slowly gets under your skin and eventually drives you nuts.

NR: A music producer and composer, this resident of Manhattan's Upper West Side got fed up with car alarms disturbing his sleep and his work. He got together with some similarly frazzled neighbors and formed a posse of sorts.

Man: We start off with a note saying, "Fix your car alarm, it's disturbed hundreds of people last night." If that doesn't help we quite often use some minor retaliatory step like breaking an egg on their windshield or on the front hood, which doesn't hurt anything but it's a little bit of a mess to clean up.

NR: The "egg man," who prefers to remain anonymous, says some vigilantes take even more drastic action. Like smearing axle grease on door handles.

Man: Another classic is to smear vaseline all over the windshield, which is incredibly hard to get off. So . . . I think in other neighborhoods there might be even broken windshields and things like that.

NR: Lucille DiMaggio was a target of vigilante retribution. It happened one night when, unbeknownst to her, the car alarm malfunctioned.

Lucille DiMaggio: I noticed something on the passenger front door. There were a lot of dent marks. It appeared to me that it looked like the heel of someone's shoe, as if someone had kicked my innocent car, because the alarm hadn't even been going off all night.

NR: The repairs cost her a couple of hundred dollars. To test the theory, Lucille DiMaggio set off her alarm for me in a restaurant parking lot. Not a single person bothered to see if a car was being broken into. Which begs the question: Are car alarms really effective? Judy Evans says absolutely not, not even when she's called the police.

JE: One night, there was a real incredible racket, and a little MG was being mutilated to death. The alarm was going off. So I called 911. Well, about 40 minutes later, the police drove up.

NR: Little remained of the car by then. Ms. Evans, who's taken to sleeping with earplugs and the windows closed, says car alarms should be banned in densely populated and already noisy neighborhoods.

Catherine Abate: The streets are much noisier than they were 20 years ago . . . even 10 years ago.

NR: New York State Senator Catherine Abate represents Manhattan.

CA: The noise affects not only their ability to sleep at night, but for the most part their ability to work during the day. And even parents have come to me and said, "What is the impact on children?" And there are more and more studies that show that young people in particular, that are exposed to a sustained amount of loud noise, have hearing loss. So it's a health issue, it's a quality of life issue.

NR: Enforcement of existing laws, along with new regulations, may be cutting down noise in some neighborhoods. It's now illegal for alarms to run for more than three minutes. After that police can break into a car to disable the alarm or even tow away a wailing vehicle. It's hoped these actions will motivate car owners to adjust their alarms, making them less sensitive so vibrations from passing trucks and the like don't set them off. Even the egg man admits the car alarm situation has improved, at least in his neighborhood. By the way, the egg man has a sidekick: his wife.

Man: When something happens outside she'll say, "Do you think that's eggworthy?" And I say, "That sounds like an egg candidate to me."

NR: For *Living on Earth*, I'm Neal Rauch in New York.

LISTENING FOR DETAILS

(*Repeat Listening for Main Ideas*)

REACTING TO THE LISTENING

Exercise 1

Excerpt One

JE: You just wait it out but you don't know if that's going to happen again. You don't know when you're going to be reawakened for a second or a third time even. . . . If one person were standing on the corner with a horn making that kind of noise, they would be arrested. They would be disturbing the peace.

Excerpt Two

LD: I noticed something on the passenger front door. There were a lot of dent marks. It appeared to me that it looked like the heel of someone's shoe, as if someone had kicked my innocent car, because the alarm had even been going off all night.

Excerpt Three

CA: The noise affects not only their ability to sleep at night, but for the most part their ability to work during the day. And even parents have come to me and said, "What is the impact on children?" And there are more and more studies that show that young people in particular, that are exposed to a sustained amount of loud noise, have hearing loss. So it's a health issue, it's a quality of life issue.

Excerpt Four

Man: When something happens outside she'll say, "Do you think that's eggworthy?" And I say, "That sounds like an egg candidate to me."

2B. LISTENING TWO: *Technology Talk*

Host: Welcome to *Technology Talk*. Our topic today is "Technological Pet Peeves." What's one thing about modern technology that really drives you crazy? Our lines are open. Give us a call. . . . Hello. You're on the line with *Technology Talk*.

Caller 1: Hi. I'm Stanley from Chicago.

H: Welcome, Stanley. As you know, we're taking complaints about technology today. What's one thing that really drives you crazy?

C1: Well, what I really hate are automated phone systems. Everyone has them these days, but I . . . um . . . think they're a mixed blessing. It's awful to try calling somewhere and getting this . . . er . . . annoying recorded voice saying, "If you're calling from a touch-tone phone, press one." Then you spend the next ten minutes making choices and you never get to talk to a real person. After all that, half the time I don't get the information I want anyway. That system drives me crazy, and there doesn't seem to be anything I can do about it. In fact, I have to call my wife at work right now. But by the time I actually get through, she'll have already left.

H: Uh-huh . . . I tend to agree with you, Stanley. But I don't know what we can do about it. . . . Let's move on to Carol from Houston. Hi, Carol.

Caller 2: Hello.

H: So, Carol, what's the one thing that really makes you frustrated with modern technology?

C2: I'm happy to get a chance to speak out. I know that a lot of people like the convenience of cellular phones, but I find them truly irritating. People don't seem to know when to leave them at home. I hate it when people use their cell phones in a restaurant or a store. It's probably none of my business, but it drives me crazy. One night in a movie theater, some cell phone began to ring and a guy behind me began to have a conversation right there during the movie! And the people who talk on the phone while they drive, well, they're putting the rest of us in danger, aren't they? There should be a law against it!

H: Well, Carol, maybe we'll be getting some response to your strong stand on cell phones. . . . Stay tuned while we see what Jessica from Brooklyn thinks of all this. Jessica?

Caller 3: Good afternoon. I just had to call to share my frustrations with remote controls.

H: Remote controls? I didn't realize they could be so problematic.

C3: In my house, we have about five remote controls.

H: About five?

C3: Yes, we're always losing one of them, and then we have to search all over the house to find them just so we can change channels. I finally bought a universal remote, which is supposed to simplify life and control everything. But to be honest, it's so complicated to work. I've given it up. Where is all this technology taking us? That's what I want to know! It was so much easier in the good old days when you could just switch the channels by hand!

H: But, then, of course, we had to get up and walk over to the TV and . . .

C3: That's true, but . . .

H: Let's take another call. Welcome, Arthur from Los Angeles.

Caller 4: Hello. I wanted to tell you about the one thing that drives me crazy. It's e-mail. I have hardly enough time already to answer letters and return calls, and now I'm supposed to answer e-mail too? What happens is that when I do open my e-mail, most of it is junk—plus messages I don't really need to read. It takes me about an hour every day to sort through it. I wish we'd never gotten e-mail.

H: I know what you mean! Well, the lines are open, folks. Let's hear what you think of our callers' comments today. . . .

3 FOCUS ON VOCABULARY

Exercise 1

[sounds of various common noises]

Exercise 2

(*Repeat Exercise 1*)

4A PRONUNCIATION: *Stressed Adverbial Particles*

Exercise 1

1. I tried to read the instructions, but then I gave <u>up</u>.

2. I asked him to turn it <u>down</u>, but he said he didn't want to.

3. Come <u>in</u> and sit <u>down</u>. You look really worn <u>out.</u>

4. I want to buy a new car. This one keeps breaking <u>down</u>.

5. I'm taking this new gadget <u>back</u>. I can't get it to work, and I'm really fed <u>up</u>.

Exercise 2

I give <u>up</u>! I've had it with these modern appliances! I bought a new alarm clock, but it goes <u>off</u> whenever it feels like it. Last night it went <u>off</u> at midnight. I got <u>up</u> before I realized what time it was. First I got angry and threw it <u>out</u>. Then I took it <u>out</u> of the garbage and decided to take it <u>back</u>. I want to get my money <u>back</u>!

The Phonetic Alphabet

Consonant Symbols

/b/	be		/t/	to
/d/	do		/v/	van
/f/	father		/w/	will
/g/	get		/y/	yes
/h/	he		/z/	zoo, busy
/k/	keep, can		/θ/	thanks
/l/	let		/ð/	then
/m/	may		/ʃ/	she
/n/	no		/ʒ/	vision, Asia
/p/	pen		/tʃ/	child
/r/	rain		/dʒ/	join
/s/	so, circle		/ŋ/	long

Vowel Symbols

/ɑ/	far, hot		/iy/	we, mean, feet
/ɛ/	met, said		/ey/	day, late, rain
/ɔ/	tall, bought		/ow/	go, low, coat
/ə/	son, under		/uw/	too, blue
/æ/	cat		/ay/	time, buy
/ɪ/	ship		/aw/	house, now
/ʊ/	good, could, put		/oy/	boy, coin

Credits

Photo credits: Page 1 The New Yorker Collection 1977 Dana Fradon from cartoonbank.com. All rights reserved; 8 ITTC Productions/Getty Images; 11 Jim Foster/Corbis; 25 Fergal O'Donnell; 43 Fergal O'Donnell; 45 The New Yorker Collection 1992 Michael Crawford from cartoonbank.com. All rights reserved; 50 Doug Menuez/Getty Images; 54 Wartenberg/Picture Press; 69 American Red Cross; 74 Alan Schein Photography, Inc./Corbis; 77 StockTrek/Getty Images; 91 reprinted with the permission of Co-op America; 93 Daniel J. Cox/Getty Images; 98 photo by Robert Espier, "Hudson River Mythic"; 113 Robert J. Baker, Habitat for Humanity International; 118 AP/Wide World Photos; 136 (left) Lynn Goldsmith/Corbis, (middle) AFP/Corbis, (right) Reuters NewMedia Inc./Corbis; 155 The New Yorker Collection 1996 Victoria Roberts from cartoonbank.com. All rights reserved; 159 Paul Seheult/Eye Ubiquitous/Corbis; 179 Bill Losh/Getty Images; 184 Arthur Tilley/Getty Images; 186 Alan Schein Photography, Inc./Corbis; 205 The New Yorker Collection 1998 David Sipress from cartoonbank.com. All rights reserved; 209 AP/Wide World Photos; 212 Don Mason Photography/Corbis; 213 The New Yorker Collection 1998 Roz Chast from cartoonbank.com. All rights reserved.

Listening Selections and Text Credits: Page 8, © Copyright NPR® 2000. The text and audio of the news report by NPR's Margot Adler was originally broadcast on National Public Radio's *Morning Edition*® on June 6, 2000, and is used with the permission of National Public Radio, Inc. Any unauthorized duplication is strictly prohibited. page 11, © Copyright NPR® 2001. The text and audio of the news report by NPR's Cheryl Corley was originally broadcast on National Public Radio's *Morning Edition*® on August 2, 2001, and is used with the permission of National Public Radio, Inc. Any unauthorized duplication is strictly prohibited. page 28, © Copyright NPR® 2000. The text and audio of the news report by NPR's Bob Edwards was originally broadcast on National Public Radio's *Morning Edition*® on March 26, 2000, and is used with permission of National Public Radio, Inc. Any unauthorized duplication is strictly prohibited. page 31, Courtesy of WWOR News, WWOR-TV, Inc. All rights reserved. page 50, © Copyright NPR® 2000. The text and audio of the news report by NPR's Michelle Trudeau was originally broadcast on National Public Radio's *All Things Considered*® on September 9, 2000, and is used with permission of National Public Radio, Inc. Any unauthorized duplication is strictly prohibited. page 54, Satellite Sisters LLC. Used by permission. page 95, used with permission of David Winston, Herbalist AHG. page 99, used with permission of Joseph Bruchac. page 118, used with permission of BarWall Productions. page 121, reprinted with permission of the Independent Sector, www.IndependentSector.org. page 142, Daniel Goleman in *Utne Reader,* November–December 1995. page 159, © Copyright NPR® 2001. The text and audio of the news report by NPR's Sarah Chayes was originally broadcast on National Public Radio's *Morning Edition*® on May 7, 2001, and is used with the permission of National Public Radio, Inc. Any unauthorized duplication is strictly prohibited. page 162, Satellite Sisters, LLC. Used by permission. page 184, as heard on PRI's *The World,* a co-production of the BBC World Service, Public Radio International, and WGBH Boston. page 188, song written by Steve Coleman 2002. www.gabrielshold.com. page 209, from *Living on Earth,* 9/27/96. © Copyright 1996. World Media Foundation and Neil Rauch, by permission.

Reviewers

Lubie G. Alatriste, Lehman College; **A. Morgan Andaluz**, Leeward Community College; **Chris Antonellis**, Boston University CELOP; **Christine Baez**, Universidad de las Américas, Mexico City, Mexico; **Betty Baron**, Johnson County Community College; **Rudy Besikof**, University of California San Diego; **Mary Black**, Institute of North American Studies; **Dorothy Buroh**, University of California, San Diego; **Kay Caldwell**, Leeward Community College; **Margarita Canales**; Universidad Latinoamericana, Mexico City, Mexico; **Jose Carvalho**, University of Massachusetts Boston; **Philip R. Condorelli**, University of Massachusetts Boston; **Pamela Couch**, Boston University CELOP; **Barbara F. Dingee**, University of Massachusetts Boston; **Jeanne M. Dunnet**, Central Connecticut State University; **Samuela Eckstut-Didier**, Boston University CELOP; **Patricia Hedden**, Yonsei University; **Hostos Community College**; **GEOS Language Institute**; **Jennifer M. Gerrity**, University of Massachusetts Boston; **Lis Jenkinson**, Northern Virginia Community College; **Glenna Jennings**, University of California, San Diego; **Diana Jones**, Instituto Angloamericano, Mexico City, Mexico; **Matt Kaeiser**, Old Dominion University; **Regina Kandraska**, University of Massachusetts Boston; **King Fahd University of Petroleum & Minerals**; **Chris Ko**, Kyang Hee University; **Charalambos Kollias**, The Hellenic-American Union; **Barbara Kruchin**, Columbia University ALP; **Language Training Institute**; Jacqueline LoConde, Boston University CELOP; **Mary Lynch**, University of Massachusetts Boston; **Julia Paranionova**, Moscow State Pedagogical University; **Pasadena City College**; **Pontifical Xavier University**; Natalya Morozova, Moscow State Pedagogical University; **Mary Carole Ramiowski**, University of Seoul; **Jon Robinson**, University of Seoul; **Michael Sagliano**, Leeward Community College; **Janet Shanks**, Columbia University ALP; **Eric Tejeda**; PROULEX, Guadalajara, Mexico; **Truman College**; **United Arab Emirates University**; **University of Minnesota**; **Karen Whitlow**, Johnson County Community College

Notes